FOREIGN INVESTMENT IN CHINA UNDER THE OPEN POLICY

Foreign Investment in China Under the Open Policy

The experience of Hong Kong companies

John T. THOBURN
School of Economic and Social Studies
University of East Anglia

H.M. LEUNG
Faculty of Business Administration
National University of Singapore

Esther CHAU
Business School
Hong Kong Baptist College

S.H. TANG
Business School
Hong Kong Baptist College

Avebury

Aldershot · Brookfield USA · Hong Kong · Singapore · Sydney

Published by
Avebury
Gower Publishing Company Limited
Gower House
Croft Road
Aldershot
Hants GU11 3HR
England

Gower Publishing Company
Old Post Road
Brookfield
Vermont 05036
USA

British Library Cataloguing in Publication Data
Foreign investment in China under the open policy: the experience of Hong Kong companies.
1. China. Foreign capital investment by Hong Kong companies
I. Thoburn, John T. (John Thomas) 1941–
332.6735125051

ISBN 1-85628-066-7

Printed and Bound in Great Britain by
Athenaeum Press Ltd., Newcastle upon Tyne.

Contents

Preface   viii
Currencies and exchange rates   x
Map 1   China   xi
Map 2   Guangdong province   xii

1.   Introduction   1
     1.1   Hong Kong firms in the Pearl River Delta   1
     1.2   The interviewing programme and the sample   4

2.   Foreign Investment in China: Investor and Host
     Country Motivations   12
     2.1   Hong Kong firms and the internationalization
           of production   12
     2.2   The value of Hong Kong investment to the Chinese 14
     2.3   Types of contract   16
     2.4   Benefits for Chinese local authorities, enterprises
           and the Chinese economy   19
           2.4.1.   Ventures with Chinese local authorities 19
           2.4.2.   Ventures with state companies   19
           2.4.3   The benefits to the Chinese economy   20

3.   The Equity Joint Venture Companies   26
     3.1   The companies and the contract   26
           3.1.1   The companies   26
           3.1.2   The equity joint venture contract   27
     3.2   The motivation and expectations of the partners   27
           3.2.1   Partnerships with Chinese companies   28
           3.2.2   Partnerships with local authorities   31
           3.2.3   Structural aspects   33
     3.3   Marketing, export, and foreign exchange issues   34
     3.4   Employment and operational issues   36

v

4.   The Cooperative Joint Venture Companies   58
      4.1   The companies and the contract   58
            4.1.1   The companies   58
            4.1.2   The cooperative joint venture contract   59
      4.2   The motivation and expectations of the partners   60
            4.2.1   Ventures with Chinese companies   60
            4.2.2   New ventures with local authorities   61
            4.2.3   Structural aspects   64
      4.3   Marketing, export, and foreign exchange issues   65
      4.4   Employment and operational issues   67

5.   Processing and Assembly, Compensation Trade, and 'Other'
      Companies   88
      5.1   The companies and the contracts   88
            5.1.1   The companies   88
            5.1.2   Processing and assembly and compensation
                    trade contracts   89
      5.2   The motivation and expectations of the partners   91
            5.2.1   Companies initiated as processing and
                    assembly ventures   91
            5.2.2   Existing Chinese companies starting
                    processing and assembly operations   93
            5.2.3   Further developments from processing and
                    assembly   94
            5.2.4   The compensation trade companies   95
            5.2.5   The 'other' companies   96
            5.2.6   Structural aspects   96
      5.3   Exporting and foreign exchange issues   98
            5.3.1   The processing and assembly companies   98
            5.3.2   The compensation trade and 'other' companies   101
      5.4. Employment and operational issues   102

6.   Locational Choices of Foreign Investors in the Pearl
      River Delta   127
      6.1   Location   128
      6.2   Labour   128
      6.3   Infrastructure   130
      6.4   Capital   130
      6.5   Technology   131
      6.6   Economic privileges   132
      6.7   Administrative efficiency   132
      6.8   Attitudes towards foreign investment   133

7.   Summary and Conclusions   144
      7.1   Experience of foreign investors with different
            types of contract   145
      7.2   Experience with different kinds of Chinese partners   147
            7.2.1   Partnerships with state companies   148
            7.2.2   Partnerships with local authorities   149
      7.3   Issues relating to foreign investment and the
            economic reforms   150
            7.3.1   The expertise of the Hong Kong partner:
                    firm-specific advantage in practice   150
            7.3.2   Taxation and the benefits of foreign
                    investment to the Chinese economy   151
            7.3.3   Exporting and foreign exchange   151
            7.3.4   Employment issues   153

	7.3.5	Management	153
	7.3.6	Other operational issues - power and transport	153
	7.3.7	Bureaucracy	154
	7.3.8	Legal issues	154
7.4		The Chinese investment climate as of 1987-8	154
7.5		The Hong Kong economy and the Pearl River Delta	155
7.6		The current austerity programme and the aftermath of 4th June	158
	7.6.1	Key features of the austerity policy	159
	7.6.2	Effects on the Chinese economy	159
	7.6.3	Effects on Guangdong	160
	7.6.4	Effects on foreign-invested enterprises	161
	7.6.5	Hong Kong investment in China	161
	7.6.6	Recent policy changes and the future	162

| Appendix | The Taxation of Foreign Investment in China | 169 |

| Bibliography | | 192 |

Preface

This study was first written over the period July 1987 to May 1989, with the aid of a research grant from the Sir Run Run Shaw Foundation, Hong Kong, which is gratefully acknowledged. The authors at the time were all based in the Business School of Hong Kong Baptist College (in Thoburn's case, on two year's leave of absence from the University of East Anglia). They would like to thank the Dean of the School, Professor Y.K. Fan, for his warm support and encouragement at all stages of the research. Publication has been delayed following the events of 4th June 1989 in Beijing, when the Chinese government ordered the forcible suppression by the People's Liberation Army of mass student demonstrations. A further visit to Hong Kong and China by Thoburn in January 1990, financed by the University of East Anglia, has provided information with which an attempt has been made to place the book's basic material, which relates to 1987-8, in the perspective of recent events.

The core of the project was an interviewing programme of Hong Kong companies in the Pearl River Delta region of Guangdong province in China in the summer and autumn of 1987. This was conducted jointly with members of the Hong Kong and Macau Institute of Zhong Shan University, Guangzhou, particularly Professors Lei Qiang, Zheng Tianxiang, and Zhang Zhongshen. Findings were discussed in several meetings in China in 1988, and January 1989, with each side agreeing on separate publication (see Lei Qiang, 1988, for a Zhong Shan University publication). We are grateful to the Friedrich Ebert Foundation for financing a project workshop in Hong Kong in July 1988, attended by most of the project researchers, and by members of the Chinese and Hong Kong business communities and some government officials (see Thoburn, Tang and Chau, 1989). Some preliminary project findings also have been published in Chinese (see Leung, Chau and Thoburn, 1988). We are most grateful to the companies and the many Chinese officials who helped us, and to Zhong Shan University's research students for their assistance in arranging interviews.

The interviews were conducted by Thoburn, Leung and Chau, with Tang providing considerable organizational backup in Hong Kong. Thoburn, as the project's Principal Researcher, brought the work to publication, and has been responsible mainly for the three central chapters (Three, Four and Five) setting out the interview results. Chau wrote Chapter Six, on locational choice, and Tang has written the appendix on taxation. Leung's main contribution has been to develop the transactions costs aspects of foreign investment and contract choice, which will be published separately (see Leung, Thoburn, Chau and Tang, 1989). The other parts of the book reflect joint efforts and discussions. We should like to thank Sue Rowell in Norwich and Viola Ngo in Hong Kong for typing the manuscript, and Phillip Judge for drawing the maps.

Of course, neither the Sir Run Run Shaw Foundation, the Ebert Foundation, nor Zhong Shan University, necessarily agrees with any view expressed here, and we alone are responsible for any errors. A similar disclaimer applies to Chris Edwards of UEA and Peter Nolan of Cambridge, both of whom we thank for some extremely helpful comments on parts of the manuscript.

Finally, and on a more personal note, I should like to thank various friends who made my stay in Hong Kong more pleasant than it otherwise would have been, particularly George and Janie Thomas, Duncan and Judy Hunter, and Graham and Annie Bowtell. George and Janie provided my wife and me with accommodation during a return visit in January 1989 and again for me in January 1990. Judy tried in a patient and kindly way to improve my Chinese, as also did Lee Siu Mei at UEA. I have learned much about China from long conversations with Zhang Leyin of the Development Planning Unit at London University; and from Chen Guangzhe, now at Harvard. I am deeply indebted to my friend Sonia Yau for many insights into the language and rich culture of the Chinese, and for much help in locating English and Chinese press material on China. June, my wife, in spite of many academic commitments of her own, always has been supportive, as have Nick and Alan in their own way.

J.T.T.
UEA, Norwich
March 1990

ix

Currencies and exchange rates

The **Hong Kong dollar** has been linked to the United States dollar since October 1983 at a fixed exchange rate of HK$7.8 = US$1. During the period of fieldwork for this book (1987-8), the Hong Kong dollar's exchange rate with Sterling was approximately £1 = HK$12 to 13.

The Chinese currency is known as the **Renminbi** (meaning People's currency), and is denominated in **Yuan**. The symbols **RMB** and **Y** are used interchangeably. During 1987-8 the exchange rate was HK$1 = Y 0.476 (US$1 = RMB3.722). The RMB was devalued in December 1989 to HK$1 = Y 0.605 (US$1 = RMB4.722). Renminbi are not normally convertible, and foreigners exchanging foreign currency have been given Foreign Exchange Certificates (FECs), denominated in Yuan at a one-to-one exchange rate with the RMB. There has been a black market both in foreign exchange and in FECs, and foreign companies in China also have been given official opportunities to trade in foreign exchange and RMB at semi-free exchange rates.

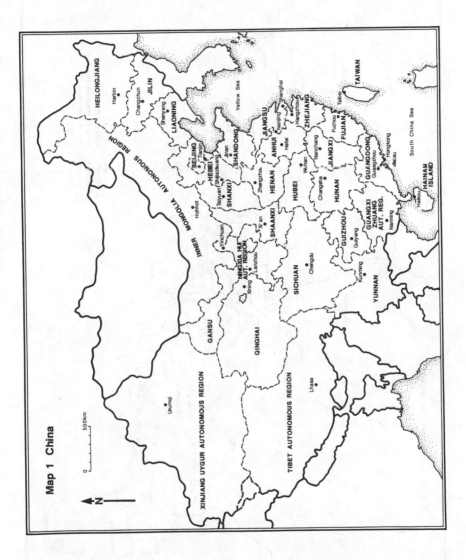

Map 1 China

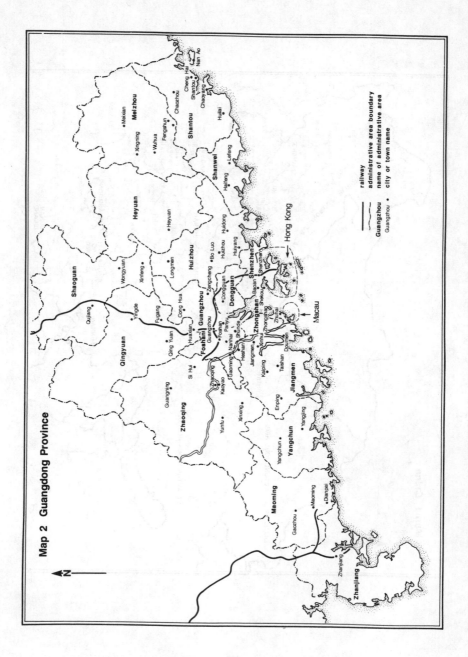

Map 2 Guangdong Province

1 Introduction

1.1 Hong Kong firms in the Pearl River Delta

Since the start of China's process of economic reform and "opening" to the outside world in the late 1970s, the attracting of foreign direct investment into China has been heavily stressed by the Chinese. This has been seen not only as a method of supplementing domestic savings, but as a means of introducing more advanced technology and management techniques into the economy.

Rather than coming from Western industrial countries, nearly two-thirds of inward direct investment has been made by companies from Hong Kong (1). Of the total inflow of foreign investment into China, as Table 1.1 shows, over a third of the realized amount has flowed into Guangdong province -- more than has been received by Beijing and Shanghai combined. China's Special Economic Zones, three of which (Shenzhen, Zhuhai and Shantou) are in Guangdong, have received the most attention overseas and are often perceived as spearheading China's drive for foreign investment. In fact, much investment has been located outside the SEZs, and particularly in the Pearl River (or "Zhujiang") Delta region of Guangdong, the economic core of the province which lies immediately adjacent to Hong Kong (2) . This Delta region has been one of the most rapidly expanding areas of the country, its combined agricultural and industrial annual growth averaging over 18% during the period 1981-6, higher than the provincial average of nearly 14%, and nearly double that of China as a whole (3). Given that China's average annual growth rate in Gross National Product over the 1981-88 period of almost 10% was one of the fastest in the world, the growth of the Delta and of Guangdong province more generally was remarkable. By 1988, however, severe strains were developing in many parts of China in the form of transport bottlenecks, power shortages, inflationary pressure and balance of trade deficits. This prompted the central government in the autumn of 1988 to introduce a set of austerity measures, especially a very tight credit policy. These measures were not in operation at the time of our research, and discussion of their effects is left to Chapter Seven.

For Hong Kong firms, the opening of Guangdong and Fujian provinces in 1979 under a special policy more liberal than that for the rest of the country offered an opportunity for investment in a culturally familiar area and one with which extensive kinship links had been maintained. This was particularly so for Guangdong, where the main language, Cantonese, is also that of most people in Hong Kong. The return of Hong Kong to Chinese jurisdiction in 1997 also has been an incentive for some businessmen from Hong Kong to try to improve their contacts with, and involvement in, China.

Hong Kong investment in China has been in the same labour-intensive industries such as textiles and clothing, electronic products, and plastics, as comprise most of Hong Kong's exports. As a tightening labour market has raised wage costs in Hong Kong and as economic expansion has made factory sites more and more expensive, the attraction of moving production to China, where wages are less than 20% of the Hong Kong level, is clear. According to the Address by the Governor of Hong Kong, Sir David Wilson, at the opening of the 1988-9 Session of the Legislative Assembly, there were between 1.5 and 2 million workers in Guangdong employed in factories either owned by, or working for Hong Kong companies, a total roughly double the manufacturing workforce of Hong Kong itself. Investment has been mainly in industry, as Table 1.2 shows, and trade and services investment was much more important in the early years of the Open Policy than subsequently.

Besides giving to foreign investors the same sort of tax concessions as those given by many Third World countries, China has been unusually flexible in the choice of investment arrangements it offers. These range from contracts for the processing of imported materials for re-export, through to several kinds of joint ventures and (sometimes) 100% foreign ownership. Tax and other incentives differ between different areas in China, but in practice, the attitudes of local officials have been as important a factor in Hong Kong businessmen's decision on where to invest. Despite the more favourable tax treatment offered by the SEZs, Hong Kong firms have been attracted to such areas as Dongguan and Shunde in the Pearl River Delta, which are noted for their helpful and unbureaucratic approach. Rising wages in Shenzhen (immediately bordering on Hong Kong) and other SEZs have also been a factor pushing Hong Kong firms to these other locations, where agricultural reform in the early years of the open policy released labour for industrial work. As wages have been pushed up in these areas too by domestic economic expansion and inward investment, the simpler processing and assembly operations have moved further afield in the province to less developed areas, and joint venture investment has become more important in the well-established locations. At the same time, as many as a million guest workers from other provinces were thought to have been in Guangdong by the end of 1987, attracted by the province's employment prospects.

Since 1985, the Pearl River Delta has been designated as one of three large special open regions, along with the Minnan Delta in Fujian and the Changjiang (Yangtze) Delta, which are able to offer investment incentives similar to those of the fourteen open coastal cities. These cities, which include Guangzhou (which, like the SEZs, is administered separately from the Delta Open Zone), were designated in 1984, and are

2

able to offer special concessions to investors, though still not as generous as those of the SEZs. (4) Within the Pearl River Delta, as between the regions of China, there is great competition for foreign investment, and this reflects the growth in the autonomy of local authorities during the course of the reforms. The Pearl River Delta Open Zone, as Table 1.3 shows, although having had only 16% of Guangdong province's population in 1986, generated a third of its industrial output and half of its fees from processing and assembly and compensation trade.

In spite of the many statements by Chinese leaders encouraging foreign investment, and of real improvements in investment conditions following the October 1986 Provisions for the Encouragement of Foreign Investment, China in recent years has been widely perceived as having a poor investment climate. This springs not only from uncertainty about the continuation of the Open Policy, given that there were struggles between reformers and conservatives for most of the 1980s, well before the 4th June events, but also from information released about foreign investment performance. For example, in 1987, the Chinese government conceded that only a third of the joint ventures started since 1979 were making profits (see Far Eastern Economic Review, 24 March 1988). There are also many stories in the press of the difficulties faced by foreign companies in China. Yet many Hong Kong companies in the Pearl River Delta are successful. By considering the difficulties they have faced, and how they have overcome them, lessons can be drawn for other investors. Where difficulties persist, and where even Hong Kong investors with their strong local contacts and special understanding of China cannot solve them, lessons can also be had by the Chinese themselves about how to encourage foreign investment effectively.

This study is mainly concerned with drawing lessons from the experience of Hong Kong companies in the Delta from the viewpoint of prospective foreign investors, and what the Chinese must do to attract them. However, a wider perspective would lead us to hope that the study also would help us to understand foreign investment as a process in relation to the internationalization of production, and to the emergence of multinational companies from newly industrializing companies. It is necessary also to consider the motivation of the host economy in attracting foreign investment, and the gains that can be realized. In this regard, policies to attract investors, such as tax concessions, may be at variance with policies to increase the gains the host economy can realize over and above those accruing through the operation of market forces; and a delicate balancing act may be necessary between the two sets of policies. Also, since foreign investment into China has been attracted usually by Chinese companies and local authorities who wish to work in partnership with foreign firms, not by the national government, possible conflicts between the interests of the host partners and those of the host nation should be considered. Also, of course, there are the interests of the home country, Hong Kong. These issues are discussed further in the next chapter. Chapters Three, Four and Five present the basic interview material, collected in late 1987. Chapter Six looks at the investment "climate" of the Delta, laying especial stress on competition between different localities for foreign investment. Chapter Seven draws conclusions, and attempts to assess how things have changed since the 4th June 1989 events, and in the light of the 1988-90 austerity measures.

1.2 The interviewing programme and the sample

This study is based on interviews with Hong Kong companies operating in the Pearl River Delta. The interviewing programme was carried out during the autumn of 1987. The places visited were -

Guangzhou (5)
Dongguan
Baoan
Panyu
Foshan
Shunde
Zhong Shan
Xin Hui
Nanhai
Jiangmen
Taishan
Bo Luo

The programme involved visits to over sixty companies, which yielded about fifty "usable" interviews. The remainder were generally very short visits, or visits to groups of companies in processing and assembly complexes for example, which, though they often produced some points of interest, do not merit being singled out as well-rounded examples of the foreign investment process. In each location the officials concerned with foreign investment were interviewed, and wherever a Hong Kong representative was present in the companies he or she was interviewed as well as the Chinese managers. In selected cases attempts were made to follow up the interviews with visits to the parents in Hong Kong, but this proved more difficult than arranging interviews in China.

Given there were thought at the time to be some 8300 factories in Guangdong working for Hong Kong companies, and another 2000 where Hong Kong companies were directly involved (see Hang Seng Bank, 1987), the sample is small in terms of the total population. More important, the study suffers from the difficulties of obtaining a truly random sample of companies in China. A researcher simply selecting potential interviewees at random from a list of foreign investors is likely to find that the response rate among the chosen companies is very low. Interviews, in practice, have to be prepared in advance through personal contacts, especially with local officials in each area, and several companies may have to be tried before willing interviewees are found. In this, our Zhong Shan University collaborators provided vital help, sending research students to each area a week or so ahead to prepare the ground, and chosing as far as possible students whose home area was in the location to be visited.

In the light of these difficulties, we attempted to stratify the sample to get a coverage of typical Hong Kong industries, and to get a representative selection of projects in the different types of foreign investment contracts available in China, which are discussed in the next chapter. However, it was not possible to stratify the sample so as to replicate the proportion of particular industries in Hong Kong exports or by their importance in different types of contract; and we cannot claim statistical significance for any quantitative results.

Table 1.4 shows the industrial coverage of the sample, also classified by type of contract. The "other" category in the table refers to a number of special cases such as a state company actively

looking for a foreign partner, a joint venture where the "Hong Kong" partner was actually a mainland Chinese-owned enterprise operating in Hong Kong, and a company in receipt of a foreign exchange loan from the Bank of China which is then classified as "foreign investment". In addition, the locations listed above represent areas corresponding to what Vogel (1989, pp.192-5) subsequently has described as representing the "three tiers" of development in the Pearl River Delta:
- areas near to Hong Kong and mainly involved in processing and assembly (Dongguan, Baoan, Panyu)
- more industrialized areas closer to Guangzhou (Foshan, Shunde, Zhong Shan, Xinhui, and Nanhai), and Guangzhou itself
- and more remote areas (Jiangmen, Taishan), distant from both Hong Kong and Guangzhou. Bo Luo is also included, which became part of the Delta after the December 1987 boundary changes (see Table 1.3).

The interviewing method did not involve the use of a detailed questionnaire. Although the analysis of foreign investment in terms of location-specific, firm-specific and internalization advantages, derived from the work of Dunning (e.g. Dunning, 1985) and used in the work on foreign investment by Hong Kong companies by Chen (1983), to be discussed in the next chapter, is illuminating as a starting point, it was decided that not enough is known about the experience of foreign companies in China to identify in advance all the promising areas of enquiry in order to formulate a questionnaire. In particular, the economic reform process in China greatly complicates the analysis. The reforms can be expected to condition the way foreign investors can operate, and the experience of investors indeed may help us better to understand the reforms (6). "Open-ended" interviews in general seemed preferable as a means of exploring the issues, rather than ones restricted by a given set of questions. Instead of a questionnaire, therefore, a guided interview schedule was used, to elicit major pieces of factual information about a company's operations and experience, but the interviews were allowed to develop in their own way so that leads into areas of interest to the particular interviewee could be followed as far as possible. Thus one company might provide most information about its efforts to reform labour practices, another might discuss problems in its relations with local authorities, and another concentrate on the distribution of foreign exchange earnings. Inevitably, some interviewees were much more helpful than others, and allowed us to check our understanding of a wide variety of issues with them.

This method of handling a research topic where not enough is known in advance to formulate all the relevant questions has gained growing acceptance in areas of social research and in business. Such **qualitative** research has the aim, ultimately, of forming new theory which is "grounded" in observation (7); but our more immediate aim here is to gain a deeper understanding of the foreign investment process.

NOTES

1. Many difficulties arise in determining the share of Hong Kong investors in total foreign investment in China. Some Western, Japanese, and Taiwanese companies operate through Hong Kong offices. Various mainland companies, especially from Guangdong, have set up Hong Kong offices and become the "foreign" partner in joint ventures in China. Pomfret's (1989) useful review of the foreign investment statistics also gives evidence of much

5

carelessness in recording nationalities of foreign investors. Nevertheless, there can be little doubt that Hong Kong investors provide the bulk of foreign investment in China. For Guangdong, the Guangdong Statistical Yearbooks give Hong Kong and Macau as the source of 73% of the province's actual capital inflow in 1987 and 63% in 1988, although this is in regard to a total inflow of which loans were 44% and direct foreign investments of the various kinds were 56% in 1987, and 50% each in 1988. For China, the Alamanacs of China's Foreign Economic Relations and Trade give the Hong Kong share of the foreign investment inflow (i.e.excluding loans) as 68% of the actual inflow for 1987 and 64% for 1988. The Macau share, now separately shown, was almost negligible.

2. The other SEZ is Xiamen, in Fujian province, immediately north of Guangdong. Hainan Island, in the far south, has been designated as a SEZ too. For a discussion of the SEZs see Thoburn (1986). To get a sense of the importance to Guangdong of investment outside the SEZs, note that the cities in which the three Guangdong SEZs are situated received only 43.9% of the province's actual total foreign capital inflow (i.e.including loans) in 1987 and 31.3% in 1988 (Guangdong Statistical Yearbook, 1988 and 1989). The four original SEZs received 28.8% of the contracted and 24.6% of the realized foreign direct investment in China over the 1979-1988 period (Beijing Review, 6-12 March, 1989). These can be compared to the figures for the share of Guangdong in Table 1.1.

3. See T.M.H. Chan (1988, p42). Another good source on the Guangdong economy, especially on its past development, is Nolan (1983). Since the first draft of the present book was prepared, there has appeared Ezra Vogel's superb study of the province under reform (Vogel, 1989), which fills in many details of places, personalities and local events. Forestier's (1989) American Chamber of Commerce guide to doing business in Guangdong also contains much useful information.

4. In fact, more and more areas were being designated as "open", as the ten coastal provinces of China were being used as the spearhead for export-orientated industrialization. For example, as of May 1988, the number of cities and counties which had been declared "open" in some sense, had risen to 288 (see South China Morning Post, 16 May 1988). In 1988,too, two more Open Zones were declared in Guangdong, covering the entire coastal area - the Han Delta Zone in the north-east, and the Jian Delta Zone in the south-west around Zhanjiang (Forestier, 1989,p.14). The Liaodong and Shandong Peninsulas in northern China have also been designated as "special open areas". In 1989 and 1990 there were signs that the favourable treatment of coastal areas was being reversed, however (see Chapter Seven).

5. Strictly speaking, Guangzhou is administered separately as a "province" in its own right, and is therefore not part of the Pearl River Delta Open Zone (see T.M.H. Chan 1988, p7). However, we felt it would provide an interesting point of comparison. There is no overall administration of the Pearl Delta Zone, unlike an SEZ, and decisions are made at the appropriate administrative level (see Forestier,1989,pp.14-15).

6. For recently published discussions of the reforms see Feuchtwang, Hussain and Pairault (1988), Perkins (1988), Riskin (1987) and Chai and Leung (1987). Perry and Wong (1985) is also still very useful. A particularly interesting work on the reforms is Reynolds (1987), which presents material based on large scale

surveys conducted by the Economic System Reform Institute of China, under the Economic Reform Commission.

7.   See Walker (1985) for an introduction to the ideas of qualitative research and "grounded theory". For an application of this to business problems see Miles (1987).

Table 1.1

Foreign Investment in Guangdong Province and China, 1979-88

(US$10,000)	1979-82	1983	1984	1985	1986	1987	1988	1979-88
China								
- contract amount	495800	191690	287494	633321	333037	431912	619072	$29.9bil
- actual amount	176900	91596	141885	195615	224373	264661	373966	$14.7bil
Guangdong								
- contract amount	481658	73557	158795	235087	117764	157634	269821	$14.9bil
	(97.1)	(38.4)	(55.2)	(37.1)	(35.4)	(36.5)	(43.6)	(49.9)
- actual amount	83983	40003	64942	65131	81280	73687	125106	$5.3bil
	(47.5)	(43.7)	(45.8)	(33.3)	(36.2)	(27.8)	(33.5)	(36.4)

Notes: Bracketed figures are percentages of respective amount in China. Foreign Investment
includes "direct foreign investment" (equity joint venture, cooperative joint venture,
and 100% foreign venture investment) and "commodity credit" (compensation trade
ventures, the value of equipment introduced under processing and assembly arrangements,
and a negligible amount of international leasing.)

Sources: Guangdong Statistical Yearbook, 1984, 1985, 1986, 1987,1988,1989
China Statistical Yearbook, 1986
Almanac of China's Foreign Economic Relations & Trade,
1987,1988,1989

8

Table 1.2
Distribution of Foreign Capital Inflow into Selected Economic
Sectors in Guangdong

(percentages of actual amounts)

	1979-82	1983	1984	1985	1986	1987	1988
Agriculture	4.3	3.0	1.3	2.9	4.5	3.8	3.4
Industry	47.9	48.2	37.7	59.9	67.4	69.0	66.4
Trade, restaurant and services	42.3	24.3	9.0	4.0	5.0	0.7	0.5
Property, public utilities and services	NA	NA	NA	23.3	14.9	6.7	4.7

Notes: The totals on which these percentages are calculated include
foreign loans. The "foreign investment" figures of Table 1.1
represented 56% of these totals in 1987, and 50% in 1988, in
terms of actual amounts.

Source: Guangdong Statistical Yearbook, 1984,1985,1986,1987,1988,1989

Table 1.3
The Pearl River Delta Open Zone in the Economy of Guangdong

Items as percentages of the provincial total

	1986	1987
Population	16.2%	27.0%
Land Area	10.8%	24.9%
Industrial Output	33.9%	40.1%
Foreign Exchange Earnings	27.8%	26.5% (sic)

- Fees from Processing
    & Assembly and
    Compensation Trade
	50.8%	NA

"Township Enterprises" Earnings	50.0%	58.3%

Notes: As of 1985 the Pearl River Delta Open Zone consisted of: Foshan City (with the counties of Nanhai, Gaoming, and Shunde, and Zhong Shan City, under its jurisdiction); Jiangmen City (with its counties of Kaiping, Enping, Taishan, Xinhui, and Heshan); Baoan county in Shenzhen City (but outside the Shenzhen SEZ); Doumen county in Zhuhai City; and Dongguan City, Panyu county, and Zencheng county. In 1986 it was extended slightly, and extended again in December 1987.

Source: Guangdong Statistical Yearbook,1987 and 1988

Table 1.4
Industrial Coverage of the Sample

	Equity Joint Ventures	Cooperative Joint Ventures	Processing and Assembly	Compensation Trade	Other
Footwear	4	1			
Textiles & Clothing	3	3	7	1	
Food & Drink	3	3		1	
Metal Products	2	1	1		
Electronics & Electrical	1	1	2		1
Plastics			1		
Toys			1		
Printing			1		
Services	2	3			1
Other					
- stone cutting	1	1			
- polythene bags		1			
- jewellery		1			
- ceramics					1
Total	17	15	13	2	3

11

2 Foreign investment in China: investor and host country motivations

2.1 Hong Kong firms and the internationalization of production

The internationalization of production among Western multinational enterprises is well-researched (see, for example, Caves, 1982; Jenkins, 1987). Of special interest for present purposes is the particular kind of vertical investment involving world-wide sourcing - the relocation overseas of subprocesses of production within a vertically integrated production chain. The pioneering work in this area, the study of the West German textile and garment industries by Fröbel, Heinrichs and Kreye (1980), argued that relocation overseas to Third World production sites was the result of rising domestic costs (especially wage costs) and intensified competition once the relocation process got underway. It was facilitated by developments in transport and communication, and also by special incentives in the form of low taxes and subsidized infrastructure in the host countries. Ozawa's (1979) work shows a similar process in various Japanese industries, hastened also by the wish to avoid controls on pollution; and in Japan, as in Germany, small and medium-sized companies were involved too (1).

The activities of Third World multinationals have been the subject of much interest (see particularly Wells, 1983; Kumar and McLeod, 1981; and Lall, 1983), and they include many companies from Hong Kong. Studies of outward investment from Hong Kong in the late 1970s and early 1980s by E.K.Y. Chen (1981 and 1983), based on interviews with the head offices of Hong Kong multinationals, provide a very useful source of information on the motivation of Hong Kong investors, and a background against which the present study can be set.

Although there has been a growing amount of Hong Kong investment in developed countries, sometimes in search of a "backflow" of advanced technology to Hong Kong, the bulk has been in Asia, particularly in Indonesia, Malaysia, Taiwan and Singapore, as well as China. Except for Indonesia, where the investment has been designed to serve the Indonesian domestic market, most of the investment has been prompted by a desire to find lower cost export bases. The desire to avoid quantitative restrictions, especially into the US market, has sometimes also been an incentive. The investment mostly has been "horizontal" (i.e. in broadly similar products to those produced in Hong Kong, though usually simpler ones). Chen suggests that Hong Kong investment in China differs from Hong Kong investment in other Asian countries in that only the labour-intensive stages were transferred to China from Hong Kong, rather than the production of the whole products, possibly reflecting a belief that China lacked the necessary technical and skill level to produce the complete product (Chen, 1983, p.112).

Chen's work explicitly uses the eclectic framework developed by Dunning (see e.g. Dunning 1985), which centres on the distinction between:

- location-specific advantages
- firm-specific advantages
- internalization advantages

to analyse the rationale for, and operation of multinational companies. Thus, the desire of a firm to operate outside of its country of origin implies that the location of its proposed investment has certain advantages (i.e. locational advantages) over its home base. These advantages may include:

- low wages in relation to labour productivity
- a stable (or more stable) political climate
- proximity to markets or to raw materials
- preferential tax treatment and other investment incentives

In these circumstances, why do not local firms in the host country market compete? The standard answer is that the multinational firm has its own advantages, usually based on the possession of exclusive technical information (developed by expenditure on R & D) or management skills, to which competitors do not have access (i.e. its firm-specific advantages). Since the firm's knowledge could in principle be transferred to a host country firm by means of a licencing arrangement for a fee, some explanation is also needed of why the foreign company chooses to undertake the production abroad itself, thus internalizing the organization of production in the different countries (Hennert, 1986). More generally, internalization has to be considered as part of a wider concern with the reducing of transactions costs by different ways of organizing a firm's activities (Leung et al, 1989).

The problem is explaining the existence of multinationals from Third World (mainly newly industrializing) countries, is that such firms are unlikely to possess the sort of firm-specific advantages on which the power of American or European firms is based, namely the monopoly of technical knowledge to engage in large scale production, or the possession of marketing power to sell differentiated, branded goods world-wide. The Third World MNCs are typically much smaller, and their advantage lies in their ability to undertake more labour-intensive tasks, often requiring labour and management skills, which give them a limited but distinct on prospective host country rivals.

In Chen's work, among the locational factors pushing Hong Kong companies abroad were high wages and, also, the sheer difficulty of recruiting unskilled workers at all in the face of the Hong Kong labour shortage. These apply even more strongly today, as does the cost or rental of factory sites. Thus China still exerts its locational advantages by having wages typically 20% or less of the Hong Kong level. Agricultural reforms have revealed the underlying labour surplus in the Chinese countryside. In the Pearl River Delta, our interviews with officials suggest, the mopping up of surplus labour was an important incentive for many localities to seek foreign investment in the early years of the "open policy". Other locational advantages of Guangdong include the common language, Cantonese; and the proximity to Hong Kong, which has often led investors to prefer places with easy access to local ports in the Delta.

In Chen's sample of 32 Hong Kong outward direct investors, the firms were large in their industries (typically with employment of 500-2000) and long-established. The industries involved - textiles, garments, electronics, electrical goods, metal, plastics and toys - mostly have mature technologies. All these industries are represented in China today. Although the firms engaged in a substantial amount of technological innovation and adaptation, they saw their firm-specific advantages as being in managerial and marketing skills, rather than production or technical knowhow. (2) These issues of firm-specific advantage are taken up again in the next section.

More recent information on the extent of Hong Kong outward investment into China is available from a sample survey in 1987 by V.F.S. Sit of nearly 300 "small and medium" size manufacturing firms (see Sit, 1989). Such firms, defined as employing under 200 workers, account for nearly three quarters of Hong Kong's manufacturing employment and two thirds of its manufacturing value-added. Of the sample small-medium companies, 18% had "outprocessing" facilities in China, defined as virtually any kind of investment or subcontracting relation, and two thirds of these companies said they had been motivated by lower wage levels in China to enter into the arrangement. In a smaller sample of 24 larger firms which subcontracted within Hong Kong to small-medium firms, 70% also had outprocessing in China, and nearly half of a sample of 31 Hong Kong/foreign joint ventures in Hong Kong had them too. Sit's study found the industries most heavily represented in the small-medium firms' outprocessing were (in order) garments, plastics, textiles, electronics, and precision equipment. Garments and textiles were inhibited in their moves to China by the need to preserve minimum proportions of value-added generated in Hong Kong to meet American "country-of-origin" import restrictions, but other industries were encouraged to go into China by the fact that China still had preferential entry into the U.S. under the Generalized System of Preferences, whereas Hong Kong had lost these privileges after January, 1988. Of the small-medium firms with outprocessing in China, nearly half said that the Chinese operation generated over half of their total output.

2.2 **The value of Hong Kong investment to the Chinese**

A convenient starting point is to ask what Hong Kong firms have to offer the Chinese. Almost thirty years of being closed to the outside world under the policy of self-reliance had left China in the late 1970s technologically backward in many areas. Emphasis on heavy industry to the neglect of all but the most basic consumer goods had made this backwardness very marked in the area of light industrial goods. Whereas agricultural reform has been primarily a domestic affair, industrial reform has been seen as requiring the importation of

14

foreign technology.

"Attract foreign investment, introduce advanced technology" (xiyin waizi, yinjin xianjin jishu) is a slogan appearing in almost all Chinese writing on industrial reform. Most of the technology imported through direct investment by Hong Kong companies has not been of a particularly advanced kind, however. The basic technology used in much of the manufacture of garments and footwear in Hong Kong, for example, is quite simple, albeit more advanced than found in those industries in China in the late 1970s. This technology is quite appropriate to Chinese conditions, particularly in the Pearl River Delta, where much industrialization has been centred on towns and villages in predominantly rural areas. Agricultural reform, which has proceeded mainly in terms of improved organization and incentives (with families under the production responsibility system able to lease land, buy equipment and sell much of their production) has resulted in large increases in output, especially of cash crops. These have found a ready market in nearby urban areas, and rural incomes have greatly increased. There has been a surplus for accumulation, which has not been creamed off by higher levels of authority, and a large reduction in agricultural labour requirements. Investment in labour-intensive industries has been an attractive proposition.

Not only is the technology used by Hong Kong investors in China often fairly simple, but it is available on the international market in the sense of being embodied in machinery which can be purchased by anyone with the requisite foreign exchange. In footwear, out of a range of techniques available on the world market, equipment from Taiwan has been developed for use in relatively labour-abundant conditions. For many garment making firms, most of the equipment simply consists of basic sewing machines. This contrasts with the situation where really advanced technology is required, which may be monopolized by particular multinational companies. Countries wanting such technology may only be able to obtain it as part of a "package", where the foreign company undertakes direct investment in China.

For light industrial investment, then, why do the Chinese simply not do the job themselves - buy the equipment on the world market, hire the short-term services of foreign technicians, and, if necessary, borrow the foreign exchange commercially?

There are several strands to the explanation:

-- first, after such a long period of being closed to the outside world China lacks both marketing expertise and a knowledge of foreign consumer tastes and quality requirements. To generate foreign exchange, either directly to finance imports of capital goods or to service foreign borrowing, the use of the Western-style marketing expertise to be found in Hong Kong is very attractive. Many Hong Kong companies can not only provide design and quality control, but also feed the output into an established customer network.

-- second, evidence suggests that the transfer of technology to China cannot simply be achieved by the installation of foreign equipment. In the early stages of reform, the same equipment in China with the same workforce as in Hong Kong or Taiwan might produce a quarter of the output. Where organizational reform and the effective provision of incentives for the workforce do not accompany the new equipment, lack of work input, wastage of raw materials, and poor maintenance will reduce labour productivity. Of course, not all the additional changes

pag 60

required are at the enterprise level. Materials supplies, and the provision of water and electricity may also be such as to reduce productivity.(3) What Hong Kong firms can offer is experience in handling labour-intensive operations with technologies that often have had twenty years or so during which improvements could be made and difficulties ironed out. Whether the Hong Kong firm can bring about the required organizational changes within the company depends much on the attitude of the Chinese partner (given that wholly Hong Kong firms are often in a better position by virtue of their cultural and linguistic familiarity with China than would be a Western company). The use of a foreign partner also provides for an enterprise better access to foreign raw material inputs, which may avoid domestic supply constraints and which are sometimes essential to achieving high enough quality for export. (4)

-- third, a major aspect of the economic changes over the past ten years has been a growing autonomy for local authorities (see Perry and Wong, 1985, chap 10). Whereas nationally run state companies may have access to foreign exchange and to the information required to buy equipment overseas, township or village-level authorities in Guangdong may choose to rely on their own personal contacts in Hong Kong, who are often relatives, to provide access to the outside world.

2.3 Types of contract

Before going on to look further at the benefits which the Chinese may obtain from foreign investment, it is necessary to consider the very wide range of contractual arrangements which are on offer in China to prospective investors. These are:

1. 100% Foreign Owned Ventures (duzi jingying)
2. Equity Joint Ventures (where some contributions are allowed from the Chinese side in kind, however) (hezi jingying)
3. Cooperative (or 'contractual') Joint Ventures (where the Chinese contribution is mainly in kind, normally land and buildings). (hezuo jingying)
4. Processing and assembly arrangements (for which fees are charged).
5. Compensation trade (where the foreign side supplies machinery and equipment, and is repaid in installments of the product). (buchang maoyi)

Table 2.1 gives statistics for these various categories for China, and for Guangdong province in comparison, both in terms of the amount of investment contracted. Table 2.2. shows their relative importance in terms of the amount of investment which has actually taken place, following the contracts.

100% foreign ventures were rare until 1988. They have been restricted to "advanced technology" and "export oriented" projects, and until 1986 they were to be found only in the Special Economic Zones in Guangdong and Fujian, and in Shanghai. In Guangdong they declined in relative importance over the 1979-86 period, and in the province, outside the SEZs, they were of little importance. However, one consequence of the credit restrictions introduced in autumn 1988 by the central government has been to make prospective Chinese partners in joint ventures very short of funds. To overcome this difficulty, the government has been trying to encourage 100% foreign ventures. As Tables

16

2.1 and 2.2 show, they have grown in importance somewhat, especially in terms of pledged investment, both in China and in Guangdong, although the Guangdong figures, it will be remembered, include the Special Economic Zones

Equity joint ventures have increased greatly in importance since the early years, rising from a mere 112 ventures in September 1983 to 2300 by 1985. They are the only form of foreign investment in China for which a (relatively) clear and detailed legal framework exists. (5) This is based on the Joint Venture Law of 1979 and elaborated in various pieces of enabling legislation, particularly the 1983 Implementation Act, which did much to encourage joint venture investment after a slow start. Foreign partners must contribute a minimum of 25% of the equity, and most contracts are for ten to twenty years. (6)

Although, as Table 2.1 shows, equity joint ventures by 1986 were contributing the largest amount of contracted investment of all the categories for China as a whole, cooperative joint ventures have been almost of equal importance in terms of investment utilized. For Guangdong province, however, cooperative (or 'contractual') joint ventures were of much greater relative importance than for China as a whole, as shown in Table 2.2. The cooperative joint venture contract is exceptionally flexible. On the one hand, it can range from an arrangement where the Chinese side contributes only nominally, leaving the foreign partner the opportunity to run a virtually 100% foreign venture, but without the constraint of the normal ten year limit on such operations. On the other hand, it can be extremely short term. For example, over (say) a five year contract period the foreign partner can receive repayment of his initial investment as a prior claim before the distribution of profits, an arrangement not far removed from compensation trade. Unlike an equity joint venture, the profit shares between the partners need not be in the same proportions as the equity contributions, and can vary over the contract's life. For the Chinese partner, no financial contribuion or foreign exchange is required, an attractive feature for a local authority investment vehicle in the early stages of cooperation with foreigners. There is also the flexibility that approval for a project can be given at a much lower level of authority than, for example, for a 100% foreign venture. All this flexibility has contributed much to the attractiveness of cooperative joint ventures, but there are some corresponding drawbacks. Compared to an equity joint venture, they have less freedom of action in practice, particularly with regard to the freedom to import inputs and to retain foreign exchange. In addition, the legal position of these ventures has been unclear. The Cooperative Joint Venture Law was not published until early in 1988, and still requires implementing legislation. In practice some such ventures have been treated as equity joint ventures - those with a legal entity are treated for tax purposes under the Joint Venture Law whereas partnerships are given the same tax treatment (under the Foreign Enterprise Income Tax Law) as 100% foreign companies as far as the foreign partner is concerned.

Wholly foreign ventures, and equity and cooperative joint ventures are referred to collectively by the Chinese as san ci ventures, san ci literally meaning "three (kinds of) investment". The remaining arrangements are known collectively as san lai yi bu; the yi (one) bu refers to the one kind of compensation trade and san (three) lai refers to the three kinds of processing and assembly contracts, of which lai liao jia gong ("bringing materials for processing" - and hereinafter LLJG is the most common). (7)

17

Compensation trade was of declining importance as far as the foreign capital actually used in Guangdong is concerned to 1986, as Table 2.2 shows, but it has picked up again in 1987 and 1988. It has been a useful way for China to acquire foreign equipment, and it has the advantage that the foreign supplier has an incentive to ensure that the Chinese recipient succeeds in making a product of acceptable quality for repayment in kind, which is particularly important given recurring Chinese problems with quality control. The foreign supplier has no interest, however, in ensuring the profitability of the Chinese operation. Compensation trade in practice is often combined with, and sometimes precedes, other arrangements.

Processing and assembly arrangements were one of the earliest forms of cooperation between Hong Kong and China. LLJG contracts are recorded in Shunde county in Guangdong before the setting up of the Special Economic Zones. The SEZs were often reluctant to accept this kind of contract, seeing it as not sufficiently "advanced", and this gave an opportunity for areas outside the SEZs to attract foreign investment. Dongguan, reputed to have one of the best investment climates in the Delta, before the Open Policy was an area known mainly for its bananas and lychees. By attracting Hong Kong investment, not least by its use of "one stop" facilities to reduce bureaucracy, it has grown in importance and has been redesignated from a xian (county) to a municipality in its own right.

LLJG contracts cover a wide range of operations. They include contracts where existing Chinese state or collective enterprises do short term contract work for Hong Kong, alongside supplying the domestic market and sometimes exporting directly. In other cases a processing and assembly operation may be initiated by the Hong Kong side on a new site - various areas in the Dongguan City administrative region, for example, actually keep a range of newly constructed factory buildings for this purpose so as to speed the introduction of new investments. Normally the Hong Kong partner will bring equipment into China, which in principle can be removed at the end of the contract. The processing fee covers the variable cost of the operation, except for the materials, which the Hong Kong partner imports. In such ventures, all output must be exported. Where the venture wishes to sell domestically, there is an incentive to move to a joint venture, usually a cooperative one for a small operation.

The choice of contract basically gives the foreign investor a choice about the degree of involvement. Even within LLJG, arrangements can vary between a Chinese company simply doing orders on contract with materials supplied by the Hong Kong side; and one where the Hong Kong side exercises a good deal of supervision and control, such that the work is to a large extent "internalized" within the Hong Kong enterprise. Joint venture contracts offer still greater scope for control and internalization, but require more input of finance and time. Sometimes joint ventures grow out of LLJG. The relation between internalization, choice of contract, and the theory of transactions costs is developed in our paper Leung et al (1989).

Table 2.3 shows the very large variation in the average size of contract as between the different types. It is noticeable that cooperative joint ventures in Guangdong, and in China as a whole, have been larger than equity joint ventures, possibly reflecting the fact that many are de facto 100% foreign ventures, although Pomfret suggests the figures are increased by the inclusion of a few large mining ventures using cooperative joint venture contracts (Pomfret,1989,pp.43-44). He also puts forward the idea that the 1986 Provisions to encourage foreign investment may have encouraged particularly the smaller, more export-orientated type of equity joint venture, which accounts for some declines in their average size, and that the distribution of equity joint ventures is bipolar with some very large projects and many much smaller ones (Pomfret, 1989,p.44, citing Campbell and Adlington,1988,p144).

2.4 Benefits for Chinese local authorities, enterprises, and the Chinese economy

Given the wide choice of contract, a variety of motivations can be accommodated on the part of the partners. These range from existing enterprises wishing to update their technology or gain foreign market access, to local authorities trying to develop their area with new companies. Since foreign-invested operations enjoy considerably more freedom of action than domestic enterprises, there is sometimes an element of rent-seeking present on the side of the Chinese partner, so that benefits to an enterprise are not necessarily benefits to the Chinese nation.

2.4.1 Ventures with Chinese local authorities

In the early years of cooperation between Hong Kong and China, and today too some extent, lai liao jia gong contracts offered many advantages to county, town, and village governments. The development could bring in capital and employ local workers. Often the investors were relatives of local people. The processing fee earned by the local authorities could be ploughed back into other investment and infrastructure, and the investors normally had no difficulty in exporting their output once quality control was achieved. The use of imported materials also meant that the local authorities did not have to worry about securing domestic supplies of raw materials. In the early years there were many problems of wastage of the raw materials, of poor quality and of unreliable delivery times, but these have grown less with experience.

A newer development, which has grown since the mid 1980s, has been the use of local authority investment companies, normally collectives, which can form cooperative or equity joint ventures with overseas partners. Sometimes these are existing companies, whose range of activities can be expanded. Where such a company was originally a state-run company it sometimes has been recognized to bring it more directly under local authority control, so as to prevent its foreign exchange earnings being syphoned upwards to higher levels of authority. Sometimes, however, provincial or national bodies (usually specialist trading corporations) join in as partners, in which case some of the foreign exchange does get syphoned upwards.

2.4.2 Ventures with state companies

Although state companies sometimes have LLJG arrangements with foreign partners, or use compensation trade, the most common arrangement is a joint venture of some sort. State companies, unlike collective enterprises, normally belong to a national hierarchy of command. They are often run in a bureaucratic fashion with a workforce of permanent workers, whom it is difficult to dismiss, whatever their performance. They are among the least reformed areas of the Chinese economy. For a reform-minded management, a foreign partnership greatly strengthens their ability not only to import foreign technology and find foreign marketing outlets, but also to introduce enterprise reform. All san ci ventures are supposed to be allowed to employ workers on contract, whose services can be dispensed with if they do not perform adequately, and local managers can learn about modern management techniques such as inventory control and accounting practices. If the Chinese company is not reform-minded, but simply wants the foreign exchange or the kudos of "following the open policy", problems can arise with the foreign partner if the partner wishes to introduce a Hong Kong (or Western) style of management. The greater freedom of joint ventures, especially equity joint ventures, is also a great attraction for state companies. This is particularly so with regard to the freedom to import and export. A joint venture can enjoy substantial tax holidays (8), and is legally separate from the original Chinese enterprise and that enterprise's parent body.

In some cases the Hong Kong partner may be a trading company in the product the Chinese partner produces, and is seeking a cheaper source of supply. In this case the Chinese side may have to handle the technology transfer itself, receiving only the foreign exchange from Hong Kong to import new equipment.

2.4.3 The benefits to the Chinese economy

The benefits to a host economy of attracting foreign investment in principle can be assessed in terms of widely accepted methods of social cost-benefit analysis, which stress the country's share of the real income (normally in terms of foreign exchange) generated by a project. This share is made up of payments to the country's factors of production, both directly and as embodied in purchased inputs, less the social opportunity cost in their best alternative use. (9) Where foreign investment activity is small (i.e. "marginal" to the economy) the gain from the investment inflow is the sum of that from individual projects; where it is not marginal, the effect of inward investment on key prices such as the wage level and the exchange rate would have to be estimated. The importation of improved technology would generate benefits directly through raising domestic factor incomes in foreign investment projects, and indirectly through diffusion effects.

The gains will be the greater if foreign investment projects generates "linkages" (raising the return on investment in other firms by buying domestic inputs, or supplying intermediate products to domestic users) and if they pay the maximum taxes consistent with leaving the foreign investor with an acceptable rate of return over the life of the project. (10) The generation of domestic employment opportunities also, of course, produces real income gains if there is an overall labour surplus in the economy.

The present project has not generated data to investigate these effects quantitatively. In any case, the situation is complicated by the wide variety of industries investing in the Delta from Hong Kong, each of which has different input-output relations and therefore somewhat different development effects.

Viewed in terms of existing theory, however, various reservations can be expressed about foreign investment in the Pearl River Delta. LLJG operations generate processing fees in foreign exchange for the services of local labour, supervision, water and power, and factory sites, but otherwise make no domestic purchases. Cases are known where the Chinese have reallocated workers trained by the Hong Kong side to

20

other enterprises, which does generate some techological spillover, but is understandably regarded by the foreign investor as unfair. Competition for processing income between different localities can drive down processing fees too, and the Dongguan City Office of Processing and Assembly, for example, tries to impose centralized approval of processing fees to prevent this.

Joint ventures too are often almost as unintegrated with the local economy as are the processing and assembly operations. Although they have the power to purchase local raw materials and intermediate products, these are often very difficult to obtain, or very expensive outside official allocations, or are of insufficient quality. Whether this lack of integration with the local economy is as undesirable as is sometimes argued (11) is, however, uncertain. The absence of dependence on local materials allows export-orientated ventures to expand without hindrance from domestic supply constraints; where domestic materials are genuinely in short supply their shadow prices would be high and their diversion to foreign firms would not necessarily be a social gain. Anyway, there is evidence that some joint ventures (12) are trying to develop domestic sources, to reduce costs and foreign exchange expenditure. Over time the degree of integration can increase.

The Chinese economy has many problems which spring from the partial nature of the reforms. While agriculture has been largely deregulated, the state industrial sector and the industrial labour market are still subject to many controls. Joint ventures allow firms, for example, to get export quotas which they could not secure as domestic enterprises. Whether such freedom is a spearheading of reform or a diversion from more appropriate action is not necessarily clear in many cases and raises all the issues of the economics of the second-best.

One very marked problem associated with industrialization centred on town and village level enterprises (xiangzhen qiye, or "township enterprises"), usually collectives (13), is that much of the income from joint ventures with them is kept at local level. While this provides great incentives for both local authorities to accommodate foreign investors, so that both sides make money, it does starve the central (and sometimes the provincial) government of funds for vital infrastructural investment. In fact, in the 1988-90 austerity programme, the central government has cut back sharply on the activities of such "rural" industry generally.

NOTES

1. More recent work has suggested that the process of internationalization may be reversible in some cases, as further technical change brings about another relocation, this time back to the home country. See Kaplinsky (1984).
2. Another early study of Hong Kong investment in China is Chai (1983). Based on a postal questionnaire to which 20 firms with investments in China (or other cooperation agreements such as processing and assembly) responded, Chai concluded that Hong Kong firms' were mainly motivated by the cost and accessibility advantages of China, and to a lesser extent by a wish to utilize existing capacity better or to gain better access to the Chinese market.
3. Differences in total factor productivity between similar plants in different countries has been the subject of some very interesting research by Pack (1987) for the World Bank. He tries

to decompose these differences into those arising from differences at task level, factory level, and the industry and national economy levels for plants in three countries in the textile industry.

4. Technology transfer by a foreign firm, then, can be in two senses. First, there is the ability of the foreign firm to utilize its firm-specific advantage effectively in China. In other words, to transfer its technology successfully but maintain control of it. Beyond this, there is technology transfer in the sense of developing the indigenous technological capability of China, which would put the foreign investor out of a job unless he moves to a new line of activity or technology. For discussion of the development of indigenous technological capacity in less developed countries see Fransman and King (1984), Lall (1987), and Katz (1987). How foreign investors can maintain their firm-specific advantages as domestic technological capacity develops is also discussed in Leung et al (1989).

5. For information on Chinese investment incentives and conditions see M.J. Moser (1987). Another useful source on equity joint ventures, and published after the first draft of the present book was written, is Campbell (1989); and also Campbell and Adlington (1988). However, most of the comments in the text on the actual operation of the regulations are from our interviews. For more detailed material on the taxation of foreign enterprises in China see Appendix.

6. Moser (1987, pp100-101). Our interviews show much variation in contract length.

7. The other two "lai's" are lai yang zhi zuo (bringing samples for manufacture) and lai liao zhuang pei (processing using assembly line operations).

8. See Appendix. Note too, however, that in 1987-8 the tax position of state enterprises was changing, as a cheng bao system was being developed, under which they contracted to deliver a certain profit level to the state and then keep the rest. For details see Chinese Economic Monthly, Hong Kong, 3/1988, pp.93-111.

9. See for example Little and Mirrlees (1974). For a discussion of this methodology applied to the appraisal of the gains from foreign investment, see Thoburn (1981, Chapter 2).

10. As noted in Chapter One, tax policy may be used to redistribute the gains from foreign investment towards the host economy. China, however, like many developing countries, has used tax holidays and reduced tax rates as investment incentives. For a classic discussion of how to use tax policy effectively as an investment incentive, see Usher (1977).

11. See for instance T.M.H. Chan (1988 pp.28-30).

12. Examples from our interviews will be shown to include firms making wool products, leather products, and footwear.

13. For a discussion of rural industrialization in China see Nolan (1988, pp.89-99 and 122-130). "Rural" industry is often actually located in small towns, hence the common Chinese description of "township enterprises".

Table 2.1

Distribution of Foreign Investment in Various Kinds of Contracts
(by Contracted Amounts)

(Percentages)	1985		1986		1987		1988	
	China	Guangdong	China	Guangdong	China	Guangdong	China	Guangdong
Equity joint ventures	32.0	19.0	41.3	19.7	45.1	19.6	50.6	39.1
Contractual joint ventures	60.9	66.6	40.8	52.5	29.7	34.4	26.2	38.5
Wholly foreign owned	0.7	1.6	0.6	1.4	10.9	25.7	7.8	4.9
Processing & assembly, compensation trade and international leasing*	6.3	10.7	14.9	16.3	14.1	20.4	14.4	17.5

Notes: * Negligible until 1988, when 3.8% of total.
Items do not sum to 100% because total includes joint oil exploration, not shown above. Over the period 1979-88 foreign investment shown above (and excluding joint oil exploration) accounted for 36.9% of the contracted, and 24.9% of the actual inflow of capital into China. Joint oil exploration figures were 3.6% and 5.3% of the contracted and actual inflows, respectively, with the balance being loans and other borrowing.

Sources: China Statistical Yearbook 1986, 1987
Almanac of China's Foreign Economic Relations and Trade, 1988,1989
Guangdong Statistical Yearbook, 1988,1989

Table 2.2
Actually Utilized Foreign Capital, by Type of Contract,
Guangdong Province, 1979-88

(Percentages)	1979-82	1983-86	1986	1987	1988	(China 1979-88)
Equity Joint Ventures	5.8	19.0	18.9	27.4	31.1	(40.9)
Contractual Joint Ventures	46.6	56.4	62.2	52.4	36.0	(33.8)
Wholly foreign owned	7.6	4.5	1.7	2.0	8.7	(2.5)
Compensation trade	12.8	7.0	4.4	7.6	11.7	(22.9)
Processing & assembly	27.3	13.2	12.8	10.7	4.2	
TOTAL (US$mil.)	829.83	2509.78	812.46	726.74	1212.26	(11,767.00)

Notes: International leasing, not shown above, was negligible (and
           is excluded from the Table's totals) until 1988, when it was
           8.2% of the foreign investment inflow (excluding loans)

Sources: Guangdong Statistical Yearbook 1984,1985,1986,1987,1988,1989
           China figures from Beijing Review, 6-12 March 1989, and
           exclude joint oil exploration.

Table 2.3

Average Size of Foreign Investment Contract in Guangdong Province, 1980-88

(US$10,000)	1980	1983	1984	1985	1986	1987	1988	China 1979-88
Equity joint ventures	888.5	102.0	99.5	91.8	62.8	51.4	66.5	116
Contractual joint ventures	466.0	154.3	113.5	129.9	148.3	95.2	93.4	205
Wholly foreign owned	6252.8	211.0	37.6	120.7	151.2	1609.9	131.3	257
Compensation trade	37.2	59.4	48.0	48.0	95.3	114.5	79.4	NA
Processing & assembly	3.2	0.75	1.36	2.0	2.6	2.5	4.3	NA

Notes: Under Processing & Assembly firms may have several contracts.

Sources: Guangdong Statistical Yearbook,1985,1986,1987,1988,1989
          China figures from Beijing Review, 6-12 March 1988

3 The equity joint venture companies

This chapter considers the motivations and expectations of the partners in seventeen equity joint venture companies interviewed, and the problems that have arisen in the course of operation. Section 1 presents details of the companies and describes the joint venture contracts. Section 2 looks at the contract partners and their motivations. Section 3 considers exports, marketing and foreign exchange, and Section 4 looks at employment and operational issues.

3.1 **The companies and the contract**

3.1.1 The companies

Table 3-1 gives an overview of the seventeen equity joint venture companies interviewed. The industrial make-up is:

footwear	4	(JV-4, JV-7, JV-10. JV-15)
textiles and clothing	3	(woolen textiles: JV-1, fur coats: JV-6, denim clothing: JV-11)
food	3	(JV-3, JV-5, JV-14)
metal products	2	(Aluminium shapes: JV-2, metal cans: JV-17)
machinery and heavy consumer durables	2	(Plastics machinery: JV-9, refrigerators: JV-16)
services	2	(Car maintenance: JV-12, removals: JV-13)
other	1	(stone cutting: JV-8)

This gives a good coverage of the well-established labour-intensive industries of Hong Kong, particularly clothing, textiles and footwear. Plastics is represented indirectly by a company making plastics machinery (JV-9), and electronics by JV-16, making refrigerators.

Most of the companies interviewed are in the medium size range, defining medium as 50 - 499 employees :

small (1 - 49 workers)	2
medium (50 - 499)	12
large (500+)	2
unknown employment	1

and even the two 'large' companies are only marginally above 500. Of the two small companies one is part of a world-wide network of removals, and the other is a high-technology, capital-intensive operation where employment gives an understatement of the size of the operation. However, if the definition of "small-medium" as recently used for Hong Kong in another study (Sit and Wong, 1988), of 1 - 199 workers, by Hong Kong standards then only a third of the sample remains in the "medium-small" range.

Roughly half the companies were heavily export-oriented, roughly a quarter were geared predominantly to the domestic market, and the rest were trying to improve their export performance. However, since joint venture are normally expected to maintain at least a foreign exchange balance (i.e. earn enough foreign exchange to cover their import costs) one would not expect too sharp a dichotomy.(1)

Virtually all the companies had used their investment funds to import capital equipment. Only in the case of the footwear industry, where most of the equipment came from Taiwan, was a clear source of technology apparent, although in other cases Japan was the most commonly appearing supplier.

3.1.2 The equity joint venture contract

As noted already in Chapter Two, equity joint ventures allow the greatest freedom of action to the partners, among all the available contracts, and are covered by the most fully-developed legislation. Among our companies contract lengths varied from 10 to 20 years (and possibly longer in the case of JV-14). Of the equity proportions, only four companies were at the permitted minimum of 25%, a third were 50% and none above it (2). Interestingly, approximately a quarter of the companies had had previous contracts of a different kind with the same partner.

3.2 The motivation and expectations of the partners

Table 3-2 gives details about the Hong Kong and Chinese partners in each of the joint ventures. No simple relation exists between motivations and expectations on the one hand, and the different types of partners, or the industries, or the type of contract, on the other. Nevertheless several ways of classifying the information obtained from our companies do yield insights, which can be combined with the standard "firm-specific, location-specific, and internalization advantages" ideas from the foreign investment literature.

The most useful starting point seems to be a distinction between those JV's which involve an well-established Chinese company (usually a state company) and ventures where the Chinese side is a local authority (either at city, county, town, or village level). Such local authorities normally work through the medium of an "economic development company" to join with a foreign partner, although sometimes they use an already existing collective enterprise, whose operations get expanded far beyond their original scope. Although there are exceptions - such as state companies with particularly reform-minded managements, and particularly incompetent or rapacious local authorities - in general, motivations are clearer, the course of foreign investment seems smoother, and expectations more often fulfilled in partnership with local authorities. In the case of partnerships with established Chinese companies, the foreign investor seems most often to find himself (or herself - many of the Hong Kong managers are women) required to be the main agent of economic reform. In partnerships with local authorities the investor more often finds himself in a position to start "from scratch" as he wishes.

3.2.1 Partnerships with Chinese companies

Individual Chinese companies may be looking for access to improved technology through importing equipment and management, or access to export markets through the prospective partners contacts with customers and through improved product quality. The greater freedom of action accorded to joint ventures to import and export, the access to foreign exchange generally, and the tax privileges compared to state companies, are also strong incentives for state companies to seek foreign partners. In a minority of cases, indeed, the "foreign" partner may be a Chinese-owned company in Hong Kong (though these have been excluded from our present seventeen firms). In such cases the joint venture becomes little more than a device to secure greater freedom of action for a Chinese company.

Where a Chinese company has a very clear idea of its technological requirements, in principle the technology could be "depackaged", in the sense that all that is required is foreign exchange to buy the new imported equipment and temporary technical assistance to install it and train the operators. It might be thought that since most of the foreign investment in the Pearl River Delta is in industries where the technology is well known in the outside world, "depackaging" might occur frequently. In practice, importation of equipment and temporary training are by no means all that is required to transfer technology to China successfully, in the sense of achieving the same levels of labour productivity would be achieved with the same equipment in other countries. This, of course, raises the issue of the firm-specific advantages of Hong Kong investors - which often lie in their ability to organize large workforces in an efficient way to get high productivity from this workforce (as well as in their export contacts). This involves all the fundamentals of economic reform in China.

One case, however, where depackaging does seem to have been attempted can be mentioned first. This is JV-11, where the Chinese partner is a very large, well-established state textile factory, which has used compensation trade in the past to develop the production of denim cloth, and where the JV-11 project is to produce denim clothing for export. The partner from Hong Kong is a trading company, who can help with marketing and in arranging finance. The basic production technology is simple and required several Hong Kong technicians to come for a short time to teach workers how to use the machines. However, the Hong Kong partner has left the brother of one of its directors to act as marketing

director based in China.   The advantages of using a joint venture over
the previous compensation trade arrangements (with a different Hong Kong
partner) were that with the JV new equipment would be obtained whereas
with compensation trade only second-hand equipment had been on offer.
The company also mentioned the advantages of a JV being able to export
directly and seek out its own overseas customers, and the joint venture
tax privileges.   In the case of JV-11, the contacts with Hong Kong were
made through relatives in the Chinese company of the Hong Kong partner.

Whether JV-11 has been successful in its "depackaging" attempts is
too early to say.   It has been achieving 30% of its output exported,
but would like to export more and has been hampered by some problems of
product quality and delivery dates.

An alternative way of acquiring new equipment and technology is
represented by JV-16, which manufactures refrigerators, and is part of
a programme of diversification by a large Chinese conglomerate.   The
Hong Kong partner has provided finance and overseas contacts, but the
technology itself comes from Japan.   The joint venture will manufacture
using the Japanese brand name under licence.   The Japanese side provides
training in its technology, but is not a partner.   The venture is in too
early a stage to make any prediction of success or failure.

A clear and more standard example of a Chinese company knowing what
it wants and searching effectively for it is JV-9.   This is the case of
a state machinery factory, in a county with a long tradition of
producing agricultural machinery, deciding it wished to start the
manufacture of plastics machinery.   It sought as a partner a Hong
Kong-owned company with factories also in Japan and Taiwan, and which
had conducted an extensive search itself for a Chinese partner, having
rejected several other areas within the country.   For the Chinese
partner, the Hong Kong technology represented not the best-practice,
but the best combination of quality and low selling price for the
machines for the Chinese markets.   Some conflict of interest arises
between the partners, however, since the foreign partner wishes to
market abroad a larger proportion of the output than the Chinese
partner.   This raises questions about the relative profitability of
exports as against domestic sales to the two sides of a joint venture,
and is taken up again in Section 3.3.

Similar in principle to JV-9, though involving a US multinational
company operating through a Hong Kong office, is JV-14.   Here the
American company (whose product cannot be identified here other than as
"food", to preserve confidentiality) sought an experienced Chinese
partner in the same line of business.   This venture has been slow in
starting owing to some disputes about factory lay out, but the
complementarity between the partners is clear.

These examples illustrate positive aspects of joint venture
operations, where the partners know their minds.   One of the least
harmonious of the JVs studied, though earning foreign exchange and not
actually unprofitable to the Hong Kong side is JV-13.   The foreign
partner, a multinational removals company, sought a Chinese partner,
having decided to extend its operations to the mainland.   Its Chinese
partner appears to have been motivated by a desire to "follow the open
policy" and earn foreign exchange.   Though a shipping company, there
was little actual complementarity between the two sides' operations
since the foreign side was essentially performing a personal service.
The Hong Kong side's complaint is that the Chinese side is basically an
unreformed, bureaucratic organization, which ignores the provisions of
the Joint Venture Law.   The disputes centre on the workforce.   The
Chinese side has insisted that workers be paid at "Hong Kong rates"

(rather than the 20-50% more than comparable state company workers as stipulated by the Joint Venture Law) in Hong Kong dollars. The workers, assigned to the joint venture by the Chinese side, are not paid these rates however, but only the same as those as other permanent workers in the Chinese partner. While the Chinese side creams off a surplus in foreign exchange, the Hong Kong side expects Hong Kong-style work practices from its workers, which they fail to produce. Other irritants include the assignment of "drivers" to the joint venture, who cannot drive and whom the Hong Kong partner is expected to train, and much bureaucratic interference with the appointment of Hong Kong staff. The foreign investor has shelved plans to set up joint ventures elsewhere in China, and uses instead much looser contractual arrangements.

Similar, workforce-centred problems affect JV-5 (whose product, like that of JV-14, can only be identified as "food" to preserve confidentiality). This is an investment by a large, diversified Western multinational which foresees a rising demand for its product as incomes increase along China's prosperous coastal region. The Chinese partner is a large state company which produces a product, a by-product of which is the raw material major input into the joint venture production. This enterprise represents many of the difficulties of introducing advanced technology into China with existing workforce and management attitudes prevailing in state companies, and will be taken up in the Section 3.4. on employment. One problem with the venture was that the foreign managers were essentially (very high-level) technicians who saw their job as the technical one of getting the machinery operating properly and ensuring product quality as a requirement for export sales (for foreign exchange balance); and they reacted with near-disbelief at some of the management practices encountered and many of the minor restrictions placed on their activities. (The foreign manager, for example, was not allowed to drive a car, and was only allowed to ride his bicycle within the factory compound. The Chinese manager followed the foreign manager around and arbitrarily changed the settings on precision machinery).

Even when the Chinese partner is reform-minded and interested in productivity gains and improved management rather than mere access to foreign exchange, the foreign investor may have to undertake much of the reform himself. JV-15, a footwear company and one of the most successful in the sample, illustrates this. Run by an American entrepreneur with a Hong Kong office, with experience in the shoe industry in the USA and Taiwan, the venture is a partnership with a state company with which the entrepreneur previously had a lai liao jia gong arrangement. Mutual dissatisfaction with the LLJG arrangement (on the American side in part because of lack of quality control, and in part because of bureaucratic restrictions imposed by the Chinese side's parent organization), the new joint venture was set up with a clear idea of what could go wrong. Unlike JV-13, the removals company, which paid its workers indirectly via the Chinese partner, JV-15 insisted on direct wage payments, on differentials for responsibility and on bonuses genuinely linked to effort. Taiwanese equipment was imported for the factory which, though not world best-practice, was highly suitable for China's relatively labour-abundant conditions. In Taiwan labour costs would be some 25% of the cost of the finished product, and Chinese labour would cost about a third of that in Taiwan. The aim of the venture was quickly to achieve product quality for export, a task made easier by the foreign side's good customer contacts in the USA; and then gradually to raise labour productivity to Taiwanese levels. Strong opposition was raised by the Chinese partner to wage differentials and bonuses, and originally to the direct payment of workers by the joint venture. However, export sales were achieved fairly rapidly and once the venture was making more profit (and in foreign exchange) than the Chinese partner's own state factory, objections dropped away, and the venture was able to expand with reinvested funds and maintain its new labour and management practices.

Reform of labour and management practices was also the key to the success of JV-12, and like JV-15, there had been a previous, not entirely successful cooperation (in this case a cooperative joint venture), which both parties thought could be improved on. JV-12's Hong Kong partner is a large car-servicing company, and the Chinese side is a car servicing collective, now diversified, and previously loss-making. Only the Chinese side of this venture was available for interview, and they stressed the introduction of new work practices such as workers clocking-in in the morning, and being fined for lateness and bad work. The company, which operates a large training programme, is highly profitable in RMB terms, and the foreign side is using the profit for expansion elsewhere in China. The Chinese side has diversified into various related activities.

3.2.2 Partnerships with local authorities

Turning to the joint ventures where the Chinese partner is a local authority, a typical example is JV-6, a company making fur coats. The county concerned has good port facilities and has a good reputation for providing appropriate conditions for investors. The investor, not a native of the area, had heard of several other ventures run by the Chinese partner with Hong Kong businessmen and, having previously had a LLJG factory in another area, decided on a joint venture. The new joint venture was given generous tax privileges for being highly export orientated. The Chinese partner is a vehicle trading company, and actually a "vehicle" for a variety of other ventures, having separated off from the county state car maintenance factory. The latter, in existence since 1949, had been part of a rigid vertical hierarchy and by reorganizing away from the state company, considerable freedom of action was gained (particularly with respect to foreign exchange retention, of which more later). The Chinese partner now comes under the county economic development general company.

The three other footwear companies (JV-4, JV-7, and JV-10) are partnerships with local authorities, though in the case of JV-7 and JV-10 a Provincial Import-Export Corporation is involved too, and for JV-7, also the National Import-Export Corporation that deals with footwear. This involvement adds a bureaucratic element to the ventures, but it seems that the major effect is not on production (where the ventures are left to themselves) but on marketing, where the higher level corporations retain foreign exchange for themselves. All these factories use Taiwanese equipment and Hong Kong style management. There is also some American customer involvement in training workers to produce footwear of acceptable quality for the US market. None has problems in exporting, and labour force problems tend to be minor. One manager commented, however, that the local workers pay much more attention to the Hong Kong manager than to the Chinese manager, who shows some unwillingness to exert any authority. So far as can be judged the three footwear and the fur companies are successful ventures in terms of export earnings, mutual satisfaction with the arrangements and generally basic profitability. Choice of location in China was determined by factors such as port facilities and knowledge of other investors' experiences. The entrepreneurs were not natives of the areas in which they invested. JV-10 gradually moved from LLJG to a cooperative joint venture and then to an equity joint venture, and stressed the latter's more favourable tax treatment and above all its ability to import new machinery compared to the second-hand equipment available under LLJG.

As will be discussed later (in Section 3.2.3.), footwear and furs are generally typical of Hong Kong labour-intensive industries migrating to China. JV-1 is an investment more like that of the internationalization of production described by Frobel, Heinrichs and Kreye (1980) (again, more on this in Section 3.2.2.). Here, the relocation to China is to produce a key raw material with an advanced process. The foreign partner is a large Hong Kong based multinational garments manufacturer, wishing to secure a supply of angora wool, most easily available from within China. This is a high-technology operation in the sense of involving a dyeing process normally beyond the capabilities of Chinese factories. The Hong Kong partner insisted from the beginning on a quality of product acceptable in Hong Kong, assuring the Chinese side that once this was achieved price competition with other countries like Japan and Taiwan would not be a problem. Of course since the Hong Kong partner planned to be the joint venture's largest customer, it had the strongest possible interest in product quality, which it felt could best be achieved by internalizing the transaction through foreign investment. The quality control necessary for this venture was achieved through the use of resident Hong Kong personnel (principally the brother of one of the Hong Kong directors) and skilled technicians from a joint venture factory in Shanghai operated by the same director. Indeed, it was this director's wide existing contacts in China which persuaded the Hong Kong partner to enter China on the first place in the belief (widely shared by other companies in our sample) that good personal contacts, especially at local level, are the most important ingredient in the success of a foreign investment project in China.

Of the four remaining companies in partnership with local authorities (in one case in partnership with the Guangzhou Economic and Technological Development Zone) two illustrate various mild problems. JV-3 is a food company, producing in a locality where the entrepreneur has strong family contacts - indeed the Chinese manager is the Hong Kong entrepreneur's brother. There the deal went through the locality's foreign economic committee and involved a partnership with the locality's trade union (an arrangement no longer allowed in China). The entrepreneur faces some marketing problem in Hong Kong and some problem with the attitudes of his city-recruited workforces. JV-2, mainly aluminium shapes, is another case of a Hong Kong investor setting up in his home town, and as yet making little profit because of poor overseas demand and difficulty in buying raw materials outside plan allocations. However, the company sees future expansion based on sales to the domestic market, and anticipates a high income-elasticity of demand for its product.

A western multinational is involved in JV-17, the manufacture of metal cans for drinks. The Chinese partners are a wide range of national and provincial organizations, as well as the local authority, and the company claims to be using world best-practice technology, for an essentially import-competing product in heavy demand in China.

Finally, JV-8 appears to be one joint venture with a local authority which could be going seriously wrong. It provided little information and, when visited, appeared to be undergoing great difficulty in starting up. Many problems have arisen even in the installation of the

machinery.   The Italian engineers on the project were reported   to
have been amazed at the number of meetings and other distractions from
what they regarded as a purely technical job, and the Chinese side felt
the Italians "disliked working in China".

3.2.3 Structural aspects

The locational advantages of the Pearl River Delta for well-established
labour-intensive export industries like textiles (3) and footwear are
clear. To the abundant, cheap labour released from local agriculture by
the agricultural production responsibility system, and the availability
of cheap factory sites, have been added a wide range of tax incentives
to attract foreign firms. What is less clear, however, is why Hong Kong
firms should have firm-specific advantages compared to local Chinese
firms.   In fact, our interviews have shown that these advantages lie at
the heart of economic reform in China.   China's closedness to the
outside world for many years has left it lacking in knowledge of western
tastes and the requirements of product quality for export, as well as
lacking close customer contacts with western buyers.   Although the
technology for such industries is easily available (to those with the
foreign exchange to buy it), simply bringing in machinery from abroad
has not been sufficient to transfer the technology in an unreformed
situation where managers and workers follow traditional state-company
practices of workers "eating from the communal pot" (the so-called da
guo fan) and being immune from dismissal whatever their performance.
    Looking at our companies on an industry basis and in terms of the
level of their technology, the four footwear companies (JV-4, JV-7,
JV-10, JV-15) seem to fit best the pattern of labour-intensive
industries relocating to China.   One (JV-15) is in fact basically a
relocation from Taiwan (where the American entrepreneur has other
operations) for similar reasons to those of firms moving from Hong
Kong. Of the other three footwear companies, however, only one (JV-10)
has virtually closed its Hong Kong manufacturing operation, whereas the
others have continued in Hong Kong while locating their expansion in
China.   Two of the four companies previously had LLJG operations, but
have chosen to internalize their marketing and technological advantages
within the more closely controlled setting of a joint venture.
    The fur company (JV-6) represents a similar level of labour-intensive
technology, although the Hong Kong partner originally was only a trading
company and did not start its own production until coming to China.
With the need for close supervision of an expensive raw material, this
operation would not simply be contracted to an existing Chinese company,
so the Hong Kong partner was obliged itself to hire skilled
management/supervisory personnel.   Like several of the footwear
companies, having had a previous LLJG agreement (though not with the
present Chinese partner), it decided to internalize within a joint
venture.   The Hong Kong partner commented that many other fur companies
were moving to China because of the shortage of young female workers
willing to do careful manual work in Hong Kong.
    Two more firms (JV-3 food, JV-2 aluminium shapes) fit the mode of
labour-intensive firms moving to China.   JV-3 indeed had a thirty year
history of production of traditional Chinese footstuffs in Hong Kong,
and has moved to the entrepreneur's home town in China, and uses a
relative as the Chinese manager.   This company has faced some marketing
problems in Hong Kong as a result of depressed demand conditions, and
the aluminium company also has not found exporting easy.   However, both
companies have also expressed strong interest in the domestic Chinese

33

market, so they are not entirely just "outprocessing". The plastics machinery company (JV-9) is interesting in this regard too in that the Hong Kong side seems to regard the venture in large part as relocation to China in order to lower costs for the export market, while the Chinese side is mainly interested in domestic sales with a highly competitive product.

The two services companies (JV-12 car maintenance, and JV-13 removals) are rather special cases, in the sense of having an obvious market-orientated locational dimension. The interesting aspect is that the former has had a sufficiently reform-minded Chinese partner and a sufficiently determined Hong Kong side to make the venture successful, whereas the latter has had difficulties.

The other joint venture companies in the sample represent higher levels of technology and types of foreign investment less specific to the Hong Kong-Pearl River Delta nexus. These may have more lessons than the earlier companies for western potential foreign investors. JV-1, the company producing dyed angora wool as part of a large Hong Kong textile multinational, have had to introduce a specialized high technology process, but we have shown it actually attributes much of its success to its previous good contacts and access to trained staff within China - a performance a western company might not be able to emulate for example.

Three other multinationals are included as partners in our companies, all western and all operating through Hong Kong offices. JV-14 and JV-17 are both geared to the domestic market. The former is in too early a stage to discuss success or failure, though there have been some (apparently now resolved) disagreements. The latter provided insufficient information about profitability for a judgment to be made, although it had clearly started production of a technically acceptable product. JV-5, is a more interesting case and we have used it to illustrate the problems of high technology equipment being introduced without the foreign investor being sufficiently aware in advance that he is not just doing a technical job but will be in the forefront of economic reform, even sometimes against the opposition of his Chinese partner. JV-8, the stone cutting operation also illustrated this point, even where the foreign technicians had been hired specifically to do a purely technical job.

3.3 Marketing, export, and foreign exchange issues

Table 3-3 summarizes the information available from our sample on the marketing, export performance, and foreign exchange issues concerning the equity joint venture companies.

The companies involved in stone cutting (JV-8) and refrigerator manufacture (JV-16) are at too early a stage to comment usefully on their export performance. JV-13 is entirely geared to the domestic market, so export issues do not arise.

The really successful exporters, selling almost the whole of their output abroad, all have foreign partners with established customer contacts. The four footwear companies, the fur company and the removals company fit this pattern exactly and the Hong Kong multinational buying wool in China is itself the joint venture's main customer.

Good customer contacts and established marketing outlets would also be available for the two food companies JV-5 and JV-14, whose foreign partners are western multinationals. In these cases, it was explained that the only problem would be getting quality to an acceptable level. In these two cases exports would be geared towards providing a foreign exchange balance, since the two companies' activities are orientated towards the domestic market. JV-17 making drinks cans as an import substitution venture appears to be in a very similar position.

The remaining four companies raise problems about exporting. JV-2 making aluminium shapes has found selling overseas difficult, though in part its difficulties are more general and due to inadequate supplies of raw materials. JV-11, a clothing company, which manages its own production technology regards itself as still learning-by-doing and expects to increase exports as it gets its quality and delivery dates right, given that its Hong Kong partner provides an adequate marketing channel. JV-3, where the Hong Kong partner was a well established food producer before moving to China, is able to sell the bulk of its output abroad, but is dissatisfied with the state of the market.

JV-9 (plastics machinery), and also JV-3 raise general issues about the incentives to export. Although one might first suppose that all parties would be keen to export and earn foreign exchange, in a situation where foreign exchange is scarce, in practice there are several complications which distort the choice.

First, where the exporting is done by the Hong Kong partner, frequently the Chinese side simply does not know the price obtained and has no independent check on market conditions. Sometimes profit is made by the Hong Kong side at the trading stage outside the joint venture - the joint venture's output may be purchased for a low price and then resold. Sometimes buyers (e.g. some US buyers of footwear) may give the Hong Kong side a commission outside of the joint venture. Second, attempts by the Chinese to determine prices may not be appropriate, however. JV-3, the food company, reported that its Chinese partner wanted all overheads included in prices whatever the volume of sales. The Hong Kong side objected that the prices should be used to cover variable costs in the first instance and overheads should be spread over a larger sales volume as market share developed.

Third, although in principle a joint venture is free to export directly and to keep its foreign exchange, in practice there is great variation from company to company. Where higher level corporations are involved on the Chinese side (e.g. the Provincial Handicraft Corporation in JV-7 and JV-10, or the Machinery Import-Export Corporation in JV-9), the higher level authority retains substantial parts of the foreign exchange earnings as Table 3-3 shows. Only three companies said they were able straightforwardly to keep 100% of their foreign exchange earnings. Also apparent was the attempt by local authorities to keep forex exchange earnings at a local level. Fairly strong evidence for this was provided by the fur company, JV-6, where the county authorities had reorganized the Chinese partner out from under the vertical control structure of a state bureaucracy (the transportation department) so as to give it financial independence to form joint ventures with a number of foreign partners.

Fourth, the exchange rate at which foreign exchange is traded for Renminbi varies between companies and seems subject to negotiation in particular cases. The opportunity for joint ventures to exchange surplus foreign exchange against Renminbi legally in recent years has been much welcomed by foreign investors, particularly those like JV-13 who have had experience of having to exchange at the official rate in the past.

All in all, there is some bias against exporting, especially from the viewpoint of the Chinese partner, JV-11 for example reported domestic sales as being more profitable, and JV-9 that the Hong Kong side was keener on exports than the Chinese side. Of course, in a still quite closed economy, the strength of market demand for a product may differ between the domestic and the international market, which complicates the relative profitability issue.

3.4 Employment and operational issues

A summary of findings is given in Table 3-4, company by company. It has been argued in this chapter that work practices, and the control of the workforce by supervisory staff and managers, lie at the heart of the Chinese reform process. A recent World Bank study of industrial reform in China concluded that the labour market was one of the least reformed areas of the Chinese economy (Tidrick and Chen, 1987 pp 113-7). In principle, joint ventures are free to hire and fire, and are expected to employ workers on contract. In practice, permanent workers are often assigned to the joint venture by the Chinese partner (if it is a state company). When JV-5 tried to hire village workers because of their better aptitude and motivation it met great opposition from the Chinese side. JV-13 has had problems because it does not hire its workers directly, and in its whole history of operation has only succeeded in having one unsatisfactory worker transferred back to his parent company. JV-15, anticipating these problems in the light of other experience in China, insisted the joint venture should hire its workers directly. Several companies such as JV-4 and JV-12 have instituted controls on the workforce such as clocking-in and fines for lateness.

Where the joint venture does not have a pool of permanent workers from its Chinese partner on which it has to draw, our study shows workers are often hired directly. As noted in earlier chapters, the labour shortage existing in the Delta has resulted in the influx of a million guest workers (T.M.H. Chan, 1988, p28). Several companies spoke of recruiting workers from outside the area or outside the province, but others recruited locally.

Most companies paid wages of 200-250 RMB a month - which is more than double that received by a university lecturer in Beijing, for example.

NOTES

1. Contrast this with the findings of Reuber's (1973) study of a large sample of Western and Japanese foreign investors where companies tended to be either almost wholly export-oriented or almost entirely geared to domestic markets. However, there does appear to be a distribution of equity joint venture companies in China which is bipolar in the sense that there are a considerable number of small, export-orientated ones and there are (a smaller number of) larger ones orientated somewhat more towards the domestic market (see Pomfret, 1989, p.44).
2. It is interesting to compare these figures with the analysis by Campbell (1989) of the official Chinese statistics for 1979-86 on 496 (non-Hong Kong and Macau) equity joint ventures. 88.5% of those companies had contracts of between ten and twenty years. Only 9.3% of them had foreign equity percentages of over 50%, and 40.3% had exactly 50%.
3. In practice the relocation of textiles and clothing manufacture from Hong Kong to China has been constrained by the need to secure quotas for entry into overseas markets, particularly the United

States (Forestier, 1989, p.59). In 1987 exports from China in excess of American and European Community quotas led to some Chinese exports being refused entry (South China Morning Post, 20 March 1987). Indeed, it has been reported that Chinese manufacturing of textiles and garments has started to move offshore itself, to locations such as the Bahamas, to avoid quota problems (South China Morning Post, 9 January 1989).

Table 3.1

The Equity Joint Venture Companies – Introductory Profiles (Sheet 1)

Company	Size	Contract	Equity Proportions (China/Foreign)	Technology	Exports	Present Venture's Previous Contracts
JV-1 Woolen textiles manufacturing	206 workers	15 years from 1984	55/45	New factory. All equipment from Japan.	80% (no stipulation in contract).	None
JV-2 Aluminium shapes manufacturing	270 workers	15 years from 1985	75/25	New factory on green field site. All machinery imported, mainly from Taiwan, some from Japan, USA and UK.	25% (contract 30%)	None
JV-3 Food manufacturing	90 workers	10 years from 1985	50/50	New company, HK partner responsible for the equipment and technology.	60% planned, but not being achieved. Achieving forex balance.	None
JV-4 Footwear manufacturing	300 workers	15 years from 1985	N/A	Production line from Taiwan – modern for the region.	90% (contract 70%)	None

Table 3.1

The Equity Joint Venture Companies – Introductory Profiles (Sheet 2)

Company	Size	Contract	Equity Proportions (China/Foreign)	Technology	Exports	Present Venture's Previous Contracts
JV-5 Food manufacturing	33 workers	18 years from 1985	50/50	Australian technology (highly capital-intensive operation).	20-25% (planned)	None
JV-6 Clothing manufacturing	220 workers	12 years from 1986	50/50 (but actually 37/63 so far)	Equipment from UK and W Germany (labour-intensive with simple machines).	100%	None
JV-7 Footwear manufacturing	510 workers	10 years from 1986	75/25	Taiwanese machinery, fairly capital-intensive by Chinese standards.	100% (contract 85%)	None
JV-8 Stone cutting factory – "marble" table-tops, etc.	Not yet in production	15 years from 1987	60/40	Equipment from Italy	Plan 60-80% but not yet in production.	NA

Table 3.1

The Equity Joint Venture Companies - Introductory Profiles (Sheet 3)

Company	Size	Contract	Equity Proportions (China/Foreign)	Technology	Exports	Present Venture's Previous Contracts
JV-9 Machinery manufacturing	130 workers	20 years from 1985	75/25	Brought technology from HK partner, and can use HK brandname. Also particular pieces of advanced equipment from Japan, and some local machines.	None at present, but planned for next year.	No
JV-10 Footwear manufacturing	500 workers	15 years from 1985	67/33	Machinery is Taiwanese. Product line moved to China from HK.	100% (contract 60%)	LLJG from 1979, then cooperative JV agreement signed for 5 years in 1984.
JV-11 Clothing manufacturing	NA (Small part of large complex)	10 years from 1987	65/35	Machinery from USA, Switzerland, W Germany.	30% (aiming at 50%)	Compensation trade to import equipment (with different foreign partners).
JV-12 Car maintenance	290 workers	10 years from 1985	60/40	Uses HK technology	None (but some local sales for foreign exchange).	Cooperative Joint Venture (1983-5).

Table 3.1

The Equity Joint Venture Companies – Introductory Profiles (Sheet 4)

Company	Size	Contract	Equity Proportions (China/Foreign)	Technology	Exports	Present Venture's Previous Contracts
JV-13 Removals	9 workers	10 years from 1985	50/50	---	100%	None
JV-14 Food manufacturing	200 planned	"More than 15 years", from 1985	50/50	All new machinery, using American blue-prints for factory.	Plan 33% exports, 33% domestic sales for foreign currency.	None
JV-15 Footwear manufacturing	455	15 years from 1985	50/50	Taiwanese equipment.	100%	LLJG
JV-16 Refrigerator manufacturing	148 workers (300 planned)	20 years from 1985	75/25	Technology from Japan under 7 year licencing agreement.	70% planned (just starting production).	None
JV-17 Metal container manufacturing	324 workers	20 years from 1986	65/35	"Some of most advanced technology in world".	50% (?) "import-replacing" domestic sales.	None

41

Table 3.2

Equity Joint Venture Companies – the Partners and the Contract (Sheet 1)

Company	Chinese side	Foreign side	Tax	Special features or comments	Other Operations in China
JV-1 Woolen textiles manufacturing (New high-technology company, with special dyeing facilities, unusual in China).	City Economic Development Corporation Guangdong-Hong Kong Corporation Guangdong Textile Import-Export Corporation Jiangsu Provincial (Textiles ?) factory (with loan guaranteed by Yuet Hoi (Guangdong Province Holding Company) in HK).	(Real HK contribution is only 15%). Large HK clothing company. Rest of "Hong Kong" share has substantial involvement by by Chinese-owned organizations.	NA	Uses Hong Kong and experienced Shanghai management/technical personnel to ensure quality. HK investor very satisfied with product quality.	Another (clothing) factory in same location, as JV between the present JV and a Shanghai company. A further factory, for woolens, is also under construction in same location.
JV-2 Aluminium shapes manufacturing - new company	City Foreign Trade and Development Company City Foreign Economic Committee	HK entrepreneur investing in home town. In same line of business in HK (?)	No income tax in first two years. 10% industry tax.	Aiming at Chinese domestic market.	None
JV-3 Food manufacturing - drinks, snacks - new company	City General Trade Union Foreign Economic Committee (Chinese manager is brother of HK boss)	HK Company previously in food manufacturing for 30 years in HK. Now maintain only a warehouse and an office in HK. Workforce now in China, 50% larger than previous workforce in HK.	No income tax for first 3 years. 7% industry tax.	With hindsight would prefer LLJG. Less hassle. Prefers equity JV over cooperative JV because former allows duty free imports. At end of contract capital equipment belongs to China.	Apparently successful LLJG in Beijing in same line, and unsuccessful venture (no profit, poor quality) in Shunde.

Table 3.2

Equity Joint Venture Companies – the Partners and the Contract (Sheet 2)

Company	Chinese side	Foreign side	Tax	Special features or comments	Other Operations in China
JV-4 Footwear manufacturing - ladies fashion shoes - new factory, with imported machinery	NA	Shoe company still manufacturing in HK. HK entrepreneur not a native of the area	NA	None	HK entrepreneur previously had LLJG in same area.
JV-5 Food manufacturing - new factory	County food factory, (a group company) - setting up new JV factory to use a major byproduct in a high-technology process.	Major multinational, with office in HK. Main interest in Chinese market, and aiming at forex balance. Introduced by Foreign Economic Committee of Guangzhou.	Tax holiday for first 3 years then 5 years of 50% tax reduction.	Special features / Receiving many preferences as a high-technology company; but many operating problems. Basic quality of product is a major concern.	Foreign partner - has JV with a shipping company. China parent does same LLJG work for one/or more US companies.
JV-6 Clothing manufacturing - furs - new factory	a vehicle trading company, now under sole control of the County.	HK company previously only in fur trading. China venture is its first production. HK entrepreneur not local. Heard of China parent through HK contact with contracts here.	3 year tax holiday then 3 years at 50% reduction (because "export-oriented"). Does not know what tax rate will be when start paying tax	Influenced in location by local port facilities. "Most fur factories are now being moved to China".	Contemplating another fur factory. Previously had a LLJG factory. China side has several other foreign cooperations.

Table 3.2
Equity Joint Venture Companies – the Partners and the Contract (Sheet 3)

Company	Chinese side	Foreign side	Tax	Special features or comments	Other Operations in China
JV-7 Footwear manufacturing - men's travel shoes - new factory	3 equally : - Beijing Handicraft Import-Export Company - Provincial Handicraft Import-Export Corporations - County Level Company	Large HK shoe company, still producing in HK. Pressure from US customers to move to China to reduce costs, and away from Taiwan. Have big factory to get substantial quota into USA if quotas are introduced. Had no previous relations with this county.	NA (not in contract).	Influenced by local port facilities. "More and more HK shoe companies are starting production in China". Uses relatively capital-intensive methods to ensure quality for US customers.	HK side - has another factory in another county doing LLJG. Also factory in Shenzhen. China side - has several other foreign cooperations.
JV-8 Stone cutting factory (very brief interview, factory still partly under-construction).	County Foreign Economic Development Company (?)	HK partner, but Italian technology.	NA	Great cultural problems between Chinese side and Italian engineers in installing equipment.	NA
JV-9 Machinery manufacturing - plastics machinery - new product line added to existing Chinese factory	County state agricultural machinery factory, with financial backing from county government to update. Wanted access to HK technology (HK less modern than Western but produces much cheaper product).	Experienced HK machinery company with factories also in Taiwan and Japan. Active search by HK side - also had considered Shanghai and Guangxi.	3 year tax holiday, 4 year 50% tax reduction.	This area has long history of producing agricultural machinery.	NA

Table 3.2

Equity Joint Venture Companies – the Partners and the Contract (Sheet 4)

Company	Chinese side	Foreign side	Tax	Special features or comments	Other Operations in China
JV-10 Footwear manufacturing - newly set up when started LLJG - Only ladies shoes being produced (because of big order). - production line for men's shoes lying idle.	- Village - Provincial Handicraft Import-Export Corporation	HK shoe company, now with only 100 production workers in HK.	3 years tax holiday then 2 years 50% tax and another 2 years 50% because export more than 70% of output.	JV gives advantage of being able to import machines (previously had cooperative JV and previous to that LLJG).	Chinese side has a nearby glue factory with another HK partner.
JV-11 Clothing manufacturing - denim clothing - new factory in existing complex	Old established, large state textile company. Updating technology and marketing.	HK trading company, with no experience in clothes manufacture. Contact made via relatives.	3 year tax holiday then 5 years at 50% (if export more than 50% of output).	Project has developed from from previous updating of factory to produce denim cloth (used compensation trade to acquire machinery) Stresses equity JV gives power to export directly	NA
JV-12 Car maintenance (existing company wishing to update equipment and technology)	Car servicing collective, now diversified.	Large car service company in HK, with many other activities too. Invested in servicing Chinese market. Brought together by External Economic Affairs Committee.	2 year tax holiday, 3rd year 50% tax.	Previous cooperation (a cooperative JV) not successful because of Chinese management problem. Present Equity JV set up with new HK-style management arrangements.	HK side has - car servicing in several major cities China side has - driver training - car rental in same location.

Table 3.2

Equity Joint Venture Comanies – the Partners and the Contract (Sheet 5)

Company	Chinese side	Foreign side	Tax	Special features or comments	Other Operations in China
JV-13 Removals (Existing Chinese company diversifying)	State shipping agency.	Multinational removals firm based in HK. Had originally considers Shenzhen, but China side was against.	NA	Not much complementarity between HK side and Chinese side's operation.	HK side - looser agency arrangements in several major cities.
JV-14 Food manufacturing	Well established Chinese food company.	Well established American food multinational with HK office aiming at Chinese market, and seeking an	NA	Both sides started with clear preference for a JV.	NA
JV-15 Footwear manufacturing - ladies casual shoes - new venture developed alongside existing factory and following a LLJG arrangement	Shoe factory under Leather Corporation under Second Bureau of Light Industry.	Independent American entrepreneur with Taiwan and US experience in the industry, and office in HK.	NA	Very careful negotiation of contract by foreign side, based on experience of earlier operations. Significant lowering of costs relative to Taiwanese operation, and attempting to achieve Taiwanese-level productivity.	Foreign side has another shoe factory in countryside nearby.

Table 3.2

Equity Joint Venture Companies - the Partners and the Contract (Sheet 6)

Company	Chinese side	Foreign side	Tax	Special features or comments	Other Operations in China
JV-16 Refrigerator manufacturing - new company in large complex	Four sides : - Large diversified Chinese state corporation. Technology being purchased from Japan. - Guangzhou Light Industrial Import-Export Corporation - Guangzhou International Trust and Investment Company - Guangzhou Foreign Trade Corporation	HK trading company. Basically providing financing and contacts with Japan, rather than production expertise.	NA	China side mentions tax being lower for a JV than for a state corporation.	NA
JV-17 Metal container manufacturing - drinks cans	- Guangzhou Beverage Industry Corporation - China National Packaging Import-Export Corporation - Zhenhua Light Industry Enterprises - an Industrial Corporation	US multinational, highly diversified, with HK office. Interested in Chinese market (counts as "import replacements").	NA	---	NA

47

Table 3.3

Equity Joint Venture Companies – Markets and Foreign Exchange (Sheet 1)

Company	Exports Actual/(Contract)	Marketing Arrangements	Competition, Domestic vs Foreign Sales	Forex Balance - raw materials	Forex retention	Other issues
JV-1 Woolen textiles manufacturing	80% (no contract stipulation)	JV has selling office in HK.	Competitive position based on quality, especially of dyeing. Main competitors are Taiwan and Japan. Almost no domestic competition.	Wool imported from Australian, considering switching to cheaper domestic supply.	100% retained."Don't have to give forex to Bank of China".	HK partner is major buyer of JV's product.
JV-2 Aluminium shapes manufacturing	? (30%)	HK side responsible for 30% exports.	Some uncertainty about foreign markets. Taiwan is major competitor abroad, with similar prices. Hope for "up-market" domestic sales.	Raw materials now from China (but some supply problems); originally from Italy.	NA	---
JV-3 Food manufacturing	60% (60%)	HK side does export marketing.	Policy of keeping prices stable to build up export market; but HK prices not very good at present; substantial domestic sales. Demand is seasonal to some extent.	Use forex to buy imports Don't need to change much into RMB. Packaging material imported from Japan.	100%	Disagreement between Chinese and HK sides. Chinese wants all factory costs included in selling price. (leads to high prices with low output).
JV-4 Footwear manufacturing	90% (70%)	HK side does export marketing	Sells to HK and USA mainly.	Most raw materials (e.g. synthetic leather from Taiwan) imported.	NA	---

48

Table 3.3
Equity Joint Venture Companies – Markets and Foreign Exchange (Sheet 2)

Company	Exports Actual/(Contract)	Marketing Arrangements	Competition, Domestic vs Foreign Sales	Forex Balance - raw materials	Forex retention	Other issues
JV-5 Food manufacturing	? (25%)	Exports through multinational parent.	Quality control essential for exports, then sales easy. France is main competitor. Export expanding, domestic market in prosperous coastal areas.	Aiming at forex balance. Basic raw materials are locally purchased.	40% can be kept by the JV. Must use account with Bank of China for buying imported equipment.	Authorities have raised no objection to use of free market to exchange RMB.
JV-6 Clothing manufacturing	100% (90%)	Exporting done by HK side.	Chinese side comments that it doesn't know overseas selling price.	All raw materials imported.	100%	Corporate restructuring carried out by Chinese side to retain profits and foreign exchange at county level.
JV-7 Footwear manufacturing	100% (85%)	Marketing and price setting done by Provincial Handicraft Corporation (one of the JV partners). HK partner acts as middlemen, with commission from US customers.	Mainly sold to US. Shoes are different quality to sort available locally.	---	40% goes to national government, 60% goes to Provincial Corporation, of which JV gets 12.5%.	---

Table 3.3

Equity Joint Venture Companies – Markets and Foreign Exchange (Sheet 3)

Company	Exports Actual/(Contract)	Marketing Arrangements	Competition, Domestic vs Foreign Sales	Forex Balance - raw materials	Forex retention	Other issues
JV-8 Stone cutting factory	No yet in production (60-80%)	HK side responsible for exporting.	Other JV factories in Guangdong make similar products.	---	---	---
JV-9 Machinery manufacturing	0 (contract?) but c.30% planned.	Export either directly using HK partner or via Guangdong Machinery Import-Export Corporation.	Very strong competition both in China and HK. Profitability on domestic sales higher.	Chinese side aiming at forex balance. HK side would like more exports.	If export directly, get forex and keep it. If export via Guangdong Import-Export Corporation, get RMB. "Forex strictly controlled in use".	Use of HK technology to produce cheaper and better machines, and use HK brand-name.
JV-10 Footwear manufacturing	100% (60%)	Either through HK partner or through Provincial Handicraft Export-Import Corporation.	Competitive position based on quality and low price.	Many materials imported (Taiwan via HK). Shoe bottoms from China.	If export directly (via HK partner) can keep forex. If export via Provincial Import-Export Corporation, get 10% of net selling price in forex, and rest in RMB at a better than an official rate.	Currently have one-year contract with US. Last year had difficulties with several different buyers all wanting fast supplies.

50

Table 3.3

Equity Joint Venture Companies – Markets and Foreign Exchange (Sheet 4)

Company	Exports Actual/(Contract)	Marketing Arrangements	Competition, Domestic vs Foreign Sales	Forex Balance - raw materials	Forex retention	Other issues
JV-11 Clothing manufacturing	30% (50%)	Product is exported to US using HK partner's quota. Has power to export directly.	Hope to increase export sales when achieve higher quality. Only one other Chinese factory produces denim for export.	HK side supplies imported raw materials. Need c.40% exports for forex balance.	"Current use of forex is strictly controlled".	Make more profit from domestic sales than from exports. If HK partner keeps profits in China government remits industrial tax and product tax.
JV-12 Car maintenance	?	Domestic sales only.	Charge higher prices, for better service, than domestic competitors. Give substantial discount to customers paying in forex.	Must import many parts. Local supplies are uncertain, and expensive; and difficult to manufacture own parts. Can obtain forex with help from External Affairs Committee or "by other, but not illegal, means".	NA	Profit repatriation not a problem because reinvesting RMB profits in expansion elsewhere in China.
JV-13 Removals	100%/(100%?)	Sales arranged through HK side.	Compete internationally by reputation and quality of service.	Few forex costs. RMB obtained for local expenditures now through legally permitted exchanges with other JVs via Bank of China. Previously had to exchange at official rate.	NA	Much of forex earnings are creamed off by Chinese partner through high payments in forex for workers.

51

Table 3.3

Equity Joint Venture Companies - Markets and Foreign Exchange (Sheet 5)

Company	Exports Actual/(Contract)	Marketing Arrangements	Competition, Domestic vs Foreign Sales	Forex Balance - raw materials	Forex retention	Other issues
JV-14 Food manufacturing	Plan 33% exports, 33% domestic sales for foreign currency, 33% domestic sales.	Export sales through the US multinational.	Expect future competition in Chinese market as other foreign investment is being undertaken in this product.	Not a problem if meet expected targets.	NA	---
JV-15 Footwear manufacturing	100%/(?)	Sales mainly to USA through entrepreneurs' previous contacts.	Price competitiveness important in US market, given quality.	Uses local pigskin. Trying to develop domestic supplies of other inputs. At beginning, almost all raw materials imported, now less than half.	NA	Very close relations with overseas customers.
JV-16 Refrigerator manufacturing	70% planned	Direct export.	Considerable competition, even within the province. Will be able to use Japanese brandname.	Royalty paid on imported Japanese technology.	NA	---
JV-17 Metal container manufacturing	50% (?)	Overseas sales by US.	Production seen as "import-replacing". Some domestic sales are for forex. Excess demand in China for this product.	Raw materials imported.	NA	

52

Table 3.4

Equity Joint Venture Companies : Employment and Operational Issues (Sheet 1)

Company	Workforce	Employment Status	Recruitment	Wages (per month)	Wages in relation to other costs	Training	Remarks
JV-1 Woolen textiles manufacturing	206 (3 shifts)	30% state cadres and permanent workers. 70% contract workers (3 years, renewable).	Directly, by advertisement. Send details to Labour Service Bureau just for information. Less than 10% of workers are from outside local area.	Y250 (last year Y200), including bonus.	Labour 4% of total costs.	---	---
JV-2 Aluminium shapes manufacturing	270	NA	Sign contract through Labour Service Bureau (though not for temporary workers). Many workers are young males from outside the area.	Y250 average, pay according to output, bonus for working complete month.	NA	Give three months training.	---
JV-3 Food manufacturing	90 (one shift, "could raise output by increasing shift working")	Mostly temporary.	Willing to fire workers.	NA	Labour over 40%.	---	Some problems with bad habits of workers and workers not knowing how to use equipment.

Table 3.4

Equity Joint Venture Companies : Employment and Operational Issues (Sheet 2)

Company	Workforce	Employment Status	Recruitment	Wages (per month)	Wages in relation to other costs	Training	Remarks
JV-4 Footwear manufacturing	300	NA	NA	Y70 while on 3 months probation, then Y140 Y180 and Y200 on piece work, with some overtime.	NA	3 months	Workers clock in and out.
JV-5 Food manufacturing	33	Mixture of permanent workers assigned from Chinese partner, and temporary workers from local village.	Permanent workers assigned from Chinese partner, and temporary workers	Y120 - 150. Workers paid directly by the JV. Basic wage + JV premium + bonus will bringwage up to Y300, but most workers are "nowhere near that".	Labour about 10%	NA	Disputes between partners about employment of permanent workers assigned by Chinese partner.
JV-6 Clothing manufacturing	220	Some contract workers, but mostly temporary.	Originally used advertisements, and then an organization to bring workers in a group from another province. More recently, existing workers introduced relations, but must go through Local Labour Service Station Very little unemployment in the local area.	Y50 during training, then Y250 on average workforce paid directly by JV.	High in relation to non-raw material costs.	3 months. Need high quality work because raw material (fur) so expensive.	Workers mainly young women.

54

Table 3.4

Equity Joint Venture Companies : Employment and Operational Issues (Sheet 3)

Company	Workforce	Employment Status	Recruitment	Wages (per month)	Wages in Relation to other costs	Training	Remarks
JV-7 Footwear manufacturing	510	All temporary	Hired directly by factory, and all local. No labour supply problem.	Average Y190. Workers work 14 hours per day and wages could "reach Y630 with overtime".	NA	NA	Workers in HK are "twice as productive" as Chinese workers in this line of business.
JV-8 Stone cutting factory	100 planned	NA	Generally young local graduates from middle school.	NA	NA	Need training to operate the equipment.	Just in trial stages, with various problems.
JV-9 Machinery manufacturing	130	Mixture of permanent and contract workers.	Some skilled workers are permanent workers from Chinese parent company.	Average currently Y200, but expect in future to reach Y300.	Labour under 10%	10 workers sent to HK for two months training.	---
JV-10 Footwear manufacturing	500 (only 1 shift)	All contract workers.	70% of workers are from outside the local area, but from within the province. Very stable workforce.	Y230 on average, but some get Y300 - 400 piece work.	Very labour-intensive. Tried to mechanize certain operations but had great difficulty.	NA	Workers mostly young women.

Table 3.4

Equity Joint Venture Companies : Employment and Operational Issues (Sheet 4)

Company	Workforce	Employment Status	Recruitment	Wages (per month)	Wages in relation to other costs	Training	Remarks
JV-11 Clothing manufacturing	NA	Trying to move towards an all-contract workforce. (3 year contracts, with 1 month's notice), but "how to make a contract worker out of a permanent worker?"	NA	Average Y200, but on piece work can get up to Y400.	Wages c.20%	NA	Will be large part of labour available from Chinese parent company.
JV-12 Car maintenance	290 (with 70 under training)	Moving towards contract system; but some workers are permanent workers from Chinese parent company.	Many from Chinese parent company. Unsatisfactory workers can be returned to parent company.	Y240, rising to Y300 with bonus. Y30 for workers under training.	NA	Workers who train must sign a five-year contract.	HK partner very keen on incentive system. (like fines for lateness or bad work).
JV-13 Removals	9	Permanent workers assigned by Chinese partner. Dismissal almost impossible.	JV has little choice about workers it gets.	All workers "paid" at "HK" levels (but actually these are payments to the Chinese partner and the workers actually get same as other permanent workers employed by parent company.	Wages are largest component of costs.	JV required to train workers.	HK partner unhappy with wage payments arrangements.

Table 3.4

Equity Joint Venture Companies : Employment and Operational Issues (Sheet 5)

Company	Workforce	Employment Status	Recruitment	Wages (per month)	Wages in relation to other costs	Training	Remarks
JV-14 Food manufacturing	200 planned	Half contract, half permanent.	NA	Y240, of which Y120 is bonus.	Wages < 10% of total costs.	NA	---
JV-15 Footwear manufacturing	NA	Most contract, some from Chinese partner's factory, some temporary. Firing never used aggressively.	Locally recruited(?)	Y200 for workers including bonus and food allowance. Workers paid directly by JV.	In Taiwan wages costs are 20-25% of total costs. JV attempting to reach Taiwanese-level labour productivity.	Heavy emphasis on developing correct attitudes among workers.	Foreign partner insisted on differentials, against initial
JV-16 Refrigerator manufacturing	148 (300 planned)	Mixture of permanent workers from Chinese parent company and (3 or 5 years) contract workers from Labour Service Bureau.	30% of workers are from technical training school.	"Highest" is Y360.	5-10% of total costs.	Some workers go to Japan for several months.	---
JV-17 Metal container manufacturing	324	Almost all contract workers.	Hired directly, not via Labour Service Bureau.	Y200 average + Y100 bonus.	Labour about 2% of total costs.	NA	---

4 The cooperative joint venture companies

This chapter tries to explore the reasons why Hong Kong firms have invested in China using cooperative joint venture contracts, and why their Chinese partners have sought such investment; and how these ventures have operated in practice. The analysis is based on information from interviews with fifteen cooperative joint ventures ("CJVs"). Following the format of the previous chapter, Section 1 sets out introductory details of the companies and discusses the CJV contract. Section 2 looks at the motivation and expectations of the partners. This section tries to introduce each company in more detail. Section 3 goes on to look at issues relating to marketing and to exports and foreign exchange. Section 4 considers employment and operational issues.

4.1 The companies and the contract

4.1.1 The companies

Table 4-1 provides summary information on the fifteen companies. The industrial coverage is:

footwear	1	(sports shoes: CJV-6)
textile and clothing	3	(clothing: CJV-1, nylon adhesive tape: CJV-4, fur coats: CJV-7)
food	3	(dried ducks: CJV-3, biscuits and confectionary: CJV-5, food: CJV-15)
metal products	1	(kitchen equipment: CJV-11)

services	3	(restaurant: CJV-9, beauty salon: CJV-10, hotel refurbishing: CJV-13)
electronics	1	(cameras: CJV-14)
other	3	(stone cutting: CJV-2, polythene bags: CJV-8, jewellery: CJV-12)

This, like the coverage of Chapter Three, provides a good spread of industries covering most of the main areas of Hong Kong industry (except plastics).

As was the case with the equity joint venture companies most are in the (small to) medium size range. This in terms of workforce:

1 - 49	1
50 - 499	11
500 +	1
Unknown employment	2

Alternatively, using 1 - 199 as the small-medium size definition:

1 - 199	9
200 +	4
Unknown employment	2

The size of company in our sample here is not very different from that of the equity joint venture sample. Of the two companies (CJV-13 and CJV-14) which did not provide employment figures, CJV-14 is almost certainly in the 50 - 499 range. CJV-13 is difficult to assess, being small in terms of its hotel management team, but probably employing a considerable number of workers in its operating company (the hotel).

Almost half of the companies were heavily export-orientated, two wished to be so but were failing in that aim, three were services orientated towards the domestic markets, and the rest were making an informed choice between exports and domestic sales.

4.1.2   The cooperative joint venture contract

Although the equity joint venture contract allows much variety of equity proportions, tax provisions, length of contract, and (in practice) foreign exchange retention, the cooperative joint venture contract can in principle cover an even wider spectrum. Contracts in our sample of CJVs have ranged from five years to thirty. No financial capital is required on the Chinese side, whose contribution may, for example, simply be a building which can be converted to a factory. Approval can be obtained at as low as county level for a CJV to be established. The division of profits between the partners need not be in the same proportions as their contributions of capital, and can vary over the project life. Normally at the end of the venture the equipment will belong to China, the foreign partner having been repaid out of gross profits prior to the distribution of net profits between the partners. Thus a CJV could in principle be little more than a compensation trade arrangement, where the foreign partner provides the equipment, is repaid quickly and the Chinese side is self-sufficient within a few years. At the other end of the spectrum, the minimal requirements for capital provision on the Chinese side could mean that (as in CJV-14, the camera manufacturer) a virtually 100% foreign enterprise could be established, yet with county level rather than (as of 1987-8) central government approval. The tax position of CJVs has often been unclear. If they were counted as legal entities they would be taxed under the Equity Joint Venture Law, with a basic rate of income tax on profits of 33% (before any special concessions to encourage location in particular areas). If counted as partnerships, however, the CJVs come under the Foreign Enterprise Income Tax Law, with progressive tax rates up to 50%. (Moser and Zee, 1987, pp. 38-63; South China Morning Post, 2 May 1988, and Appendix).

The new Cooperative Joint Venture Law, published in April 1988, promises to resolve some of the uncertainty, but its details still await the subsequent publications of various sets of implementing regulations.

4.2 **The motivation and expectations of the partners**

The distinction between ventures with existing Chinese companies, and those which are new ventures with the investment vehicles of local authorities, proves less useful for our sample of cooperative joint ventures than it was for the joint venture companies of the previous chapter.   This is in part because there are fewer ventures with existing companies in the CJV sample, but also because the new ventures set up by local authorities provided a more diversified experience than was the case with the equity joint ventures.   Since cooperative joint venture contracts can be quite short (remember a third of the present sample are 5 - 8 years only) and the equipment normally belongs to Chinese at the end of the contract (the foreign side having a prior claim on profits in order to repay its equity contribution) it is more likely that the Chinese side will attempt "depackaging" of the technology and finance, and generally wish to be (competently) independent more quickly.   Cooperative joint ventures are also easier to start, requiring no financial capital on the Chinese side and requiring a lower level of official approval.   In these circumstances, the role of the foreign partner, and in particular whether it is utilizing some firm-specific advantage or merely providing finance, becomes particularly interesting and may vary between ventures more than in equity joint ventures.   Table 4-2 give details of the partners and the contracts.

4.2.1   Ventures with Chinese companies

As with equity joint ventures, existing Chinese companies may use cooperative joint ventures to acquire technological expertise, marketing outlets, or the foreign exchange for importing equipment, and also to acquire greater freedom of action from the planning system.

CJV-1, a collective clothing factory, is a standard case, where a clothing factory has joined with a Hong Kong partner in the same line of activity.   The Hong Kong side does the designs and the marketing, while having run down its own production but retaining enough production capacity in Hong Kong to do certain parts of the orders. The Chinese side is a collective under a larger parent collective organization owned at town level, and the venture has imported equipment and quadruple the size of its labour force.   Though successful at exporting, the company has faced labour force problems which result in low productivity and wastage of materials, but did not go into detail on these issues at interview.

CJV-5, producing biscuits and confectionary, appears, in contrast, to have "depackaged", but not to be a very successful exporter because of heavy competition in foreign markets. It comments that in its previous lai liao jia gong (processing and assembly) arrangement it did not have adequate machinery to provide good quality output, and the CJV has been a means of acquiring equipment. The Hong Kong partner is in electronics, the same line of business as the CJV's parent; and takes no part in the running of the business. The parent, a state company, was originally in confectionary but diversified into electronics during the Cultural Revolution (!). The confectionary company was helped to find a cooperative joint venture partner by the Local Foreign Economic Committee, and preferred a CJV to a JV because it lacked capital. The company claims to be profitable. Its preference for domestic sales is taken up in Section 4.3 and does not necessarily seem to reflect any failure of the depackaging.

Of the other two existing Chinese companies going directly into CJV's, CJ-9 is a restaurant in a large city run by a resident Hong Kong team of manager, accountant and chef. In attempting to move towards a Hong Kong standard and compete more effectively (especially for the custom of tourists from Hong Kong) it clearly relies on Hong Kong expertise, from a Hong Kong company in the catering business. Again the choice of CJV results from a lack of its own funds. The Hong Kong side pays rent for the premises and then takes the bulk of the profits. The restaurant has expanded its seating capacity from about 100 to 700 over the past three years. CJV-13 similarly has a Hong Kong partner with appropriate expertise. This is in hotel refurbishing and the venture is renovating a well-established hotel with apparently successful results.

Two more companies in the sample can be considered under the present heading, but are new ventures started by large existing companies as part of diversification. CJV-10 is a beauty salon, set up by a Guangdong film studio in association with a Hong Kong partner related to members of the studio. The Hong Kong partner provided finance for importing equipment, takes no part in management, and (unusually) is guaranteed by the film studio repayment of his capital within three years. The motivation on the Hong Kong side is a purely financial return while the Chinese side gains a certain useful freedom of action for foreign transactions (through less than under a JV).

CJV-11, making kitchen equipment for restaurants, is the only company in the group being discussed in this subsection, to have had serious difficulty. It is a new factory set up by a machinery company under a very large and diversified conglomerate. Its main problem is that its Hong Kong partner, though in the restaurant business, has failed to generate export orders and local buyers refuse to pay foreign exchange since there is considerable competition in the industry. After reorganization and the appointment of new Hong Kong and Chinese managers the venture makes an RMB profit, but, feels it is burdened by various payments it must make to its Chinese parent and complains about the need constantly to bargain with tax and trade authorities. This company felt an equity joint venture would have given it for more freedom of action.

4.2.2   New ventures with local authorities

Discussion of the nine remaining CJVs can usefully start with two

61

where the initiative seems clearly to have come from the Chinese side as much as from the foreign partner. In CJV-4, a Hong Kong investor set up a factory in his family's home town in China to produce nylon adhesive tapes used in fastenings on such items as sports bags, with machinery imported from Taiwan. The Hong Kong investor was purely engaged in trading, and mastering the technology was left to the Chinese side. Unfortunately for the venture, some complex chemical technology is involved in the dyeing of the raw materials and the factory is in an area where skilled workers are few and technical education insufficient. Several workers have been sent for training to Shanghai, but some have not returned. Purchasing already-dyed tapes from domestic sources raises problems of a product quality too low for exports, yet failure to export results in a shortage of foreign exchange to buy the better quality (but much more expensive) imported raw materials. This venture, working at 30% capacity and making losses, seems to be foundering on the inability of either side to transfer technology.

In CJV-3, in contrast, virtually no new technology other than the peripheral use of refrigerators and motor vehicles is required, since the process (the production of dried ducks, a well-known Chinese delicacy) is traditional and the factory is in an area of China long renowned for this activity. The Hong Kong partner is in this trade and was looking for a product source in China, and had also considered Dongguan. The motivation of the Chinese side (a town-level trading company) was very straightforward - ducks require an export quota, which would be obtained more easily for a foreign cooperation than for a domestic enterprise. (The quota is decided for each province by the national poultry corporation and the quota for companies would be decided at county level).

One technical worker from Hong Kong stays in the factory, but otherwise it is wholly Chinese run. The venture thus has a short run contract (five years) and the Chinese side would wish to dispense with the Hong Kong partner (who is said to be very satisfied and keen on the cooperation to continue) if they can get a quota for themselves at the end of the contract. In the meanwhile the Chinese side feels it receives inadequate information from the Hong Kong side about export prices received. In general the venture is dissatisfied with exporting, and also because of the exchange rate it receives for its forex earnings (see Section 4.3). Difficulties are experienced with the customs authorities when importing food stuffs (over 10 "chops"- authorizing stamps- are needed to import), although exporting is easier since it goes directly via Jiangmen City; Jiangmen, like Foshan, having its own "open gate" to the outside world.

Another venture, CJV-8 (polythene bags), where a local authority, a village, has tried to set up a new venture in an attempt to reduce localized youth unemployment and to make use of funds from land sales during agricultural reform. In this case the Hong Kong partner is a trader in the machinery used in the venture, and there was a strong feeling in the village (with hindsight) that they had been overcharged for the equipment. Many problems have been encountered with the lack of labour force skills and the Hong Kong manager recently left along with several skilled workers. In 1987 the venture was expecting to make a loss though it had started to export. One official commented that the village authority had not sought any outside advice about the venture and had indeed tried to keep its activities towards foreign investors confidential.

CJV-12, making jewellery, again is a local authority initiative, this time in a village near Guangzhou and with Hong Kong partners related to the villagers and experienced in the jewellery industry. This is also a minority involvement by the Guangzhou City Handicraft Company, a state organization. This venture illustrates a common pattern. The village (of about 8000 people) moved into rural industrialization following the agricultural reforms and the open policy. During the early days of the Open Policy it was very easy to set up processing and assembly operations, and the present venture started as a LLJG operation in 1980 with the Hong Kong relatives. The move towards a CJV came because the Hong Kong partner also wanted some sales within China, which are not allowed under LLJG contracts. In practice certain features of the LLJG contract remain, and the Hong Kong side pays rent and a processing fee to the Chinese side. As the venture has progressed the Hong Kong partner has played less and less part in routine management and supervision and is mainly confined to export marketing. The village leadership is involved in the venture and the village collective has several other enterprises too. The Chinese manager commented that unless the leaders take a positive attitude there is no point in doing business. The venture has welcomed recent central government decisions to treat CJVs like equity JVs for tax purposes. It commented that setting up a CJV, however, was much more time consuming than establishing LLJG, and many government departments had to be considered.

CJV-6 (footwear) and CJV-7 (furs and leather) are similar to many of the equity joint ventures discussed in the preceding chapter. Both are ventures where the Hong Kong side has expertise in marketing, design and production and has relocated to China for reasons of cost. In the case of CJV-7, a further motive is that fur products exports from China are not subject to US import restrictions whereas those from Hong Kong are. In CJV-6, the Hong Kong entrepreneur was a classmate of the county's communist party secretary, and the secretary persuaded him to come to this county rather than to Jiangman City. Both factories sell almost 100% of their output abroad. In the shoe factory there are some skilled workers from Hong Kong and a deputy general manager from Hong Kong who comes frequently. The Hong Kong side would have preferred the clearer tax position and greater freedom of action of an equity joint venture, but at the time of signing the contract a JV would have required provincial level approval whereas a CJV could go through at county level, facilitated by the Hong Kong side's good relations with the county CP secretary. In the fur factory (soon also to branch out into producing leather) the Chinese side preferred a CJV to a LLJG because they felt the Hong Kong side would feel a greater obligation to provide orders. The Hong Kong side is actively involved in management and supervision, and has six people resident in the factory. Style is of obvious importance in the marketing of fur coats and the Hong Kong entrepreneur is also a fashion designer. Adding leather goods to the fur coat operations is a sign of increased confidence in the running of the operations as mistakes on leather work cannot be corrected as they can with fur coats (which are made up of numerous separate very small strips).

Of the remaining three CJVs in the sample, CJV-2 (stone cutting) and CJV-15 (food) did not provide a great deal of information but appear straightforward. CJV-14 (cameras) is a venture where both sides, but especially the Hong Kong side, are dissatisfied.

CJV-2 quarries granite to be cut into such items as tops for coffee tables. The technology is western European, and the previous chapter showed a case (JV-8) where attempts to introduce similar machinery into another county had gone wrong. In CJV-2 the foreign investor (about whom there was little information other than that he was from Macau), has good personal contacts with the Chinese partner (about whom, however, little information was available except that it was a "travel company" owning hotels and amusement parks). The venture was in operation, though in its early stages. CJV-15, making an up-market food product according to French designs and taste, was in a very early stage and still experimenting with product quality. It was a CJV between a Hong Kong trading company and the Guangzhou Economic and Technology Development Zone and the product is one for which at present there would be little domestic demand except in foreign-run hotels.

CJV-14, the camera factory, is situated on a large municipally-owned industrial estate. Both sides claim it is de facto a 100% foreign enterprise, but since such an enterprise should have required central government approval it went through as a CJV instead. Although hoping to sell its cameras in China for RMB, at present the venture only exports, but is not making an operating profit. The company contrasts the degree of cooperation it receives from the Chinese side unfavourably with that of another factory it has (in Dongguan). The company suffers problems form power cuts and poor quality accommodation provided by the Chinese side for workers, and for Hong Kong staff. The Chinese side felt the Hong Kong staff, however, were constantly undertaking "unreasonable" expenditure.

Several companies (e.g. CJV-6, CJV-12) commented that in practice they were run like equity joint ventures, with considerable freedom of action. Others, like CJV-3 and CJV-11, bemoaned their lack of flexibility compared to equity JVs, especially in their relations with the trade and tax authorities, though the tax position is less ambiguous now that the Cooperative Joint Venture Law has been published (April 1988). Where the CJV has developed from an earlier processing and assembly arrangement, in some cases (e.g. CJV-12) the foreign partner still pays a processing fee to the Chinese side. The flexibility of the CJV contract is well-illustrated by CJV-12 in fact, where at the end of the contract the equipment will be divided among the partners (like a JV) instead of belonging to the Chinese side (as in a normal CJV). The company which was regarded as virtually 100% foreign (CJV-14, camera) was one which was the most dissatisfied about the cooperation it received from the Chinese side.

Such information as would be gathered on tax payments is shown in Table 4.2. CJV-2, CJV-6, and CJV-10 appear to be taxed under the Foreign Enterprise Income Tax Law, whereas CJV-5, CJV-12 and CJV-15 appear to be receiving Equity Joint Venture treatment. The widespread use of tax holidays, except for the shortest contracts is apparent.

4.2.3   Structural aspects

The range of firms in our sample differs from that of the JVs in the previous chapter in so far as **no Western or Japanese multinationals are included,** reflecting the general tendency of such multinationals to go for equity joint venture arrangements. Companies such as CJV-6 (footwear), CJV-9 (fur coats), CJV-12 (jewellery) represent out-processing by Hong Kong firms where the firms have internalized through a closer arrangement than LLJG to maintain greater control. In the case of CJV-1 (clothing) and CJV-5 (biscuits), LLJG arrangements with existing Chinese factories have developed into CJVs, and CJV-12 (jewellery) developed first as a new LLJG venture, and later became a CJV.

CJVs also seem to have been commonly used by relatively inexperienced local authorities trying to attract inward investment, often from relatives or people with personal contact with the area, under the open policy. By no means all of these have been successful, and CJV-4 (nylon adhesive tape) points to the problems which can, arise when the Hong Kong partner is not able to provide whatever expertise the Chinese lack.

In general, although CJVs appear to have been suitable vehicles for inexperienced Chinese partners, lacking capital, often they have been chosen because they are easier to get approval for, and the lack of freedom of action compared to equity joint ventures is widely commented on. For some of the Hong Kong companies, the CJVs were relocations of most of their production to China e.g. CJV-1, clothing, where the Hong Kong partner's Hong Kong operation now deals mainly with design and samples, and CJV-11 (fur coats) which have cut its Hong Kong operation from 100 to 20 workers. CJV-6, however, continued to produce shoes in Hong Kong. Compared to the equity joint venture companies, however, more of the CJVs were genuinely new ventures rather than relocations from Hong Kong, indicating that it is often the **expansion** of production which has been located in China.

4.3 **Marketing, export and foreign exchange issues**

Table 4.3 sets out a summary of information for the sample of CJVs on marketing and foreign exchange issues. As in other areas of this research, some companies provided merely routine information whereas other gave good insights into particular issues.

The level of exports of a company will depend on overseas demand conditions, on the Chinese level of costs relative to overseas competitors, and on product quality. The choice between exporting and domestic sales will depend on the relative state of competition in the export and domestic markets, and will be influenced by the behaviour of the foreign partner with regard to export policy and by the share of foreign exchange received by the CJV, and the exchange rate at which it can exchange forex into Renminbi.

In our sample of CJVs, six of the companies export the bulk of their output:

CJV-1	Clothing	CJV-8	Polythene bags
CJV-6	Footwear	CJV-12	Jewellery
CJV-7	Furs and leather	CJV-14	Cameras

Of these six, the footwear company, exporting all of its output in a situation of strong demand, is planning to expand its capacity. It uses a cost plus mark-up system of pricing, which in the joint venture companies in the previous chapter was resisted by the Hong Kong side. Foreign exchange is retained completely and is being used for expansion. The clothing factory which, like the footwear company, has a Hong Kong partner with good customer contacts, feels it is competing on price rather than high quality, and is worried by rising prices of imported equipment. It chooses to sell domestically 10% of its output to acquire RMB for buying domestic inputs and paying wages, and fashionable western-style clothing is in strong demand within China.

Neither CJV-6 nor CJV-1 expressed reservations about its Hong Kong partner's pricing policy, a theme familiar from the previous chapter.

This arises in CJV-12, the jewellery, which appears to be a successful and amicable cooperation, but where the Chinese side feels it has no choice but to place great trust on the Hong Kong side's goodwill about the prices charged. This is particularly acute since the jewellery is not at all standard, and requires individual pricing and apparently frequent price changes. All the profits on exporting go to the Hong Kong side, which pays the Chinese a processing fee in spite of the venture being a CJV rather than a LLJG. One interesting feature here is that the company regarded the overseas market for jewellery as much less competitive than the domestic market and therefore was exporting 90% of output less by choice than by necessity. The latter feature also characterises the camera company, CJV-14, which found itself unable to compete on the domestic market but could sell abroad. The camera company was making losses however, but was paying rent for its factory site to its Chinese partner (who provided no other capital contribution).

Competitive pressure in foreign markets was strongly felt by the polythene bags manufacturer, CJV-8, whose raw materials prices were rising faster than those for its product. It was also developing direct exports, alongside those undertaken by its foreign partner.

All these six companies have been "successful" in achieving a high proportion of gross foreign exchange receipts in total sales, and only in the case of the camera company is this in the context of a clear failure to sell in the domestic market. Two other companies - CJV-4 (nylon adhesive tapes) and CJV-11 (kitchen equipment) illustrate that even success in this simple sense should not be taken for granted. The nylon tapes factory has been unable fully to master the technology required to achieve acceptable quality for export, and the kitchen equipment factory's Hong Kong partner has failed to achieve the export orders he promised.

Some companies produce products which are necessarily export-orientated, in the sense of being outside the tastes or beyond the income range required for sale in the Chinese domestic market. In these cases problems on the export side have to be "absorbed" by the business and if those problems are too great the business fails. In other cases, if anti-export biases (discussed in Chapter Three) arise, companies may be able to switch in part to the domestic market. In this regard, the question of foreign exchange retention, the exchange rate for forex into RMB, and the pricing policy when the foreign partner is responsible for export sales are major influences. A company "tied" to exports is the fur coat company, CJV-7. Since the price of a fur coat may be in excess of the lifetime earnings of many Chinese workers, domestic sales are hardly likely to be large and mainly take the form of substandard products sold off in the summer months when export sales are weak. CJV-7 commented that the exchange rate it received on its forex earnings would determine the difference between profits and losses. Since the company buys many of its furs locally, it must acquire RMB. Since even the "street" rate for foreign exchange in 1987 and 1988 was 50% more than the official rate (RMB75 per HK$100 instead of RMB47), a company at the border line of profitability at the official rate would have over a 30% mark-up on turnover at the "free" rate. CJV-7 commented that recent opportunities for it to sell forex for RMB to other enterprises at "free" rate under the new internal adjustment system had proved most helpful.

Two companies which seem to have made a choice to move more towards the domestic market, while earning enough foreign exchange to buy imported inputs and pay the foreign partner for capital equipment charges, are CJV-3 (making preserved ducks, a traditional delicacy) and CJV-5 (making confectionary and biscuits). Both face heavy competition in overseas markets (in these cases principally Hong Kong itself). For biscuits and confectionary heavy expenditure on advertising and packaging is necessary in the Hong Kong market, and domestic profits are higher. The dried duck factory also has problems with the export price it receives (via its Hong Kong partner) which at the official exchange rate often does not cover the RMB costs of production. This factory has had many difficulties with foreign exchange. It can get back only 30% of the forex earned, and earnings are defined narrowly as only including profit. It only gets the official rate for these earnings, and when it requires forex (e.g. to pay for imported feedstuff) the Bank of China is slow to provide it. In this case the anti-export bias seems strong.

Since CJVs have been expected to achieve a balance in foreign exchange (though now there are legal opportunities for foreign-invested companies to exchange at free rates) CJVs geared towards the domestic market may face forex problems. CJV-9, the restaurant earns a proportion (16%) of its revenue in forex by catering to tourists. CJV-15, the hotel management company, earns an unspecified amount of its revenue in forex. The beauty salon, CJV-10, set up by a film studio as a diversification, earns no forex. Its Hong Kong partner sometimes buys Chinese goods with his RMB profits for resale in Hong Kong, and the film studio parent company has some activities of its own to forex apparently.

Of the two remaining companies insufficient information was provided by CJV-2, the stone-cutting factory, to explain its choice of 50% exports. CJV-15 making a sophisticated food product for export, is currently at a trial stage developing its product.

For most companies the net foreign exchange earnings will have been substantially less than the gross forex receipts. Remission of import duty on imported inputs when used in the production of export products facilitate the export processing of such inputs. Some companies (e.g. CJV-4 making nylon adhesive tapes) had real problems with the quality of local inputs whereas a few others (e.g. CJV-2, CJV-7 had developed some local supply sources).

4.4 Employment and operational issues

Table 4.4 give a summary of material from the companies on issues relating to employment and other operational matters.

Labour practices and the motivation of workers received less comment from the cooperative joint venture interviewees than from the joint venture companies in Chapter Three, perhaps because among the CJVs were no western entrepreneurs to whom Chinese work practice would be unfamiliar. CJV-1 (clothing) and CJV-8 (polythene bags) mentioned problems with the lack of skills of ordinary workers, and CJV-8 referred to the continuation of an "iron rice bowl" mentality among its workforce (even though they were from outside the area and had come seeking employment). They were unwilling, for instance, to work without bonus during the training period. Many workers in the sample were on piece rates, and CJV-8 commented that in Hong Kong workers would not have required piece rates to motivate them. CJV-4 (nylon adhesive tapes) suffered from a shortage of skilled workers.

Many factories had recruited workers from the countryside,

including CJV-4, CJV-6 (footwear), generally recruited directly. Only JV-11 (kitchen equipment) and JV-12 (jewellrey)) used Labour Service Bureau for recruitment. More than two thirds of the sample employed workers on contract, though in a few cases this only applied to very temporary workers on certain categories (e.g. CJV-7's inspectors). The labour shortage in the Pearl River Delta in 1987-8 was reflected in comments on high labour turnover, which CJV-1 dealt with by paying higher wages and CJV-6 by keeping 10% of wages back until workers had finished their contract. Only CJV-3, in a small town, referred to local unemployment. CJV-12 was in a village where foreign investment had been sought at the start of the Open Policy to deal with a labour surplus, but now had a labour shortage.

Two thirds of the sample companies paid wages of a little under Y200 per month, most of the rest paid more. CJV-3, where there was local unemployment, said its wages were almost double that of domestic Chinese companies in the town.

Some companies with large Chinese partners (or Chinese parent companies) had special problems of their own. CJV-11, making kitchen equipment, found much of its profit creamed off by excessive payments for labour benefits to its large parent company. CJV-7, the fur coat company, had started by employing various relatives of personnel in its Chinese partner, but had gradually "let many of them go".

Most factories had resident Hong Kong managers and some skilled workers. Generally it had been possible to reduce the Hong Kong staff after the initial stages. Some ventures, such as CJV-12 (jewellery) felt this operation ran better now that the Hong Kong manager visited only at intervals. Only one company (CJV-15, food) had had equipment set up by Western technicians. CJV-11 had had disputes between the Chinese and the Hong Kong managers, now resolved by replacing both.

Other operating issues concerned the problems of power supply which affect many companies in China. CJV-14 complained of power cuts, as did CJV-3. CJV-8 operated three shifts to make use of electricity when it was available. CJV-15 complained of high fees charged for water and power.

Table 4.1

The Cooperative Joint Venture Companies -- Introductory Profiles (Sheet 1)

	Company	Size	Contract	Equity Proportions; Profit Sharing Proportions (China/Foreign)	Technology	Exports	Present Venture's Previous Contracts
CJV-1	Clothing Manufacturing	300 workers	10 years from 1985	c60/30+; NA NA	Equipment imported through Hong Kong (origin uncertain).	90%	Also have LLJG with same Hong Kong partner.
CJV-2	Stone cutting factory	100 workers	10 years from 1986	50/50; 50/50	Equipment from West Germany, some from Italy.	50%	None.
CJV-3	Dried duck processing	70 workers	5 years from 1985	50/50; 55/45	Basically traditional technology.	30-40%	None.
CJV-4	Nylon adhesive tapes manufacturing	60 workers	5 years from 1985	70/30; NA/NA	Taiwanese equipment, said to be 'advanced'. Factory felt it lacks technical knowledge	20%	None.
CJV-5	Confectionary manufacturing	68 workers	6 years from 1983	Equity shares NA 50/50 for first three years, 55/45 for last three years.	Packaging machinery, imported from Japan.	'very small'.	LLJG 1981-83

Table 4.1

Cooperative Joint Venture Companies -- Introductory Profiles (Sheet 2)

Company	Size	Contract	Equity Proportions; Profit Sharing Proportions (China/Foreign)	Technology	Exports	Present Venture's Previous Contracts
CJV-6	Footwear manufacturing	300 workers	10 years from 1985	50/50 50/50	Equipment from Japan.	100%	None.
CJV-7	Leather and Fur manufacturing	120 workers	10 years from 1985	50/50 NA	New equipment (source?)	Almost 100%	None.
CJV-8	Polythene bags manufacturing	200 workers	10 years from 1986	60/40 NA	Machinery from Taiwan.	'Heavy export orientation'	None.
CJV-9	Restaurant	600 workers	contract length ~? from 1984	NA 10/90	Hong Kong style restaurant supervision.	16% of turnover is in forex.	the second CJV for this restaurant.
CJV-10	Beauty parlour	c20 workers	5 years from 1985	NA 40/60 for three years, then 60/40.	Hong Kong styles.	0	None.

Table 4.1

Cooperative Joint Venture Companies -- Introductory Profiles (Sheet 3)

	Company	Size	Contract	Equity Proportions; Profit Sharing Proportions (China/Foreign)	Technology	Exports	Present Venture's Previous Contracts
CJV-11	Kitchen equipment for restaurants manufacturing	55 workers	8 years from 1985	NA Three years repaying capital then 40/60 for 2 years, 50/50 for 1 year, 60/40 for 2 years.	NA	'low'	None.
CJV-12	Jewellery manufacturing	180 workers	10 years from 1985	29/71 56/44 over and above repayment of capital to HK side.	Hong Kong designs.	c90%	Previously LLJG (1980-85)
CJV-13	Hotels company	NA	15 years from 1985	90/10 NA	Hong Kong management style.	Some revenue in forex.	NA
CJV-14	Camera manufacturing	NA	10 years from 1985	NA (but de facto 100% foreign) 30/70 (of net profit).	NA	100%	No previous contracts at this site.
CJV-15	Food company	85 workers	30 years from 1987	'Almost all capital is from HK side'. NA	French technology.	NA	None.

Table 4.2

Cooperative Joint Venture Companies -- The Partners and the Contract (Sheet 1)

Company	Chinese side	Foreign side	Tax	Special Features or comments	Other operations in China
CJV-1 Clothing manufacturing - existing company	Collective, under the town government.	Hong Kong clothing factory, doing designing, and some parts of the orders.	No income tax for 3 years. 5% product tax. 150% import duty on raw materials for local sales.	Has expanded from employment of 70 before the foreign investment.	Chinese parent has several companies employing 600 workers.
CJV-2 Stone cutting - new company	State travel company.	Macao company, whose head is "old friend" of the Chinese partner's management.	No product tax for first year, then 5%. 55% profits tax, "after several years".	Also 10 years loan from People's Bank of China (to be repaid in forex).	Chinese parent has some hotels and amusement parks.
CJV-3 Dried duck processing - new company	Town trading company.	Hong Kong trading company, dealing with dried products.	NA	Hong Kong partner wants to diversify next year into meat production (dried ducks produced only in winter), and to continue beyond the five year contract.	None at present. Chinese side plans to set up a factory for duck by-products (will be 100% Chinese).
CJV-4 Nylon adhesive tapes manufacturing - new factory	Town trading company.	Hong Kong trading company. HK entrepreneur's family from this town.	Free of income tax for first three years. 5% product tax.	Capital on Chinese side borrowed from a Shanghai finance company. Have to buy forex at above official rate to repay this company.	None.

Table 4.2

Cooperative Joint Venture Companies — The Partners and the Contract (Sheet 2)

Company	Chinese side	Foreign side	Special features or comments	Other operations in China
CJV-5 Confectionary manufacturing - existing factory	State electronics (sic) company, (produced confectionary until the Cultural Revolution!)	Hong Kong electrical company. No experience in confectionary. Introduced by City Foreign Economic Committee.	City has 20% discount on the 33% profits tax. (This is the standard Open Zone tax concession)	Guarantee repayment of capital and interest to HK side whether or not the CJV is profitable. If profitable the interest comes out of HK's profits share. First CJV is first to import machinery in confectionary industry. Chinese side wishes to renew contract.	State company still in operation (with 739 workers), and CJV is only a part of it. Also engages in LLJG(?)
CJV-6 Footwear manufacturing - new factory	Collective under town government.	Hong Kong shoe company, still in production in Hong Kong. HK entrepreneur is classmate of communist party secretary of the county.	Initial tax holiday (two years?) then 5-graded profits tax. Duty free in parts of raw materials because output is exported.	Want to change to an equity JV. Profitable and reinvesting the profits. Would have preferred equity JV in the first place, but this needed provincial level approval (county level approval for CJV).	The town collective has 30 other companies.
CJV-7 Leather and fur manufacturing - use existing factory building provided by Chinese partner.	City Housing Authority.	Hong Kong fur company, previously with 100 workers in Hong Kong; now only 20, doing design and samples. The HK entrepreneur and the Chinese manager are originally from same village.	NA	Wanted CJV from the beginning rather than LLJG because Chinese side felt HK side would take more interest.	None for HK side. NA for Chinese side.

Table 4.2

Cooperative Joint Venture Companies -- The Partners and the Contract (Sheet 3)

Company	Chinese side	Foreign side	Tax	Special features or comments	Other operations in China
CJV-8 Polythene bags manufacturing - new factory	Village government agency.	Hong Kong company which trades in machinery for polythene bags production.	Three year tax holiday.	Some feeling on Chinese side of having been overcharged for the CJV's machinery by the HK side. Village had considerable spare funds from agricultural reform and land sales. Unemployment in village, despite the area's general labour shortage.	NA
CJV-9 Restaurant - already in existence before the CJV.	Garden Forest Office (sic) is parent company.	Hong Kong company with fast food shops in HK.	NA	First CJV was one of Guangdong's first. Chinese side claim first partner was confidence trickster.	The CJV has diversified into hotel management and bakeries.
CJV-10 Beauty parlour	Film company	Hong Kong partner is related to film studio people. Provides finance only, no management.	"No tax holiday on five year contracts", but HK side pays 20% tax on its 60% of the profits (over and above capital repayment).	HK side guaranteed repayment of capital over first three years of operation, over and above their share (60%) of profits. Guarantee from Chinese parent. Unusual tax provisions.	Film company is diversifying, and seeking freedom of action of a CJV. Film processing operated by CJV in same building.

74

Table 4.2

Cooperative Joint Venture Companies — The Partners and the Contract (Sheet 4)

Company	Chinese side	Foreign side	Tax	Special features or comments	Other operations in China
CJV-11 Kitchen equipment for restaurants manufacturing - new company	Machinery company, under a large industrial conglomerate.	Hong Kong restauranteur.	5.5% output tax, 3.5% sub contract tax, 25% income tax.	-Disputes with tax authorities over depreciation period (CJV wanted 3 years, and tax authorities 8 years). -Feel CJVs have much less freedom of action than JVs. -Need constant negotiations with trade and tax authorities.	Chinese partner's parent is highly diversified, with other JVs.
CJV-12 Jewellery manufacturing - new company for first (LLJG) contract	Village collective, (with Guangzhou City Handicraft Company owning minority (12%) shareholding and getting 12% of net profits).	Hong Kong company experienced in jewellery manufacturing, whose entrepreneur has relatives in the village. Chinese side stresses importance of good relations with village authorities.	Profits tax - 3 year tax holiday then 2 years at 50%. (counts as an export orientated venture). But only profits on domestic sales are reported to tax authorities.	-CJV refers to a "new policy" of treating CJVs like JVs for tax purposes. -When the venture finishes the partners share the joint assets like a JV. -Wanted change from previous LLJG because HK partner wanted some sales in China. -HK side appears to supply materials and pay the Chinese side a processing fee like LLJG.	The village collective owns 6 other enterprises with foreign involvement.

Table 4.2

Cooperative Joint Venture Companies -- The Partners and the Contract (Sheet 5)

Company	Chinese side	Foreign side	Tax	Special features or comments	Other operations in China
CJV-13 Hotels company - refurbishing hotels	National Handicraft Company and Tourist board of a major northern city.	Hong Kong partner experienced in fitting out hotels.	NA	10 year loan from bank in Hong Kong, with two year initial grace period. Venture has also set up a finance company in Hong Kong to borrow funds. Complicated structure of ownership and control.	NA
CJV-14 Camera manufacturing	Large industrial estate owned by city government.	Hong Kong company with real estate as well as camera operations in HK.	NA	Claim to be de facto 100% foreign company. At end of contract equipment will belong to China except for certain items which are on loan.	Chinese side has many other foreign cooperations. HK side has a profitable camera factory in Dongguan. Also

Table 4.2

Cooperative Joint Venture Companies — The Partners and the Contract (Sheet 6)

Company	Chinese side	Foreign side	Tax	Special features or comments	Other operations in China
CJV-15 Food manufacturing	Guangzhou Economic and Technological Development Zone.	Hong Kong company	Two year tax holiday then 50% for next three years.	-	had a LLJG Operation in Foshan by same HK company to produce raw materials for this CJV. operation in Shenzhen, started 1978 and finished before contract. Also have factory in Zhuhai which stopped production.

Table 4.3
Cooperative Joint Venture Companies -- Markets and Foreign Exchange (Sheet 1)

Company	Exports Actual/(Contract)	Marketing Arrangements	Competition Domestic vs Foreign Sales	Forex Balance - raw materials	Forex Retention	Other Issues
CJV-1 Clothing manufacturing	90(?)	Hong Kong side does export marketing.	Competitions based on price rather than quality. Local sales to secure RMB. Customs duty on raw materials for domestic is an incentive to export.	NA	50% goes to Chinese parent, 50% kept by CJV, which can remit overseas through Bank of China.	Problem of rising prices of imported equipment, and shortage of capital ("hard to borrow from banks").
CJV-2 Stone cutting	50(90% "planned")	Macau side does marketing.	"No problem with demand".	50% of raw materials imported originally, now all from China.	70% retained, 30% given to government.	
CJV-3 Dried duck processing	30-40%(?)	Hong Kong side does marketing. Get Chinese export quota because they are a CJV.	Production depends heavily on state of HK market. Chinese side lacks information on HK prices. Won't export if export price less than domestic price or less than costs. Frequent export price changes in China, can't easily sell in another county.	Much duck feed is imported. Just achieving a forex balance, to cover raw materials and depreciation to HK partner.	30% retained by factory, 70% to various levels of government. Can actually get back the 30% only on their forex profits, not gross forex receipts.	Bank of China slow in providing forex, if they need it, and factory gets RMB against forex receipts only at official rate. Problems with customs duties and procedures.

Table 4.3

Cooperative Joint Venture Companies -- Markets and Foreign Exchange (Sheet 2)

Company	Exports Actual/(Contract)	Marketing Arrangements	Competition Domestic vs Foreign Sales	Forex Balance - raw materials	Forex Retention	Other Issues
CJV-4 Nylon adhesive tapes manufacturing	20%(50%)	Hong Kong side trades this product along with leather products.	Get little information on market conditions from HK partner. Operating at 30% capacity because poor demand, and HK side has not received any profit yet. Now many other factories in China producing similar product.	Raw materials all local, and would be import duty problems if imported materials.	NA	Local materials have colour control problems. Imported materials more expensive. Chinese side thinks export prices too low. Making losses.
CJV-5 Confectionary manufacturing	Only "small" proportion exported.	Hong Kong side does marketing.	Need heavy advertising expenditures for HK sales. Competition on quality and packaging. Claim to be very profitable. Profits lower on exports than domestic sales.	Packaging materials are imported from Japan and Korea.	100% retained during repayment period.	
CJV-6 Footwear manufacturing	c100%(contract?)	Sell through HK partner. Sell according to direct cost + machinery.	Have more overseas orders than firm can meet. Price according to direct cost irrespective of demand.	Raw materials imported duty free.	Retain 100% (town uses this to develop factory and import equipment).	Designated an "export enterprise". In process of doubling factory area to meet growing demand.

Table 4.3

Cooperative Joint Venture Companies — Markets and Foreign Exchange (Sheet 3)

Company	Exports Actual/(Contract)	Marketing Arrangements	Competition Domestic vs Foreign Sales	Forex Balance - raw materials	Forex Retention	Other Issues
CJV-7 Leather and fur manufacturing	c100%(contract?)	Sell through HK partner. Avoid USA import duty by producing in China. Sell only rejects in China, especially during off-season.	Exchange rate received on forex sales is crucial to profitability. No shortage of foreign orders, but demand is seasonal. Sell mainly to USA and West Germany, some barter trade with Italy.	Some furs are from China, for which company must acquire RMB.	100% retention, but RMB shortage for domestic raw materials.	Working capital is a problem.
CJV-8 Polythene bags manufacturing	"Heavy export orientation".	90% done through HK partner, 10% directly. Make according to customer specifications e.g. for West German supermarkets	Raw materials prices rising faster than output prices.	Domestic raw materials are poor quality, so they import (mainly from Japan).	100% retained until repayment period finishes.	Expect to make losses this year until venture more fully developed.
CJV-9 Restaurant	16% of turnover is in forex.	Serves domestic market.	Quality of service important, especially for visitors from HK.	NA	NA	Chinese side takes a rent for the site, CJV makes about 10% profit on turnover.

Table 4.3

Cooperative Joint Venture Companies – Markets and Foreign Exchange (Sheet 4)

Company	Exports Actual/(Contract)	Marketing Arrangements	Competition Domestic vs Foreign Sales	Forex Balance - raw materials	Forex Retention	Other Issues
CJV-10 Beauty parlour	0	Serves domestic market.	Hong Kong styles are important in attracting customers. Cheaper than in big hotels.	Need 33% forex to repay HK side (sometimes Hong Kong partner takes goods instead).	Must obtain forex to repay HK side from Chinese parent company.	-
CJV-11 Kitchen equipment for restaurants manufacturing	"Low"/35%	Hong Kong partner responsible for exports. Had hoped, unsuccessfully, local hotels would buy paying foreign exchange.	Heavy domestic competition (e.g. 30 similar factories in Guangzhou). Much competition on quality.	Pay HK partner in RMB. No import duty on raw materials imported for use in exports. Use local materials (mainly steel) unless customer wants especially high quality.	NA	Making RMB profit, now quality and delivery dates are better than previously.
CJV-12 Jewellery manufacturing	90/70	Hong Kong partner sets export prices, which need changing frequently ("requires trust").	More competition in domestic market. Export sales mainly to Middle East. On exports HK side "gets all the profit". Only share profit on domestic sales.	Raw materials mainly imported. (Local ones not high enough quality). Pay 60% duty on materials imported for use for domestically sold products.	NA	Planning to expand into related products like buttons.

Table 4.3

Cooperative Joint Venture Companies – Markets and Foreign Exchange (Sheet 5)

Company	Exports Actual/(Contract)	Marketing Arrangements	Competition Domestic vs Foreign Sales	Forex Balance - raw materials	Forex Retention	Other Issues
CJV-13 Hotels company	NA/NA	---	The hotel, in northern city, has well-established clientele, mainly Japanese.	Some receipts in forex.	NA	Planning to diversify into renovating restaurants.
CJV-14 Camera manufacturing	100/60	Hong Kong side does own marketing in what is in effect a 100% foreign company.	Easier to sell in HK. Want to sell in China to obtain RMB for workers' salaries.	NA	Must go through Bank of China.	Not profitable. HK side dissatisfied with cooperation received from Chinese, and compares this CJV unfavourably with its operation in Dongguan.
CJV-15 Food manufacturing	Plan to be mainly export oriented.	Marketing done by Hong Kong side.	Quality very important. Strong competition from France and Hungary.	Much of basic raw materials are local.	NA	-

82

Table 4.4

Cooperative Joint venture Companies -- Employment and Operational Issues (Sheet 1)

	Company	Workforce	Employment Status	Recruitment	Wages (per month)	Wages in relation to other costs	Training and Supervision	Remarks
CJV-1	Clothing manufacturing	300	60% are "contract" workers, but very short term, and move from factory to factory.	Direct advertisement, don't use Labour Service Bureau.	Y180 including bonus on average, on piece work.	20% (raw materials 40%).	One technical worker from Hong Kong helps training.	Low output and wastage of raw materials because workers insufficiently trained. Keep wages high to reduce labour turnover.
CJV-2	Stone cutting	100	"Mainly on contract".	Workers all newly hired for the venture.	Y300 on average.	10% (raw materials 30%) but 60% of 'costs' are repayment of equipment and loan.	Frequent visits by Macau partner.	Some problems with unskillful workers.
CJV-3	Dried duck processing	70	All contract.	NA	Y170 - 200 (total) on average. No bonus, but can use residual output to make sausages (sic!) to sell.	NA	One HK technical worker stays in factory.	In an area where still some unemployment. Average wage in town about Y100. Some power supply problems.
CJV-4	Nylon adhesive tapes manufacturing	60	All contract.	Most workers are former peasants.	Y160, on piece rate.	Less than 20% (raw materials 60%)	Sent workers to Shanghai for training (but don't always return).	Town very short of technical workers.

Table 4.4

Cooperative Joint Venture Companies -- Employment and Operational Issues (Sheet 2)

Company	Workforce	Employment Status	Recruitment	Wages (per month)	Wages in relation to other costs	Training and Supervision	Remarks
CJV-8 Polythene bags manufacturing	200 (three shifts, to lessen pressure on electricity supply).	Mainly contract(?)	60% of workers are from outside the City area (they can be paid lower wages, and are more stable than local workforce.	Y130 - 140 on average, but skilled workers get Y200 on piece rates (in HK "do not need piece rates to make workers work").	NA	Initially used 6 technicians from HK, but this proved too expensive. Now only one General Manager is from HK. Local workers not keen to work without bonus during training period.	25% of the workforce is in administration. Much of an "iron rice bowl mentality" in the factory, say the managers. Unskilled labour is venture's main problem.
CJV-9 Restaurant	600	Contract(?)	NA	Basic Y100 + Y100 bonus on average.	NA	Staff need to be watched carefully. Have five permanent HK staff (including general manager, chief accountant, and head chef).	Has expanded from employment of 100 over last three years.

Table 4.4

Cooperative Joint Venture Companies -- Employment and Operational Issues (Sheet 3)

Company	Workforce	Employment Status	Recruitment	Wages (per month)	Wages in relation to other costs	Training and Supervision	Remarks
CJV-10 Beauty parlour	c20(?)	CJV has "complete freedom in hiring and firing.	NA	Basic Y80 + 10% of revenue so skilled staff get Y4 - 500 (more than manager, who comes from film studio, but who keeps his fringe benefits as a permanent worker).	30 - 40% of total costs, (materials 10%).	NA	-
CJV-11 Kitchen equipment for restaurants manufacturing	55 (including 7 technicians).	Pay workers directly.	Through Labour Service Bureau. HK manager has absolute right to hire and fire.	Over Y400 on average, including a Y140 productivity bonus. Company must also pay Machinery Company (parent) Y170 per month for various benefits, and Y30 to Labour Service Bureau ("for nothing")	Wages + Overheads 30% Materials 60% Profits 10%	Initially were over 15 people from HK, last year 4, now only 1 (the general manager).	Disputes about how to run the business between the previous managers.

Table 4.4

Cooperative Joint Venture Companies -- Employment and Operational Issues (Sheet 4)

Company	Workforce	Employment Status	Recruitment	Wages (per month)	Wages in relation to other costs	Training and Supervision	Remarks
JV-12 Jewellery manufacturing	180 (including 40 part-time)	140 are permanent workers, 40 part-time workers are on contract.	Use Labour Service Bureau (pay Y30 per worker per month). CJV feels this isn't fair because as a collective their workers do not get any fringe benefits out of this. Village now has labour shortage.	Permanent workers get Y180 on piece rate. Use welfare fund to pay for annual holiday as fringe benefits.	NA Wages are 56% of the "processing fee" received by the Chinese side.	Originally close HK supervision, now only occasional visits.	-
CJV-13 Hotels company	Management team of about 10 at head office.	NA	NA	NA	NA	A condition of the bank loan was to have an internationally reputed manager for the hotel.	Interview with management company, not operating company (i.e. the hotel).

Table 4.4
Cooperative Joint Venture Companies -- Employment and Operational Issues (Sheet 5)

Company	Workforce	Employment Status	Recruitment	Wages (per month)	Wages in relation to other costs	Training and Supervision	Remarks
CJV-14 Camera manufacturing	NA	Contract(?)	Must try to employ from Guangdong first - where still unemployment, but many potential workers are peasants with low educational level. Recruit by direct interview.	Y150 - 200	NA	NA	Problems in running factory because of power cuts.
CJV-15 Food manufacturing	85	Virtually all on (one-year) contract and paid directly.	Can hire and fire directly, just informing the Labour Service Bureau. Most workers are peasants from nearby village.	Range from Y180 to Y800. CJV must pay 16% of wage to Labour Service Bureau.	NA	French technician in early stage, and Hong Kong management.	Problem of high fees for water and power.

5 Processing and assembly, compensation trade, and 'other' companies

This chapter considers foreign investment in the form of various processing and assembly arrangements and compensation trade. It also discusses a small number of companies which could not be classified under any of our headings, but which raise issues of interest. The analysis is based on interviews with thirteen processing and assembly companies, two compensation trade companies, and three "other" companies. The chapter's layout is basically similar to the preceding two chapters. Section 1 sets out introductory details of the companies, and discusses the processing and assembly and compensation trade contracts. Section 2 introduces each company in more detail with a view to looking at the motivation of the partners and the provisions of their contracts. Section 3 looks at exporting and foreign exchange issues, and Section 4 considers operational and employment questions. As in Chapters Three and Four, more detail about each compny is presented in a comparative form in tables, whose headings correspond to each main heading of the chapter.

5.1 The companies and the contracts

5.1.1 The companies

Table 5.1 gives a summary of information about the companies. For processing and assembly companies, the industrial coverage is:

textiles and clothing   7   (leather gloves: PA-1, underwear: PA-4,
                                 textiles: PA-5,   clothing: PA-6,
clothing:
                                 PA-9, knitwear: PA-12, clothing: PA-13)

metal products   1   (metal pipes: PA-3)

electronics   2 (tapes:PA-8, digital watches: PA-10)

plastics   1 (PA-2)

toys   1 (PA-7)

printing   1 (PA-11)

The two compensation trade companies were a brewery (CT-1) and a
factory making cardboard boses (CT-2). The "other" companies were a
company making washing machines and hoping to sign a joint venture
contract (0-1), a shipping company whose "Hong Kong" partner was
actually a mainland-owned company (0.2), and 0-3 was a large ceramics
company which counted as a "foreign investment" because it had a
foreign currency loan from the Bank of China.

In terms of workforce, the processing and assembly companies were in
the medium size range using the 50-499 definition:

        1-49   0
        50-499   9 (+CT-2,0-2)
        500+   4 (+CT-1,0-1,0-3)

Using the 1-199 definition of small-medium:

        1-199   3
        200+   10 (CT-1,CT-2,0-1,0-2,0-3)

most did not qualify.

These companies then, and surprisingly, are on average rather larger
than either the equity or cooperative joint venture companies
interviewed. Although our samples cannot claim to be random, there is
no reason to suppose a bias in favour of large companies in processing
and assembly and small companies in joint ventures (1). The greater
size in terms of workforce to some extent is a reflection of the
importance of labour intensive operations in processing and assembly,
but also of the rapid growth which companies in such operations have
experienced.

As would be expected from this form of operation, most processing
and assembly operation were entirely export orientated, and those that
were not will be discussed below.

5.1.2 Processing and assembly and compensation trade contracts

The basic feature of processing and assembly operations is that the
Hong Kong side supplies raw materials from abroad to be made in China
into a final product which is to be exported. The Hong Kong partner
often supplies machinery for the venture, and this machinery in
principle can be taken back to Hong Kong at the end of the contract.
Often too the venture is entirely new. The administration of Dongguan
City, for example, one of the areas most successful in attracting
processing and assembly investment from Hong Kong, has built a number
of new factory buildings in anticipation of new contracts, which can
then be started very rapidly.

Although entirely new ventures, set up by the Hong Kong partner, are
the most common arrangement, processing and assembly contracts are
also used by existing Chinese companies to export part of their

production, using materials supplied by an overseas customer, while at the same time exporting through other channels and selling on the domestic market. Such companies sometimes have started their activities with a more general processing and assembly contract, and have moved to a partial arrangement when the initial contract was finished. This is most frequently the case where the company has acquired ownership of the foreign machinery through a compensation trade agreement (see below) running in parallel with the processing and assembly contract. Such partial processing and assembly arrangements can be very short-term, and with several customers simultaneously. Fully fledged contracts were, for our companies usually 3-5 years, though often renewed. With a fully fledged contract (i.e. where the company is set up by a single Hong Kong partner and works for no one else), the Hong Kong partner is not allowed to sell any output in the domestic market. This has been a reason why, in our earlier two chapters, companies wanting domestic sales have moved to contractual, and occassionally, equity joint ventures.

Under processing and assembly, the Hong Kong partner pays the Chinese side a processing fee in foreign exchange, and the Chinese partner is responsible for paying labour and other costs. Some companies (like PA-1: industrial leather gloves) have been given back the processing fee, and make their own payments to workers and for locally purchased inputs - this is a cheng bao arrangement (2), and the owner of PA-1 mentioned it had been started two years previously, but had been discontinued for new ventures by the autumn of 1987. Nanhai county authorities mentioned they operated two kinds of processing and assembly systems. The first was the normal kind with a processing fee; the other, from which they actually received a larger income, was there input and output prices were agreed, and the foreign investor kept the difference.

In general the control by the Hong Kong side varies between companies. In PA-1's case, the Hong Kong owner took a very direct part in establishing and running the factory, making frequent visits, while the factory is run by a Hong Kong trained Chinese manager. In other cases the arrangement is more like a subcontracting one. Processing and assembly arrangements are of three kinds:
- lai liao jia gong - "bringing materials for processing"
- lai yang zhi zuo - "bringing samples for manufacture"
- lai liao zhuang pei - similar to lai liao jia gong but with production involving an assembly line.

Of these, lai liao jia gong (hereinafter LLJG) is by far the most common, and all of our interviewed companies had this arrangement.

Processing and assembly operations and compensation trade are referred to collectively in Chinese writings and statistics as san lai yi bu - the "san (three) lai" referring to the three kinds of processing and assembly, and the "yi (one) bu" to the one kind of compensation trade.

Compensation trade (buchang mayoi) is where the foreign party supplies machinery, for which it is repaid by supplies of the product. It most frequently appears in combination with other contracts, but sometimes entirely on its own, as in the brewery in our sample, CT-1.

Processing and assembly arrangements are subject in principle to the Foreign Enterprise Income Tax Law and the Consolidated Industrial and Commerical Tax, but it has been argued (Moser and Zee, 1987, pp.4 and 106) that they generally have not actually attracted any tax in China. Information on tax payments proved very difficult to collect in our interviews and, such as it is, is presented in Table 5.2. It is also discussed for individual companies (including the compensation trade and "other" companies) later in this section. In practice it seems that LLJG companies are given tax holidays, and contracts often are renewed under different company names to get another tax holiday, with the knowledge and cooperation of the local authorities. Several otherwise helpful Hong Kong interviewees were unclear about tax arrangements. However, as Sectin 5.3 will show, there is considerable implicit taxation falling on the Chinese partners in processing and assembly operations. This arises when they receive Renminbi at the official exchange rate against that part of the processing fees retained by higher authorities (and paid by the foreign partner in foreign exchange), when the "free" rate for foreign exchange is much higher.

5.2   The motivation and expectations of the partners

Processing and assembly operations were the earliest kind of economic cooperation to develop between Hong Kong and China after the start of the reforms. The first contract was in Shunde county im 1978, even before the Special Economic Zones were set up.

For the Chinese side, especially local authorities in the countryside, processing and assembly has been a way of attracting foreign capital and foreign exchange at little cost. The foreign partner would bring in the machinery, and supply the raw materials. Of course, the importation of raw materials minimized the backward linkage effects of investment, lessening the operations' contact with the host economy. However, in an economy characterized by many supply shortages, and with difficulties in getting raw materials either though plan allocations or the free market, a supply of raw materials from the foreign investor, with a contractual commitment to sell the output abroad, made the production much easier to organize. Importation of high quality materials of kinds often not available locally sometimes has been an essential requirement or successful exporting. There has been considerable competition between different localities for this kind of investment, although the Special Economic Zones have discouraged it to some extent. The Dongguan City area, one of the largest recipients of processing and assembly operations, has tried to steer them to the countryside while attracting higher techology, joint venture investment to urban locations. It has also tried to impose uniform processing fees between its constituent local authorities, to prevent undue competition.

For the foreign side, virtually always Hong Kong companies, processing and assembly has been a way of locating operations in China with minimal risk, as the machinery could be removed at the end of the contract. In fact, as we shall show, the degree of involvement of the Hong Kong side varies considerably between undertakings.

Compensation trade has been a way whereby Chinese companies could acquire foreign equipment without having to accumulate foreign exchange in advance. Also, the foreign side has had an interest in ensuring that the product was of sufficient quality to meet export requirements, so as to ensure repayment in kind.

5.2.1 Companies initiated as processing and assembly ventures

Companies PA-1 (industrial leather gloves), PA-2 (plastic toys), and

91

PA-4 (garments - underwear) typify processing and assembly operations, all LLJG, where the company is engaged in production of the product in Hong Kong, and has been pushed into the move to China by rising costs and compensation from companies who have already moved. PA-1, one of the most useful interviews, where the proprietor allowed us to accompany him from Hong Kong to visit his factories in China, illustrates this. This company, originally set up a leather gloves factory on a five-year contract in the Shenzhen Special Economic Zone in 1979. When the Chinese side refused to renew the contact in Shenzhen, because the authorities needed the buildings for another purpose, the venture moved to the proprietor's family's home town. At the time of the initial relocation from Hong Kong to Shenzhen, wages in the Chinese operation were only 10% of what had been paid in Hong Kong, and the proprietor commented on the skill with which the Hong Kong workers had always made wage demands at a time when the factory had had rush orders. Located in a small town, the factory is a new building put up by the Hong Kong side, who also supplied all the machinery. The operation is managed by a Chinese manager, trained by the Hong Kong side, but the proprietor makes frequent visits and appears to keep a very close control over the operation. The Hong Kong company has closed its leather gloves operation in Hong Kong, although it does still have Hong Kong manufacturing operations in another activity (scrap metal).

Also illuminating was a visit to another factory owned by the same Hong Kong company, in a nearby village, to which the Hong Kong side had been recommended by business friends. This factory in the countryside prepares the leather from imported semi-cured hides for the gloves factory. The location is away from urban areas because it is quite polluting, and the village was also chosen because it had a good supply of water (for washing the hides). The hides factory is run by a resident Hong Kong manager, who is expected eventually to be replaced by a Chinese counterpart, and the factory is staffed by workers introduced by the village authorities. The workers are mostly male, and are former agricultural workers. They leave the factory for about two weeks a year to bring in the harvest, otherwise the women in their families do the agricultural work. This operation has a ten year contract, long for LLJG. The Hong Kong side did all the construction itself, as well as bringing in the machinery. Although the factory has benefitted from the surplus labour released by the agricultural reforms, the proprietor mentioned that in the preceding two years wages had risen 50%, driven up, he thought, by other Hong Kong operations in the area.

PA-2, making plastic toys, is in the same industrial complex as PA-1's leather gloves factory. This company previously had 200 workers in Hong Kong, but following the move to China to this, and one other factory in a nearby area, its Hong Kong operation has been reduced to design and paper work. Significantly, and a frequent feature in the companies interviewed, the Chinese operation is now substantially larger than the Hong Kong operation ever was, showing how the move to China has permitted expansion rather than mere survival. The Hong Kong proprietor, unlike that of PA-1, has no family connection with the area, but the manager commented how the official in this area were much more helpful, and less bureaucratic, not only than those of the SEZs, but also those of Guangzhou. The manager of this factory was from Hong Kong, though he commented that Hong Kong companies often found it difficult to persuade Hong Kong managers to live in China.

PA-4, making underwear, and the smallest LLJG factory we

92

interviewed, is in a small town in a rather poor area. In the area there was still some localized unemployment in spite of the general economic expansion of the Pearl River Delta, and it had not strated to attract foreign capital for rural industrialization until 1984. Several other garment factories operate in the area, and this factory has chosen its location in the light of their experience through contacts with them in Hong Kong. The factory owner, originally from the pre-1949 textile industry in Shanghai, has had a long history of production in Hong Kong, and operations still continue there. The present venture had been in operation for only six months, and the severe problems which it had faced in recruiting workers in Hong Kong had been behind its move to China. The resident Hong Kong manager commented on the large number of other garment factories which were moving to China. The machinery, mainly simple sewing machines, had been brought in from Hong Kong, and the factory was housed in an existing site, not purpose-built as a factory.

PA-12, a knitwear factory, estimates that it achieves a 40% reduction in costs by producing in China, but has to face a problem of variable quality. After an initial three year contract, the venture changed its name to obtain another three year tax holiday. This is a device frequently encountered in our interviews - PA-11 (see below) is another example.

A less successful venture has been PA-10, making digital watches. This company, established in 1985 by a Chinese close relative of the Hong Kong partner, expanded rapidly at the beginning, and opened an additional two factory sites, and moved from manufacturing watch components to manufacturing the whole watch. More recently, the operationm has been hit by a fall in demand in Hong Kong. The machinery is "borrowed" from the Hong Kong partner and the contracts have been annual, much shorter term than the three other companies mentioned in this section so far. This is a purely LLJG operation, with all the raw materials supplied from Hong Kong, and all the output exported. There have been some disputes about the processing fee, as the Hong Kong side would not pay more when the venture moved from producing watch components to making the whole watch.

5.2.2 Existing Chinese companies starting processing and assembly operations

The five companies in Section 5.2.1 represent a common pattern, but existing Chinese companies too have used LLJG, sometimes to change their operations completely. One such is PA-8, which is now wholly engaged as a subcontractor to one of the largest Hong Kong conglomerates, and makes video and cassette tapes. Owned by the district foreign economic company of a large city, which also manages other foreign cooperations, it has used compensation trade to import equipment for making video tapes, and the Hong Kong partner was about to invest in reconditioning the rest of its equipment. Although managed by Chinese personnel, the management in pratice is much influenced by the Hong Kong partner, which maintains an office in the city.

PA-5, a knitwear company whose Chinese partner wa originally a virtually unmechanized operation, which joined with an experienced Hong Kong company still in this line of business in Hong Kong, to build a new factory under the guidance of the county industrial corporation. Although of 1960s vintage, the equipment represents a considerable technical advance on the earlier operation, and the Hong

Kong side provided training, design and marketing.

PA-11, a printing factory in a less developed part of the province, also was formed as a new factory, with an existing printing works joining with an experienced Hong Kong partner. Initially the Hong Kong side brought in second-hand machinery, but later invested in modern equipment. When this expansion was made, the Hong Kong side was allowed by the Chinese authorities to change its name so as to get another three year tax holiday.

PA-3, producing various kinds of electrical conduits and galvanized steel pipes, is a very different case to those encountered so far, and shows how processing and assembly can be a first stage for a reform-minded Chinese company to seek links with the outside world. This company was an offshoot of a state chemical engineering enterprise, which is still in production on a nearby site. The manager of the state venture wished to set up a reformed organization (with differentials between the workers, supervisors and managers, and with the manager having the right to manage effectively), and, with the help of the Guangdong Petrochemical Bureau found a foreign partner willing to advise on the purchase of modern equipment (bought from Italy with a Bank of China loan). Although the company would much prefer a joint venture, it has only succeeded in getting a LLJG contract from the foreign partner, through which it exports 20% of its output using raw materials supplied. It also exports through the provincial Mineral and Metal Corporation, and claims to have received many commendations (including a written one from a Hong Kong government body, shown to us) for the quality of its products.

5.2.3 Further developments from processing and assembly

One worry, sometimes expressed in Hong Kong, is that when current contracts have expired, the Chinese may be able to run the operation themselves and the foreign investor will be out of a job. In the case of LLJG operations, the Hong Kong side can remove its equipment, but in practice this is often acquired by the Chinese side through compensation trade. SInce more than a decade has passed since the first processing and assembly contracts, and since such contracts are usually quite short-term (3-5 years, as we have seen), our interviews gave us an opportunity to observe companies who had long since finished their initial contracts. Although some have renewed, others have developed in different directions.

PA-13 claims to have been the very first processing and assembly venture in China. This company makes denim clothing, for which there is now a ready market within China as well as overseas. Prior to the cooperation, the company was already in operation as a garments factory. It originally signed a six-year contract, running from 1978, involving a mixture of processing and assembly and compensation trade, but was able to repay the Hong Kong partner within three years, and then concluded the contract by mutual agreement. Recently reorganized as an industrial corporation, with give factories under its jurisdiction, the company still engages in some LLJG operations, and maintains the original Hong Kong partner as a customer. After the original contract was finished, the company started to export via the customer contacts of its own. When it exports, it uses imported denim; when it sells on the Chinese market, it uses domestically produced material, which it regards as lower quality.

PA-9, also making garments, has followed a similar pattern through on a much smaller scale. Having acquired its machinery through compensation trade while doing processing and assembly, it undertakes a number of very short-term LLJG contracts with a variety of customers, as well as domestic sales.

Two much larger operations are PA-6 and PA-7, both in the same location and both operated by the same Chinese parent company. The parent company was, until 1979, in a totally different line of activity (importing cashew nuts), in which it was experiencing some supply difficulties. PA-6 was to some extent started on the initiative of a well-know Hong Kong garments manufacturer, with strong personal connections with the area, and who was attracted to the site (among other reasons, for its good fengshui!), and who arranged the venture via the town's Foreign Economic Department. The Chinese operation is now one of the largest garment factories in the area, and works for a number of customers, including the original Hong Kong partner. The provincial textile import-export corporation is a partner in this township enterprise, and also provides some export outlet for this mainly export-orientated company. The venture started with making shirts, and has branched out in many other garments, even including foreign army uniforms. Some machinery has been purchased by the provincial corporation, and some has been obtained through compensation trade. PA-7, also started in 1979 by the cashew nuts company, makes cloth toys, and toy clothes (sic), to the highest standards of Western design. The workforce has grown to over 4000, and another 1000 people are employed indirectly as outworkers. Given the very Western designs, and a product wholly exported, the company stressed the importance of the LLJG contract as a means of securing high-quality raw materials from abroad, and suggested that without this reason they might have dispensed with the foreign partner. The original Hong Kong partner arranged the training of the workers, and had had a similar (but small) factory in Hong Kong, but now does only designing work with imported materials. One reason for the very fast growth was the development of a network of Hong Kong traders among business friends of the Hong Kong boss as customers, once the quality of the products became established, and these friends also have provided machinery to the factory. The ultimate markets are mainly in North America, and most of labelling and packaging was supplied by the customer.

5.2.4 The compensation trade companies

The two companies here are rather different ventures. The brewery, CT-1, is a state company under the First Light Industrial Bureau, set up with a view to introducing foreign advanced technology to produce beer mainly for the local market. Using technology for a well-known Belgian beer, whose equipment is supplied from France with a largely tied loan guaranteed by the Bank of China. The brewery, when visited, was in production but was still having quality problems and had not yet exported. It planned 20% exports to repay the loan.

CT-2 is a collective under a town industrial corporation, and the cardboard box factory is one of three financially interrelated operations. It had borrowed within China 70% of the cost of the Japanese equipment it had imported, and the Macau partner in the agreement had supplied 30% of the cost and would be repaid in product. The company complained that it had to pay a premium of more than 60% over the official exchange rate for the foreign exchange which it purchased with the (RMB) loan within China. It used some of the proceeds from its export sales to finance the purchase of equipment for a third venture, the production of sanitary towels. The company's first compensation trade agreement - for Italian equipment to make zips, which the foreign partner (also from Macau) had only provided 20% of the finance - had been very unsuccessful. The equipment was too advanced for their needs and they could not use it properly. The Macau partner, when investigated by the company on a visit to Macau, proved to be very small. He had been mainly interested in selling them expensive equipment, and had virtually no customer contacts for the product. They subsequently found a more satisfactory partner, in Hong Kong, through whom they imported more suitable equipment from Taiwan.

5.2.5   The 'other' companies

The three companies included under this heading are quite disparate, and their inclusion in this chapter is arbitrary, but they raise a few interesting points.

O-1 is a company making washing machines, legally a collective under a city government, and has imported Japanese equipment under a leasing arrangement with the China International Investment Company. The washing machine company gradually pays back the cost of the machines as a loan, and then acquires ownership of them. They were currently negotiating with a Japanese investor in the same line of business, who was proposing to supply them with his company's technology, and the Chinese side would produce the machines for sale in Japan.

O-2 is a shipping company, operating hyrofoils between a port in the Pearl River Delta and Hong Kong. It had borrowed money from a mainland-Chinese owned operation in Hong Kong, which became its joint venture partner. It is often claimed that many "joint ventures" in Guangdong have as "foreign" partners companies which have been set up in Hong Kong by mainland Chinese organizations, who can then use joint venture import and export privileges to acquire foreign exchange.

0.3 is a group company (jituan gongsi) set up recently to administer a large complex of some forty operating companies making ceramics. This counts as a "foreign investment" because it is in receipt of a foreign currency loan from the Bank of China to import Western equipment, for example for the manufacture of tiles. What is interesting for our purposes is that the organization has its own research department, which copies the machinery and makes prototypes of its own; and claims it can master the imported technology quite well by itself without needing a foreign partner.

5.2.6 Structural aspects

As in Chapters Three and Four, this subsection is used to draw out some common features of the operations of the companies in the chapter as they relate to questions of industrial structure and development.

All of the foreign partners directly involved in the processing and assembly operations were Hong Kong companies, in contrast to some of the joint ventures where the foreign partner was a Western or Japanese multinational with a Hong Kong office. Overwhelmingly the companies were in the textile and garments industry, although Hong Kong light industries were represented too. In Hong Kong these industries are heavily export-orientated, and we found evidence in a number of cases that the ultimate foreign buying groups took a considerable interest in the production of the product, and there was a widespread use of Western labels and sometimes packaging.

Of the thirteen processing and assembly companies, three were in Guangzhou, one was in the urban areas of another city, and the rest were in small towns (zhen), except for the tannery owned by PA-1, which was in a village. Many city and town authorities mentioned to us that equity and cooperative joint ventures were steered towards the more urban areas, especially the equity joint ventures, whereas processing and assembly operations were mainly associated with the "rural industrialization" for which China is well known, especially since the reforms. "Rural" in this context includes small towns, but many processing and assembly operations have gone to villages, and several village authorities were interviewed. Onbe village in Baoan county (administered by Shenzhen City, but outside the Shenzhen SEZ) can be cited here as an illustration. Baoan in part because of its close proximity to Hong Kong, has been very successful in attracting foreign investment.

This village, who had sent people to Hong Kong as early as 1979 to investigate possibilities for attracting Hong Kong investors, got its first processing and assembly factory in 1982, making artificial flowers. A second factory, making electrical goods, was set up in the same year, having tried and failed in Guangzhou because of the unproductiveness of the workers. This factory was a key factor in their expansion, as the American buyer brought in a large group of visitors to inspect the factory, and the confidence which developed among potential investors seeing profitable operations in the village led to the village attracting nearly twenty new companies. The village has also been helped by the policy of the county authorities in centralizing information about local investment opportunities as an exhibition with a staff in a hotel in Shenzhen City, where each locality can maintain a staff member and negotiate with prospective investors.

The village's population in 1979 was just 2300 but by 1987 it was employing 4000 workers from outside the province, with local village workers being mainly in management. Additional workers from outside the area were normally recruited through the personal contacts of existing workers, not through any government agency.

The village's industrial operations are run by a collective industrial development company (later changed to a "group company"), which has issued shares, available for purchase not only by villagers but by people in Hong Kong. The village makes about 15-20% profit on the processing fees after all payments have been made, and a factor in the village's expansion through foreign investment has been the ploughing back of profits into infrastructural improvement, especially electricity generation. All the foreign exchange earned through the processing fees has to be passed over to the county, and the village gets back RMB at the official rate of exchange. However, another village in the same area said that its foreign exchange earnings were distributed:

village: 15%
Baoan county: 60%
Shenzhen City :   15%
Guangdong Province: 10%

Availability of cheap labour was an important factor, of course, in the early development of processing and assembly. Also important was land availability. The first village under discussion explained that, under the reforms, once it had met its grain deliveries to the state, it was free to use land not needed for grain for other purposes. It first developed fish ponds as a sideline, later attracting Hong Kong investment in fish processing, but basically the land was then free for industrial use, and land rents far lower than Hong Kong's could be offered.

Processing and assembly contracts, usually lasting five years, have been the only kind of foreign investment. Some investors have expressed interest in joint ventures, but the village feels its officials do not have good enough knowledge of product or raw material prices, or of marketing in general, to take part in a joint venture, which they therefore regard as pointlessly riskly. The second village mentioned, had recently signed one cooperative joint venture, after about twenty processing and assembly contracts, because the Hong Kong company wanted access to domestic raw materials (cotton in this case) and for sales (of garments) to the domestic market, neither of which were possible with his LLJG contract.

The first village thought it would be give or six years hence before it would feel capable of participating in any joint venture project. The common idea that processing and assembly is necessarily a stepping stone to joint ventures was also questioned by officials in one city authority. They thought that joint ventures often lacked the marketing skills of the processing and assembly operations, which were more geared directly to serving export markets.

Finally, it is worth recalling how important processing and assembly operations are in all the areas we considered outside of Guangzhou in terms of the total employment provided by foreign investment. In Dongguan City 150,000 were employed in processing and assembly compared to 5000(?) in joint ventures. The figures for Shunde county were 15,000 in joint ventures and 45,000 in processing and assembly. Nanhai had just over 50 cooperative and equity joint ventures, but 400 factories engaged in processing and assembly.

5.3   Exporting and foreign exchange issues

5.3.1 The processing and assembly companies

Of all the Chinese foreign investment arrangements, processing and assembly operations seem the least likely to raise export marketing problems. Where a Hong Kong company with an established market in Hong Kong or overseas decides to set up a processing and assembly operation in China, sales should be no problem once production in China is running smoothly and product quality is established. Four companies in our sample are wholly export-orientated LLJG operations of the most familiar type, where the factory has been set up on the foreign investor's initative, with a local authority investment vehicle as partner, in order to serve a market already mapped out by the Hong Kong side's existing production. These are:

PA-1: industrial leather gloves
PA-2: plastic toys
PA-4: underwear
PA-10:digital watches

An additional four operations, through an existing Chinese company took an active role in setting up the venture, neverthless found Hong Kong partners of the same kind as the first four, in other words with existing markets already served by their own production. These are:

PA-5: knitwear
PA-7: cloth toys
PA-8: video and cassette tapes
PA-12:knitwear

Although the foreign investors are all from Hong Kong, many of the
ultimate customers are from further afield. Western brand names are
to be found on some of the products, like PA-1's industrial gloves or
the very Western-style toys made by PA-7, and the foreign customers
sometimes take a quite direct interest, sending representatives to
China to check on product quality.

Of these eight companies, only two complained of marketing problems.
PA-10 had experienced initial success but later the demand for its
product in the Hong Kong market had fallen.   PA-8 commented that the
degree of competition in the international market for tapes was very
intense, and it was making video tapes initially at a loss, and cross-
subsidizing with profits from cassette tapes, as it gained production
experience. Whilst LLJG operations could be conceived as "in-and-out"
activities, where the foreign investors can pull out their equipment
if market conditions change, and the Chinese workers can move to other
employment, the Chinese side sometimes acquires capital equipment
through the operation and thereby commits itself in a riskier way. A
frequent comment from Chinese interviewees was that they were still
heavily dependent on the Hong Kong partner for marketing information,
even in ventures which had been going for some years.   They sometimes
were unsure whether the processing fees they received were reasonable,
in the sense of allowing them some share of the profits of successful
activities.

Some LLJG operations, surprisingly, have faced problems of securing
export licences from the Chinese authorities, although by no means all
products are subject to export licencing. (see Moser, 1987, pp.14-17)
One such was PA-1, who would like to have expanded further, but had to
go to considerable trouble to get a licence.

Under the contracts of the wholly LLJG operations we interviewed, it
is normally stipulated that the raw materials must be supplied from
abroad, and may not be obtained in China.   PA-1 mentioned, however,
that in spite of this it was sometimes allowed to buy its basic raw
material, semi-cured hides, within China, and also chemicals.   PA-7,
established for almost a decade, said that there were simply no
suitable raw materials to be had within China, and that the Hong Kong
partner's access to supply sources was a key reason for continued
cooperation.

Of the other companies, PA-12 did not provide information about its
exporting, but, as a printing operation, it may well have been geared
towards China and had used processing and assembly as a way of setting
up a new factory beside its old one in order to update techologically.
Here, LLJG was used to obtain foreign exchange.

PA-3, making pipes, had used LLJG as a way of seeking foreign advice
for updating technologically, and particularly with a view to breaking
into export markets.   Its actual foreign exchange initially had come
from a Bank of China loan.   It would have preferred a closer relation
with its Hong Kong partner.   Having become known among customers
abroad, it also marketed independently of the Hong Kong partner
through a provincial trading corporation.   It felt itself to be mainly
in competition with two companies in Beijing and Suzhou, who had

imported Japanese equipment and felt that its Italian equipment made a better quality product.

Three companies in the sample had moved beyond the initial LLJG contracts and now exported in other ways:

PA-6: clothing
PA-7: clothing
PA-13:clothing

PA-9 used LLJG contracts on a purely short-term basis and was mainly geared twoards the domestic market using the equipment it had obtained through compensation trade during its original processing and assembly contract. It also exported independently using local materials.

PA-6, set up in 1979, maintained good contracts with the original Hong Kong partner, and had also branched into short-term LLJG contracts with business friends of his. However, the provincial textile company was heavily involved as a partner in this large venture and many export sales were made through that corporation. Some 5% of output was marketed within China, to the relatively sophisticated market served by big shops in major cities.

The provincial corporation also was the major export outlet for PA-13, who felt it was put under pressure to export even though there was a good market within China for its fashionable denim clothing. It had acquired machinery while undertaking its processing and assembly contract. A substantial part of its foreign exchange earnings were spent on imported raw materials, which it always used when it wished to export.

Strong complaints were made to us by one company about the import regulations for equipment. If they are "lent" equipment by the Hong Kong partner (the normal LLJG practice), they must leave a deposit with the customs authorities. If the Hong Kong partner gives them the equipment, they must pay a hefty duty. Only, they said, if the machinery was obtained under "normal" san lai yi bu arrangements was it duty-free, and presumably they refer here to compensation trade. Machine spare parts were a particular problem, and if officially imported were subject to duty; so the company arranged for its people to purchase such parts as individuals wherever they visited Hong Kong on business.

Foreign exchange retention rights, and the rate at which forex earnings can be exchanged into Renminbi are contentious, as under the other forms of contract discussed in the preceding two chapters.

Officials in one city government explained that the normal division of forex earnings for processing and assembly operations in their area was:

Guangdong province: 60%
City government: 15%
County government: 10%
Enterprise: 15%

and that the provincial government gave back Renminbi only at the official exchange rate. This indeed was a major cause of the city's administrative area having a balance of trade payments deficit in spite of buoyant export earnings. In a county in another area, officials said that "locals" (enterprises) could keep 12 ½% of their forex earnings as of right, whereas before they had to apply to keep it. As mentioned in subsection 5.2.6, a village in Baoan county said the distribution was: village: 15%, county: 60%, city: 15%, province: 10%. In other words, there is great variability!(3)

Information from the enterprise level confirms the 15% of forex earnings for the enterprise from PA-4 and PA-6 among the seven for which information could be obtained about forex retention. PA-5, also retained 15%, but its situation was complicated by loan repayments, and the proportions for the other recipients differ from those above even though it is within that same city's area of jurisidiction. PA-12, in a different area, says it retains 12% even though it thinks it "should" get 15% and says the province gets 18% (and "should" get 15%). PA-13 told us it gets only a "small" share of its forex earnings, but much of its exports are through the provincial textile corporation. PA-8 and 9 each have different arrangements, although they are in the same location. Both receive their processing fee in RMB, via the Bank of China, which keeps the forex, but PA-8 can buy back up to 30% of its processing fee earnings at official rate of exchange, whereas PA-9 says it can buy back only 12½%, to purchase equipment from abroad.

5.3.2 The compensation trade and 'other' companies

Companies using compensation trade necessarily must become export-orientated to pay in kind for the equipment supplied by the foreign partner, who then has a strong interest in seeing that the equipment is used efficiently to ensure adequate product quality for its own markets. CT-1, the brewery, undoubtedly had secured a partner of considerable expertise, the supplier of the machinery for a well-known brand of continental European beer, although adequate quality had not yet been achieved when the enterprise was interviewed. Once the brewery had achieved sufficint export sales to pay for its equipment, it then planned to serve the buoyant domestic market. It mentioned that it was allowed to import the equipment duty-free, and also had been exempted from all but 5% of the 25% Industrial and Commercial Tax it would otherwise have had to pay. The first compensation trade partner of CT-2, the supplier of zip-making machinery, did not have the same degree of expertise, and did not have the same incentive to help with export marketing since he had made profit on the machinery sale and only had committed himself to financing 20% of the cost. Here the basic safeguard to the Chinese side from compensation trade - the interest of the foreign partner in the equipment working successfully had been lost. Although CT-2 was not willing to supply details of its forex retention provisions, it seemed that from its subsequent and more successful compensation trade arrangements for zips and cardboard box manufacture it was able to generate enough forex for its own use to import additional machinery. It exported a third of its box output, and commented that domestic sales normally were more profitable because of poor exchange rate received when it converted its forex receipts into RMB. However, very recently, it said, domestic market conditions for cardboard box sales had been difficult, as Taiwanese manufacturers had dumped production onto the Chinese market, unhampered by any effective import controls.

Among the "other" companies, O-1, the washing machine factory, mainly sold within China, where there is (as of late 1987) excess demand for most consumer durables, although it had made some exports to South East Asia. It commented that it was allowed to retain its foreign exchange earnings to pay the leasing costs of its imported equipment, and was unsure what would be the forex retention provisions after the repayment had been completed. CT-2, the shipping company, had used its partnership to import advanced equipment (hydrofoils), and would receive foreign exchange from its ticket-sales in Hong Kong, although it provided no further information. CT-3, the ceramics group company, was selling products some of which were Western style (especially tiles) and needed to be be of Western quality, besides traditional Chinese ceramics, for which there is a ready market in Hong Kong both among local people and to some extent among tourists. The company has the right to export directly, and its operating company each make over one third of the production to the group, which then helps them to export. Of the remaining two-thirds of output, it is planned for the operating companies to sell half domestically and half overseas, but the overseas sales are slight as yet. The group company says it gets some concessions on import duty on imported equipment, but was not willing to give details. Some quality problems were encountered with raw materials, all obtained locally.

5.4 Employment and operational issues

Table 5.4 gives a summary of the material from the companies relating to employment and operational matters.

In the two preceding chapters we have shown that foreign companies were most likely to encounter operational difficulties when going into partnership with existing Chinese state companies. This was especially where they had no choice but to employ permanent workers from the Chinese partner, who frequently were hard to manage or to motivate.

Most processing and assembly ventures in this sample, involved the setting up of new factories. In the case of

PA-1: industrial leather gloves
PA-2: plastic toys
PA-4: underwear
PA-10: digital watches

these were entirely new ventures and the Chinese partner was simply a local authority, usually operating through an industrial holding company. One city government told us that in such cases they give the foreign investor a completely free hand to recruit, and subsequently to run the factory. Not alllocal authorities were as flexible as this, and this authority initially had had some criticism from the provincial authorities for its attitude. Nevertheless the recruitment of workers released by the agricultural reforms, who had not previously worked in industrial enterprises, was common. In some cases, workers left the factory to work in the fields at harvest times (e.g. PA-1's tannery), in others (e.g. PA-7: toys and clothes) the factory recruited additional workers from nearby rural areas when the factory had heavy orders. Given the labour shortage in Guangdong at the time of our interviews, several ventures recruited from outside their immediate area. PA-5 (garments) got 20% of its workers, mostly the skilled ones, from other countries. PA-7, which could not get enough young women to work on its toys in itw own small town, recruited some 50% of its workforce from neighbouring Guangxi province. Men, it said, were not willing to work in this activity. Indeed, over the whole sample, especially in the garments factories, the workforce was predominatly female. As research on the agricultural reforms has shown (e.g. Nolan, 1988) it has been women in particular who have been relieved of agricultural employment and have moved into sideline production and, in our cases, industrial employment.

Although former peasants may be well-motivated, they need substantial training, and several companies mentioned problems caused by the low educational level of rural workers. PA-4, making garments in a small town, said that after its first few months of operation it still was getting less than half the output that it would have achieved in Hong Kong with the same equipment, and that it sometimes had problems with the garments being dirty or not packed in the correct quantities. Most companies paid piece rates to motivate the workers.

Where an existing Chinese company was involved in the partnership, the processing and assembly ventures in our sample nevertheless all involved the construction of entirely new factories. PA-11, the printing factory, mentioned it employed a number of permanent workers transferred from the old factory. Two companies which had completed their original processing and assembly contracts and had moved on to shorter term and partial contracting, PA-9 and PA-13, both garments factories, now had the bulk of their workforce as permanent workers. Many companies spoke of their need to treat workers well so as to prevent them seeking employment elsewhere, and laid especial stress on providing welfare benefits. Only PA-4, the newly established garments factory, said it had a waiting list of workers wishing to join it. One strong complaint received from PA-1, which in many respects was very satisfied with the investment environment in the small town in which it operated, was that it had trained some workers at its own expense, and then the local authorities had succeeded in moving these workers to other (presumably Chinese-run) factories without any compensation to the foreign investor. No processing and assembly company made the kinds of complaint about worker motivation found in some equity and cooperative joint ventures. PA-1 mentioned its cheng bao arrangement, which allowed it to pay for workers and other inputs directly, but even this company said it had difficulties with the local authorities about making direct payments of bonuses to give the workers extra motivation. The level of wages among the sample's processing and assembly companies is a little lower than among equity and cooperative joint ventures. More than a third paid under 150RMB per month, and only PA-3, a more technologically advanced company employing a more skilled workforce to make various kinds of piping, paid an average of over 200RMB.

NOTES

1. However, in the light of the discussion of the average size of contracts in Chapter Two, recall that equity joint ventures, and cooperative joint ventures too to some extent, were divided into large numbers of fairly small projects and a small number of large projects, often import-substituting. We did not seek out any of the very large projects, which, in any case, are mostly not located in Guangdong.

2. The term "cheng bao" normally means making oneself reponsible for doing something, and is the term used in the various kinds of responsibility systems in China.

3.   For a discussion of foreign exchange retention and its
      variability, see also John Kamm's contribution in Vogel (1989, Chap.11).

Table 5.1

Processing and Assembly, Compensation Trade and 'Other' Companies – Introductory Profiles (Sheet 1)

Company	Size	Contract	Chinese Contribution	Foreign Contribution	Technology
Processing and Assembly Companies					
PA-1 Industrial Leather Gloves	150 workers	5 year LLJG (Cheng Bao), first started 1979.	New factory shell only.	All equipment.	From Hong Kong.
PA-2 Plastic Toys	300 per shift (3 shifts)	5 year LLJG, from 1986.	Buildings.	All equipment.	From Hong Kong.
PA-3 Metal Piping	325 workers	10 year, partial LLJG, from 1984.	All buildings, plant and equipment.	Technological advice, and help in locating source of equipment.	From Italy, turn key project, financed by loan from Bank of China.
PA-4 Garments	50 workers	5 year LLJG, from 1987.	Buildings.	All equipment.	New from Hong Kong.
PA-5 Knitwear	690 workers	6 year LLJG, from 1986.	Buildings.	Equipment.	1960's vintage from Hong Kong.

Table 5.1

Processing and Assembly, Compensation Trade and 'Other' Companies – Introductory Profiles (Sheet 2)

Company	Size	Contract	Chinese Contribution	Foreign Contribution	Technology
PA-6 Clothing	Originally 200, now 1600 workers.	Partial LLJG, with some compensation trade.	Factory site (previously occupied by another factory).	Basic equipment.	Sewing machines supplied from Hong Kong, but main contribution to technology was reorganize a new agreement with division of labour between workers.
PA-7 Toys and Clothes	Originally 50, now 4200 workers.	LLJG, started 1979.	Buildings.	Equipment.	Design is particularly important, and quality of raw materials (all imported).
PA-8 Cassette and Video Tapes	300 workers.	3 years (renewed) LLJG from 1982, for video tapes + compensation trade for cassette tapes equipment.	Buildings of existing factory.	Foreign side currently reinvesting in more modern equipment.	Design currently via Hong Kong.

Table 5.1

Processing and Assembly, Compensation Trade and 'Other' Companies – Introductory Profiles (Sheet 3)

Company	Size	Contract	Chinese Contribution	Foreign Contribution	Technology
PA-9 Clothing	140 workers.	Partial, short term LLJG. Full LLJG, 1982-6.	Buildings, purchase of equipment using processing fees.	Supplied machinery under two compensation trade agreements (now complete).	Japanese equipment.
PA-10 Digital Watches	260 workers.	One year (renewable). LLJG since 1985.	Buildings (have set up three factories).	Equipment.	Moved from component manufacture to manufacture of whole product.
PA-11 Printing	470 workers.	Four years LLJG from 1984.	Existing printing factory.	Hong Kong partner originally supplied second-hand machinery. Now both sides wish to expand factory with new investment.	NA
PA-12 Knitwear	240 workers.	Three years LLJG from 1986.	NA	New machinery.	NA

107

Table 5.1

Processing and Assembly, Compensation Trade and 'Other' Companies – Introductory Profiles (Sheet 4)

Company	Size	Contract	Chinese Contribution	Foreign Contribution	Technology
PA-13 Clothing	930 workers	Started LLJG in 1978. Now contract completed for original factory, but some subsidiaries still do LLJG work.	Buildings of existing clothing factory.	Loan for equipment.	American, Japanese, German
Compensation Trade Companies					
CT-1 Brewery	700 workers.	7 years from 1983.	Everything except the imported equipment.	Only technological, not managerial.	Equipment mainly from France, "know-how" mainly from Belgium.
CT-2 Cardboard Box Factory	200 workers.	7 years from 1985.	Already existing factory.	Technological and marketing.	Japan.

Table 5.1

Processing and Assembly, Compensation Trade, and 'Other' Companies – Introductory Profiles (Sheet 5)

Company		Size	Contract	Chinese Contribution	Foreign Contribution	Technology
"Other" Companies						
0-1	Washing Machines Factory	570 workers.	Currently discussing a joint venture with Japanese partner.	Japanese company would provide designs and access to Japanese market.	Had had an earlier technology (compensation trade) contract with Japan, now completed.	Japan mainly, also USA, France, Italy.
0-2	Shipping Company	200 workers.	JV contract, 20 years from 1984.	Buildings.	Foreign side is Chinese-owned company in Hong Kong.	Hydrofoils, from from Hong Kong.
0-3	Ceramics Company	16,000 workers.	7-year Bank of China loan to import equipment.	Chinese side fits new equipment into existing production facilities.	None. Can absorb technology of imported equipment within needing a foreign partner.	Equipment from West Germany, Italy, Japan. Have copied some of it.

Table 5.2

Processing and Assembly, Compensation Trade and 'Other' Companies – The Partners and The Contract (Sheet 1)

Company	Chinese side	Foreign side	Tax	Special Features or Comments	Other Operations in China
Processing and Assembly Companies					
PA-1 Industrial Leather Gloves	Township processing and assembly office.	Multi-product (originally bricks, then scrapmetal) company in Hong Kong, family run. Moved glove production to China because of Hong Kong labour shortage.	Finished a three-year tax holiday.	- Under Cheng Bao contract HK side is given back the processing fee and can make wage payments, etc. directly. - Township ploughs back processing fees into new factory building to attract foreign investors.	- Hong Kong side has tannery preparing leather; also a banana chips factory. - Local authority has had other LLJG operations.
PA-2 Plastic Toys	Same as PA-1.	Hong Kong plastics company previously employed 200 workers in HK, now less, and doing mainly paper work.	---	HK side originally had factory in Guangzhou, but present location has lower costs and less bureaucracy.	- HK side has another plastics factory in same city area.
PA-3 Metal Piping	State factory built 1984, as technologically advanced offshoot of a similar factory set up in 1979, under the Guangdong Petroleum Chemical Bureau.	Hong Kong trading company, which sells 20% of the company's output abroad.	3-year tax holiday, then tax at a rate not yet decided.	Chinese company is actively looking for a JV partner	---

Table 5.2

Processing and Assembly, Compensation Trade and 'Other' Companies – The Partners and The Contract (Sheet 2)

Company	Chinese side	Foreign side	Tax	Special Features or Comments	Other Operations in China
PA-4 Garments	Township Industrial Company	Clothing company with 20 years history of production in Hong Kong. Still producing in HK, with up to 80 workers (fluctuates with market conditions). HK boss originally from Shanghai.	3-year tax holiday, then on profits at progressive rate.	Chose the location on advice of other HK firms already in the area.	- HK side has a compensation trade factory in Dongguan. - Town Industrial Company runs four other LLJG and two CJVs and eight local industrial collectives.
PA-5 Knitwear	County Investment Company (a collective under the County Foreign Economic and Trade Committee).	Hong Kong knitwear manufacturing company, still in operation in Hong Kong.	3-year tax holiday.	Contact with Hong Kong partner made via provincial government.	---
PA-6 Clothing	Township enterprise, under Provincial Textile Import-Export Company.	Several since 1979. Originally set up by a Hong Kong clothing manufacturer.	Several factories build one after the other, each getting a 3-year tax holiday.	Very large and successful factory complex, in an area with many other clothing factories.	On Chinese side, set up by same company as set up PA-7.
PA-7 Toys and Clothes	Township enterprise.	Hong Kong company, now only doing designing, but but originally had a small factory.	---	Major expansion started 1984.	On Chinese side, set up in 1979 by same company as set up PA-6.

Table 5.2

Processing and Assembly, Compensation Trade and 'Other' Companies – The Partners and The Contract (Sheet 3)

	Company	Chinese side	Foreign side	Tax	Special Features or Comments	Other Operations in China
PA-8	Cassette and Video Tapes	City District Foreign Trade Company	One of the largest Hong Kong conglomerates.	5% industrial and commercial tax (+ 2% management fee to Chinese parent). No profits tax because the company is "new".	Making losses on video tapes while trying to develop this line of production. Subsidizing from cassette tape production.	NA
PA-9	Clothing	Collective under a city district foreign trade company.	Originally Hong Kong contact was a worker's relative. Now have a wide range of customers.	5% product tax (+ 2.5% management fee to Chinese parent).	LLJG work, using imported materials, is seasonal.	NA
PA-10	Watches	Collective.	Hong Kong electronics company. Hong Kong partner is relative of Chinese manager.	NA	---	---
PA-11	Printing	Existing, county-owned printing factory, wishing to update equipment.	Hong Kong printing company.	NA	---	NA
PA-12	Knitwear	County External Trade Committee and Labour Bureau.	Set up by earlier Hong Kong partner, who withdrew after first contract expired.	NA	Considering setting up a joint venture, with Provincial Textile Import-Export Company as a partner.	Hong Kong partner has two other factories in China.

Table 5.2
Processing and Assembly, Compensation Trade and 'Other' Companies – The Partners and The Contract (Sheet 4)

Company	Chinese side	Foreign side	Tax	Special Features or Comments	Other Operations in China
PA-13 Clothing	Collective, now a holding company for five subsidiaries.	Hong Kong garment company.	NA	Used compensation trade to import equipment, and finished the original 6-year contract after three years.	---
Compensation Trade Companies					
CT-1 Brewery	New state company, under city government, under 1st Light Industry Bureau.	French and Belgian suppliers of equipment and technology.	Free of 25% industrial and commercial tax (except for first 5%).	Loan from France, via Bank of China, largely tied to purchase of French equipment.	NA
CT-2 Cardboard Boxes	Town industrial holding company.	Macau company.	NA	Early failures in compensation trade. Close links (e.g. cross-use of forex earnings) between the holding company's three factories.	Town holding company has related factories making zips and sanitary products.
"Other" Companies					
0-1 Washing Machines	Collective company, previously producing agricultural machinery (up to 1976).	Japanese company negotiating with them.	55% Profits Tax (no other taxes paid).	---	---

Table 5.2

Processing and Assembly, Compensation Trade and 'Other' Companies – The Partners and The Contract(Sheet 5)

Company	Chinese side	Foreign side	Tax	Special Features or Comments	Other Operations in China
0-2 Shipping Company	City port office.	Chinese-owned shipping company in Hong Kong. Also loan from Bank of China.	NA	---	NA
0-3 Ceramics Company	A state "group company" (reorganized into present form in 1987).	None. Bank of China provides foreign exchange loan.	55% Profits Tax.	Counts as a "foreign investment" because of foreign currency loan from Bank of China.	Parent company has 42 companies under its control.

114

Table 5.3

Processing and Assembly, Compensation Trade and 'Other' Companies – Markets and Foreign Exchange (sheet 1)

Company	Exports(%) (Actual/Contract)	Marketing Arrangements	Competition Domestic vs Foreign Sales	Forex Balance – Raw Materials	Forex Retention	Other Issues
Processing and Assembly Companies						
PA-1 Industrial Leather Gloves	100/100	By Hong Kong side. Some marketing of products under customer brand names.	NA	Raw materials supplied by Hong Kong side, under LLJG.	NA	–
PA-2 Plastic Toys	100/100	By HK side. Mostly to USA and Europe.	NA	Raw materials supplied by HK side under LLJG.	NA	–
PA-3 Metal Piping	50/NA	50% of production is marketed independently, 30% through the Guangdong Mineral-Metal Corporation, and 20% via LLJG sales by Hong Kong partner.	Complete on basis of very high technical specifications. Have replaced imported galvanised water pipes in Chinese market.	Some raw materials supplied under LLJG, but steel comes from within China.	In practice, Bank of China retains the forex to repay the loan.	–

Table 5.3

Processing and Assembly, Compensation Trade and 'Other' Companies – Markets and Foreign Exchange(Sheet 2)

Company	Exports(%) (Actual/Contract)	Marketing Arrangements	Competition Domestic vs Foreign Sales	Forex Balance - Raw Materials	Forex Retention	Other Issues
PA-4 Garments (underwear)	100/100	All products are sold to West Germany.	Hong Kong market buoyant for these products.	---	15% of forex is retained by the factory.	-
PA-5 Knitwear	100/100	All sold by Hong Kong partner.	NA	All raw materials supplied by Hong Kong partner.	25% of forex goes to repay a loan. Of the remaining 75% - factory retains 15% points, county retains 10%, nearby city retains 5%, Guangdong province retains 45%.	

Table 5.3

Processing and Assembly, Compensation Trade and 'Other' Companies - Markets and Foreign Exchange (Sheet 3)

Company	Exports(%) (Actual/Contract)	Marketing Arrangements	Competition Domestic vs Foreign Sales	Forex Balance - Raw Materials	Forex Retention	Other Issues
PA-6 Clothing	95/NA	Originally sold to USA (shirts), now a wider range of products sold world-wide (including Japan, Canada, Europe). Not all exports are via LLJG. Some are through Provincial Textile Import-Export Corporation.	Buoyant export markets.	Raw materials supplied by LLJG customers, and sometimes bought in China with forex supplied by Hong Kong boss. Problems with customs duty on machine parts.	Company can get back 15% of the processing fee as forex, but at the official rate.	LLJG orders, and machinery, are from a variety of Hong Kong customers. Must pay import duty on machinery given by customers.
PA-7 Toys and Clothes	100/NA	Main market is North America. All marketing is done by Hong Kong side.	Buoyant overseas market. Chinese side very satisfied with marketing arrangements.	Materials from Japan and South Korea. No suitable materials in China.	NA	Hong Kong side prepared a processing fee to allow Chinese side to buy machinery, and was repaid by being allowed to buy product at a discount.

Table 5.3

Processing and Assembly, Compensation Trade and 'Other' Companies - Markets and Foreign Exchange (Sheet 4)

Company	Exports(%) (Actual/Contract)	Marketing Arrangements	Competition Domestic vs Foreign Sales	Forex Balance - Raw Materials	Forex Retention	Other Issues
PA-8 Cassette and Video Tapes	100/100	Marketed by Hong Kong partner.	Very intense overseas competition in market for video tapes. No sales in China because raw material costs high and demand is low. Cassette tape sales subsidize video sales at the moment.	Raw materials imported, generally from Singapore, to maintain quality.	Hong Kong partner pays processing fee in forex to Bank of China, who gives company RMB at official rate to cover its costs. But company can buy forex at the official rate, up to 30% of the processing fee, to buy imported equipment.	
PA-9 Clothing	20/No contractual figure	Not all exports are through LLJG. Also export using local materials.	Higher profits on exports.	For local sales basic materials are from China. High cost of Japanese machine parts because of high Yen.	Bank of China receives forex for processing fee and gives company RMB. Can buy back 12.5% at official rate to buy machinery.	Seasonal demand.

Table 5.3

Processing and Assembly, Compensation Trade and 'Other' Companies – Markets and Foreign Exchange (Sheet 5)

Company	Exports(%) (Actual/Contract)	Marketing Arrangements	Competition Domestic vs Foreign Sales	Forex Balance - Raw Materials	Forex Retention	Other Issues
PA-10 Digital Watches	100/100	All marketed by Hong Kong partner.	Hong Kong market conditions much less favourable than in mid-1980s. Main competitor is another factory in Guangdong.	All materials are from Hong Kong, under LLJG.	NA	-
PA-11 Printing	NA	All marketed by Hong Kong partner.	NA	NA	NA	-
PA-12 Knitwear	100/100	All marketed by Hong Kong	Sell to USSR, USA, Canada.		Factory gets 12% Guangdong province	-
PA-13 Clothing	70-80/No contractual figure	Generally sell through Guangdong Textile Import-Export Corporation. Still have a Hong Kong partner, but sometimes find own customers too.	Can sell in Chinese market using poorer quality (local) raw materials.	Many raw materials bought abroad (takes 50% of forex earnings), when planning to export.	Get paid in RMB. Can get a "small amount" of forex back, but must spend through Bank of China.	-

119

Table 5.3

Processing and Assembly, Compensation Trade and 'Other' Companies – Markets and Foreign Exchange (Sheet 6)

Company	Exports(%) (Actual/Contract)	Marketing Arrangements	Competition Domestic vs Foreign Sales	Forex Balance - Raw Materials	Forex Retention	Other Issues
Compensation Trade Companies						
CT-1 Brewery	0/20% planned	Sell domestically under well-known local brandnames. Quality not yet high enough for export.	Excess demand in China for good quality beer.	Buy raw materials from Australia, through Bank of China, and not using own forex.	Plan to use any forex to repay French loan. At present must buy forex at free market rate.	-
CT-2 Cardboard Box Factory	33/33	Part of exports sent to pay for compensation trade, and part through the City Light Industrial Products Import-Export Corporation.	Intense domestic competition. Need to keep costs low. Domestic sales are more profitable.	Use imported materials (higher quality) for products to be exported. Part of forex for equipment was borrowed from town government.	Exports provides enough forex to finance the compensation trade and to import new equipment in another line of activity. Exchange rate received is "not" favourable to exports.	-

120

Table 5.3

Processing and Assembly, Compensation Trade and 'Other' Companies – Markets and Foreign Exchange (Sheet 7)

Company	Exports(%) (Actual/Contract)	Marketing Arrangements	Competition Domestic vs Foreign Sales	Forex Balance - Raw Materials	Forex Retention	Other Issues
"Other" Companies						
0-1 Washing Machine Factory	NA/plan 10% exports	1985-6 mainly sold within China. 1987 exported some production to South East Asia.	Excess demand for washing machines within China.	Imports of parts from Japan and Europe, but some made locally.	Any forex earned is repaid to pay for the leasing of equipment.	Japanese interest in a joint venture because of rise in Yen exchange rate.
0-2 Shipping Company	NA/NA	Much traffic originates in Hong Kong and pays in forex.	Little alternative transport to this location.	NA	Loan repayments made in forex.	-
0-3 Ceramics	33/66 planned	Member companies give one-third of production to the group company, which has the right to export (and import). Of the remaining two-thirds, members plan half domestic/half foreign sales.	Well-established market for these well-known products to both in China and in Hong Kong.	Raw materials mainly from within China. Get some tax concessions on importing equipment.	Retain "some" forex over and above loan repayments to Bank of China, in order to import equipment.	

121

Table 5.4

Processing and Assembly, Compensation Trade and 'Other' Companies – Employment and Operational Issues (Sheet 1)

Company	Workforce	Employment Status	Recruitment	Wages (per month)	Wages in relation to other costs	Training and Supervision	Remarks
Processing and Assembly Companies							
PA-1 Industrial Leather Gloves	150 workers (single shift).	Workers paid directly by HK side (under Cheng Bao contract).	NA	Y160 for experienced workers (Y6-7 per day, and Y3-5 per day for new workers).	Total direct costs in China almost the same as wage costs alone in Hong Kong.	Problem that workers trained by the factory may then be removed by the local authority.	Wages in the district are said to average Y150 for LLJG operations.
PA-2 Plastic Toys	900 workers (3 shifts)	Workers paid directly.	Mostly directly recruited.	Y140	NA	Hard to get suitable HK staff to come here in supervisory/training roles.	Wages are less than 20% of Hong Kong level, but workers less efficient.
PA-3 Metal Piping	325 workers	Mostly contract workers (3 year contract)	Factory manager can hire and fire. Mostly recruited directly by advertisements in local area.	Y250 + Y50 medical benefits.	Raw materials are approximately 75% of total costs.	Initially a team of up to 15 Italian engineers supervised installation of new machinery and staff training. Strong stress on new factory giving manager more freedom of action.	Mostly young workers. Wages higher than most of the area.

Table 5.4

Processing and Assembly, Compensation Trade and 'Other' Companies – Employment and Operational Issues (Sheet 2)

Company	Workforce	Employment Status	Recruitment	Wages (per month)	Wages in relation to other costs	Training and Supervision	Remarks
PA-4 Garments	40-50	All temporary, though factory wishes to retain them for long period.	Hiring and firing done by Chinese partner. All workers are local. Waiting list of workers wanting to join factory.	Y130 average (Basic Y80 + price rate).	10% of costs are labour, 60% raw materials.	3 technical workers from HK work in the factory. Two weeks training for workers. Low education level of workers is a problem.	Many of the workers are the children of local cadres.
PA-5 Knitwear	690	Contract workers. Some workers come in only at peak times, and otherwise work in agriculture.	80% of workers are local. Skilled workers are mostly from outside the county.	Y125 (piece rate).	Wages 50% of costs.	Manager from Guangzhou, is HK partner's grandson.	–
PA-6 Clothing	1600	Mostly on three-year contracts.	Mostly local workers, mostly former peasant women.	Over Y150 on average. Piece work, with bonuses for quality and speed.	NA	Management "similar to HK" except cannot fire workers.	

123

Table 5.4

Processing and Assembly, Compensation Trade and 'Other' Companies - Employment and Operational Issues (Sheet 3)

Company	Workforce	Employment Status	Recruitment	Wages (per month)	Wages in relation to other costs	Training and Supervision	Remarks
PA-7 Toys and Clothes	4200 and another 1000 outworkers. (normally one 10-hour shift, but 12-13 hours if busy).	Mainly contract workers, 10% temporary workers, because work is seasonal. 90% of workers are unmarried women.	Half workers are recruited from other provinces (e.g. Guangxi).	Y180 average, paid on piece rate.	Of the processing fee, 30% is for labour, 50-60% for other costs. Leaving 10-20% profit.	Two HK representatives work in the factory. Many individual households already had sewing machines in this area, which made training easy; although town did not have a garment industry prior to the Open Policy.	-
PA-8 Cassette and Video Tapes	300	Two-thirds are contract workers.	Workers almost all young women.	Y135 (piece rates), including bonus.	Percentages of output: Wages - 40%; Material fees - 40%; Profit - 20%.	Managers all local, though operation tightly controlled by Hong Kong partner's China office.	-
PA-9 Clothing	140	100 permanent, 40 temporary workers.	Permanent workers directly hired, some from country side. Must take a technical examination to get employment.	Y100 basic + Y50 bonus on average.	Percentages of output: Wages and Salaries - 13%; Materials - 45%; Product Tax - 5%; Management fee - 2.5%; Profit - 35%.	Foreign partners have no say in management.	-

Table 5.4

Processing and Assembly, Compensation Trade and 'Other' Companies – Employment and Operational Issues (Sheet 4)

Company	Workforce	Employment Status	Recruitment	Wages (per month)	Wages in relation to other costs	Training and Supervision	Remarks
PA-10 Digital Watches	250	7 permanent, 20 contract workers. Rest are temporary.	NA	Y150-200.	Labour is two-thirds of total costs.	NA	-
PA-11 Printing	470	Combination of permanent workers from old printing factory, and some new contract workers.	NA	Y200 + for technicians.	NA	One technician from Hong Kong works in the factory.	-
PA-12 Knitwear	240	90% temporary.	Recruited from rural areas.	Y115 on average.	NA	2 workers from Hong Kong. Quality problems with Chinese workers.	-
PA-13 Clothing	930 (9-hour shift, no night shift).	Two-thirds are permanent workers. But after one year workers get treated like permanent workers (or else they will go elsewhere!).	10% of workers are from other provinces.	Y150-200 on average (piece rates).	NA	NA	

Table 5.4

Processing and Assembly, Compensation Trade and 'Other' Companies – Employment and Operational Issues (Sheet 5)

Company	Workforce	Employment Status	Recruitment	Wages (per month)	Wages in relation to other costs	Training and Supervision	Remarks
Compensation Trade Companies							
CT-1 Brewery	700 (planned: 594)	Mainly contract workers.	Workers frequently assigned to company by city government.	NA	Percentage of cost: Labour: < 10%; Raw materials: 30%.	NA	Company feels it has excess labour.
CT-2 Cardboard Box Factory	200	Permanent workers, plus 150 temporary workers spread over this and the two other factories (zips, sanitary products).	NA	NA	Percentage of cost: Labour: < 10%; Raw materials: 75%.	NA	-
"Other" Companies							
O-1 Washing Machine Factory	570 (three shifts).	NA	Workers recruited "in market".	Y200 average (no bonus at present).	NA	Some of the factory's engineers were sent to Japan for training.	-
O-2 Shipping Company	200 (including 24 on the ships).	Half permanent workers, half contract workers.	Some of the permanent workers were hired from other companies.	Average Y200 on land, Y300 on sea.	NA	NA	-
O-3 Ceramics	16,000	65% are permanent workers. All new workers are employed on contract.	NA	NA	NA	Company has large research department to absorb foreign technology.	-

6 Locational choices of foreign investors in the Pearl River Delta

Our interviews have shown clearly that there is considerable variation in the attractiveness of different areas within the Delta for foreign investors. Though the Shenzhen Special Economic Zone was the earliest area that was opened to foreign investors in 1979, the first foreign industrial cooperation (a lai liao jia gong operation) was not found in Shenzhen but in Shunde xian (county) in the Pearl River Delta. Why did investors choose to locate their LLJG operations in Shunde and not in Shenzhen which is so much nearer to Hong Kong and offers more economic privileges? Why after a few years, did Dongguan, which was a county famous mainly for the production of bananas and lychees, become the most popular site for LLJG operations instead of Shunde? Also, why is Baoan, which had insignificant industrial output before 1984, now famous for the establishment of small industrial villages in nearly all of its towns and has become a major competitor to Dongguan in attracting LLJG operations? In this chapter we will try to investigate the locational advantages that the various counties or cities possess in attracting the different forms of foreign investment. Moreover, as time goes on, some of the specific advantages that a county or city orginally possessed may be acquired by others and this means that counties or cities will be facing keener competition in the future in attracting foreign investment. We will conclude the chapter with some suggestions as to what counties and cities can do to enhance their competitive edge to attract investors.

There is general agreement that the main reason why Hong Kong firms invest in China is to reduce their cost of production, namely, the labour and land costs. However, apart from the labour and land costs, there are other factors that enter into the decision of choosing a plant site. For example, the reliability of electricity and water supply, an efficient transportation and communication network, prepared factory buildings, local government cooperation and so on. In the following sections we will look into these factors in more detail with respect to the various counties and cities in the Pearl

River Delta.

6.1 Location

From Map 2 we can see that all the counties and cities are located along the delta with Baoan being the county and Dongguan being the city (except for Shenzhen) nearest to Hong Kong. Baoan is 40 km and Dongguan is 100 km from Hong Kong, there are also waterways linking these places to the ports in Hong Kong (see Table 6.8). With such an advantage of proximity to Hong Kong, it is not surprising to find that over 40% of the processing fees earned during 1979-1986 were from these two places.   Other counties such as Taishan, Enping, Hesan, Gaoming, which are located further away from Hong Kong, are thus less attractive for foreign investment.   (see Table 6.2).   From the transportation point of view there are more likely to be foreign manufacturing operations located at places that are more easily accessible either by land or by water so that raw materials and final products can be transported to and from Hong Kong at a lower cost. However, since the manufactured goods produced are mostly light industrial products such as textiles, garments, toys and electronics which are not bulky, transportation is therefore not a significant cost in the entire cost structure. Therefore, even though Shunde, Nanhai and Foshan are further from Hong Kong (over 200 km), investors are still willing to locate their plants there if other advantages outweight the cost of transportation. Moreover, if the counties are of the same distance from Hong Kong and one can be accessed by land and the other by sea, the transshipment cost will make the latter less attractive as a location.   To reduce the transshipment cost, Shunde has recently opened a port at Rongqi, and the area around the port is zoned to be an export processing zone replacing the previous development zone near its county capital Tailung which is some distance from the waterway.

6.2 Labour

The availability of abundant labour is believed to be the major reason for the enormous shift of production operations from Hong Kong to the Pearl River Delta.   Hong Kong has been a labour-intensive manufacturing centre since the early 1950s and labour has certainly played an important role in the growth history of Hong Kong. However, as Hong Kong grows, the changing economic structure has resulted in increasing wage differentials between the industrial and tertiary sectors, so that, together with an increase in education level, workers are attracted to the tertiary sector.   The number of manufacturing workers peaked at 1981 at 900,000 and since then there was a gradual decline. Though China started to "open" in 1978, most of the production operations in the Pearl River Delta have been established only in more recent years.   The depreciation of the US dollar has meant that Hong Kong products have become more competitive than those of its neighbours such as South Korea, Taiwan and Singapore.(1) The rapid growth of export demand combined with the falling number of manufacturing workers have led to a serious labour shortage in Hong Kong, which is the main reason that pushes investors to establish processing and assembly plants in the Pearl River Delta, which has become a hinterland for Hong Kong industrialists.   With relatively large populations (see Table 6.7) it is not surprising to find Zhongshan, Nanhai, Shunde, Dongguan, Panyu and Zengcheng have become the most popular locations for labour-intensive processing plants. The abundant supply of labour has resulted in wage rates that are as low as 10% of the average wage paid to a worker in Hong Kong.(2) However, why then does Baoan, with a population one fifth of that of Dongguan, still manage to attract an enormous number of foreign firms there? Does it mean that the availability of labour is not important? Surely not. If we look at Baoan carefully, we will find that in 1985 over 160,000 workers were employed from outside the region which was two third of its local population.(3) In fact, with more and more LLJG operations, some cities and counties in the Delta started to experience labour shortages and the monthly wage of workers has gone up to RMB 500-700 in areas like Baoan and Dongguan. In order to ease the labour shortage, it is now a common practice for localities to import cheap labour from outside the Delta. It has been estimated that the size of outside labour or guest workers working in the Delta was about one million which amounts to over 10% of the total local population. For instance, in Dongguan City, the number of guest workers was between 150,000 to 200,000, which is about 12% to 16% of the local population. (T.M.H. Chan, 1988, p28) In Foshan, there were about 300,000 guest workers which is roughly equal to its own local population.(4) However, the import of cheap labour will cease one day as there is a limit to the size of population that a city or county can hold (especially in the provision of food and lodging). Also, when wages continue to rise, investors will find it more profitable to locate their operations further away in areas with more labour supply. In fact, more and more processing plants are moving away from Dongguan to areas such as Boluo to take advantage of the lower labour and land costs. Moreover, apart from the wage paid to the workers, there are other labour costs that investors have to consider when they choose their plant location. For instance, the wage paid to the workers may be the same in the Shenzhen Special Economic Zone as in Baoan, but investors may still prefer Baoan to Shenzhen despite the fact that Shenzhen is nearer to Hong Kong. One reason may be that the labour cost is more higher in Shenzhen because the employer has to pay the Employment Bureau extra money to cover the accommodation and welfare benefits of the workers. In smaller Pearl River Delta localities, either there is no need to provide accommodation for the workers because they are from the nearby villages, or, if they are guest workers, there are no strict regulations concerning the accommodation payments; and even if there are, the investor can always obtain a better deal from the local government.

The labour issues relating to foreign investment comprise not only the labour cost, but the freedom of hiring and dismissing employees, and the efficiency of the labour force. The management's right of hiring and dismissing employees is affected by three factors, that is, Chinese traditions and customs, bureaucratic intervention and the lack of labour market. (Wang, 1988, p32). The degree of bureaucratic intervention differs among enterprises. In some cases, the Chinese partners may favour those who have special relationships with them disregarding their actual qualifications as employees. As for labour efficiency, since most of the production activities located in the Pearl River Delta are of a labour-intensive type and the technology is not of advanced kind, workers can be trained fairly quickly.

6.3   Infrastructure

Apart from having low labour costs and proximity to Hong Kong, the provision of a transportation and communications network, water and electricity, and prepared factory sites/industrial villages are also important considerations for investors in choosing a plant location. Most cities and counties in the Pearl River Delta have direct telephone links with Hong Kong which is very important in speeding up the information flow between the parent and sub-contracting firms (see Table 6.8).   Also in terms of areas under construction (excluding residential areas), and of road construction, Zhongshan City, Nanhai, Shunde and Dongguan are among the top in the Delta (see Table 6.7). Their high percentage of non-residential building may mean that these cities and counties will have more prepared factory buildings and thus are more attractive for industrial activities.   The supply of electricity is another major problem for most investors. As a result of frequent power cuts, factories have to have their own-back up generator which adds to operating cost.   In order to guarantee the supply of electricity, some localities such as Panyu have built their own electricity plant instead of just relying on the provincial electricity network.

6.4   Capital

The availability of capital is not a significant factor in affecting the choice of foreign investors in choosing their partners in compensation trade and LLJG contracts as the foreign partners will be responsible in providing the necessary equipment and raw materials. What is needed from the Chinese side are labour and factory sites.   In Dongguan and Baoan where local governments (at various levels) have the capital to construct prepared factory buildings, Hong Kong investors can just rent the factory and employ the necessary labour, and start the production solely by themselves.   Very often the Chinese side, normally a development company, will provide the investors with administrative personnel to deal with the labour and import and export matters.   Thus, for processing and assembly activities, even if a county or village does not have an industrial base, if the local government can obtain capital to build factory sites and provide the necessary infrastructure, it will attract foreign investors.   In fact this is how Dongguan and Baoan became the most popular locations for LLJG operations. The choice of location for industrial joint ventures is quite different, however, in that they have to look for a place with a stronger industrial base.   This is why there are more joint ventures located in Shanghai and Tianjin.   In the Pearl River Delta, Foshan (5) and Shunde were considered to have had a stronger industrial base even before the influx of foreign investment.   For instance, Foshan had a annual industrial growth rate of 14% during the period 1949-1978, which was higher than the average for the whole of China and this rapid growth has continued (see Table 6.6).   Shunde also has a high level of industrial output (see Table 6.1) and its rural industrial development is ahead of others.   Shunde, being one of the main producers of silk in the past, had accumulated experience in the manufacturing of textiles and garments; thus, it is not surprising to find that the first foreign industrial cooperation (LLJG) contract was signed with a garment factory in Shunde in 1978.   Apart from textiles and garments, machine tools were another major industry in

Shunde. In fact, it is based on the industrial experience of producing machine tools that Shunde has developed into a major producer of electric fans in China in recent years. The industrial development of Shunde does not stop at the town level. In order to help village industries to grow, for instance, the electric fan factories in Kuaizhou subcontracted some parts of the product to enterprises at the village level. In so doing, the electric fan factories were able to become more specialized in their operation and thus increase production efficiency, and, at the same time, to transfer technology and machinery to the village level (see Table 6.9 for information on village-level industrial output). This increases the economic and industrial power of the entire xian and thus, is more attractive to foreign investors when they are looking for a Chinese partner (especially for joint ventures) who has both capital and industrial experience.

From Table 6.3 we can see that of the cooperative joint venture contracts signed between 1979-1986 in the Pearl River Delta, 23.5% was in the industrial sector. Apart from the frquently cited locations such as Foshan, Zhongshan, Nanhai, Shunde, Dongguan and Baoan, we find that Kaiping, Xinhui, Jiangmen and even Heshan have considerable number of industrial cooperative joint ventures. The distribution of industrial JVs seems less concentrated than that of LLJG operations. One of the reasons may be due to the previously mentioned factor that the industrial JVs have to look for partners that have both economic and industrial power. Even though Kaiping, Xinhui, Jiangmen and Heshan may be relatively further away from Hong Kong, if these localities possess suitable enterprises for cooperation, they are still attractive to foreign investors. In addition, for JVs, their markets are not confined to exports, and thus, proximity to Hong Kong is less important as compared to LLJG operations. However, after all, Foshan, Zhongshan, Shunde and Dongguan still top the list of joint venture investment during the period 1979-1986. (refer to Table 6.5).

6.5   Technology

As with capital, the technology level is not a significant factor in affecting the choice for processing and assembly plants since the level of technology used in these plants is relatively low and it is easy for the workers to learn. However, for industrial joint ventures, the availability of technical and management personnel is more significant. From Table 6.1 we can gain an overview of the kind of industries which are most important for each locality. There are six major industries in the Delta, namely, machinery, construction materials, food-processing, textiles, garments and construction. For instance, the small towns of Foshan (excluding the city of Foshan, ie. only including the surrounding small towns) are well-known for the manufacturing of construction materials such as bricks and tiles, whereas Nanhai's major industries are food-processing and textiles. When we look at the industrial output as percentages of that of Guangdong small towns in 1986, we find that Shunde had the greatest percentage share of industrial output in Guangdong (about 10%). Being the major machinery producer in the Delta (excluding the city of Foshan and Jiangmen), the technology level of Shunde is believed to be among the highest in the Delta. (6) Thus, again it is more likely that Shunde will attract JV partners.

6.6   Economic privileges

Apart from constructing factory buildings and infrastructure to attract foreign investment, governments in different cities or counties can offer different economic privileges to the foreign investors at their own discretion. Before the State Council of China promulgated the Provisions for the Encouragement of Foreign Investment on October 11, 1986 (the 'Provisions'), there were only general policies laid down by the central government, and their interpretation and implementation were subject to the discretion of local administrative bodies.   For instance, in the area of taxation, in order to be qualify for the preferential treatment stipulated in the Provisions for export-oriented and technologically advanced enterprises, an enterprise had to apply to, and be examined and confirmed by, the relevant   Chinese authorities as satisfying the necessary requirements.   Prior to the Provisions, local authorities could more easily offer preferential treatment to foreign investors as there was no precise definition for the categorization of enterprises. However, there are still areas where local governments can grant foreign investors special privileges so as to increase their own competitiveness in attracting foreign investment. For instance, there is currently no national law regulating land-use fees. Such fees are therefore determined by the local governments in accordance with the conditions of their respective localities.   Though there is a standard as to the amount of land use fees that the local authorities can charge, if they desire, they can reduce the fees at their own discretion so as to promote foreign investment.   In addition, the Provisions allows local governments to exempt foreign-investment enterprises from paying land use fees for certain periods of time. (Wang, 1988, p.61). In order to attract foreign investment, individual localities in the Delta have offered special policies to foreign investors.   For instance, in Shunde, the local authority offers other special advantages to foreign investors, such as exempting them from paying miscellaneous fees (7), extending the tax holidays for local tax payments, giving them priority in the supply of water and electricity and charging the fees at state-owned enterprise level. (8) In order to encourage export-oriented investment, the officials in Baoan give back to the factory for re-investment purposes that part of foreign exchange reserves that belongs to the county. In other localities, the authorities may help the factories escape tax payments after the first three years of tax exemption by allowing the factories to register under a new company name. Also, there may be cases where the relatives of the foreign investors get priority when they apply to migrate to Hong Kong if a certain amount of investment is invested in the locality. Thus, to the foreign investors, it is more attractive to invest in localities in the Pearl River Delta because they can offer more economic privileges and flexibility than the Special Economic Zones and large cities such as Guangzhou.

6.7   Administrative efficiency

One of the most commonly cited problems in foreign investment is the complicated and time-consuming administrative procedures that investors have to go through.   There may be as many as 20 to 30 offices that one has to go through before the actual production can take place. In order to facilitate foreign investment, Dongguan was

the first county in the Pearl River Delta to establish a Processing &
Assembly Office. This consists of officials from various government
departments including the Planning Committee, Economic Committee,
External Economic Relations & Trade Committee, banks and other
industrial and commercial departments who deal with the processing of
LLJG contracts and the actual setting up of the factories. The Office
also deals with the negotiation of processing fees, import and export
matters, application for vehicle purchases, foreign exchange, etc. In
addition, sub-offices have also been set up at the town level in
Dongguan. The formation of this office and its sub-offices have
greatly improved administrative efficiency and encouraged foreign
investment. The processing fees in Dongguan have increased from
US$2.34 million in 1979 to US$62.68 million in 1986, and the average
annual growth rate was greater than the provincial level. (T.M.H.
Chan, 1988, p44) Of the 29 small towns in Dongguan, over three
quarters of them have an annual processing fee over US$1 million. In
fact, Boluo has followed the example of Dongguan in the setting up of
a Processing and Assembly Office. On the other hand Baoan, instead of
setting up a single office, has arranged for all the relevant offices
to be located in a hotel in Shenzhen. In addition, each small town
also has an office in the Hotel so as to facilitate the investors
choosing their plant location without actually travelling to the
different towns. However, the improvement in administration can be
more easily made for LLJG contracts than the JVs because the latter
are always projects involving larger amounts of capital, which if
exceeding a certain amount, have to be approved at a higher level. In
order to escape the more complicated administrative procedures at the
higher level, some joint venture projects are signed within the limit
that can be approved at the county level but in fact, the actual
amount of investment may far exceed the contracted amount. Again, the
flexibility at the lower level of the hierarchy has made for an easier
procedure for foreign investors.

6.8   Attitudes towards foreign investment

The most important factor that affects the choice of location is often
the attitudes of government officials and the Chinese partners towards
foreign investment. If the officials have confidence in the open door
policy, they will be quick in responding to the policy by actively
carrying out such changes to attract foreign investment. Such changes
include the establishment of previously mentioned Processing and
Assembly Offices to improve administrative efficiency, the spending of
money on infrastructure and the offering of economic privileges.
Those localities whose officials are quick in response reap the
benefits first. For example, although Baoan is nearer to Hong Kong
than Dongguan, due to the active attitudes of the officials, Dongguan
became a major location for LLJG operations in the early 1980s, which
was four years' earlier than Baoan. As Dongguan became prosperous,
other xians started to follow. In our interviews, some officials in
Panyu admitted that it was due to the conservative attitudes of the
former leaders that Panyu, which used to be ranked together with
Shunde and Nanhai, is now lagging behind them. If the local officials
are open and ready to learn and change, investors will have more
confidence in locating their investment there. The positive attitudes
of the officials towards foreign investment will mean that they will
try their best to accommodate the requests of the investors.

Moreover, the attitudes of the Chinese partners are such that they are unwilling to carry out reforms, foreign partners will find it very difficult to cooperate with them in the joint ventures. In places where the local people have more contacts with Hong Kong, they tend to be more receptive to new ideas and changes. Thus, the number of overseas Chinese originating from a particular area is often being quoted by the local authorities of that area as one of the factors that improves the foreign investment climate.

NOTES

1. The Hong Kong dollar was linked to the US dollar in October 1983. The depreciation of the US$ after 1985 meant that Hong Kong products became more competitive in the world market.

2. For instance, the average wage paid to a garment worker in Boluo, a county included in the Delta in late 1987, was RMB 120-150 per month, which was about HK$300. Unskilled Hong Kong workers would rarely have been earning less than HK$3000 per month.

3. Information gathered from authors' field trip in December 1987.

4. Information from Hong Kong television TVB news, 28 December 1988. The same broadcast suggested that the number of guest workers in Dongguan had risen to 300,000, equivalent to about a third of the local population.

5. The administrative region of Foshan City includes four xians, namely, Shunde, Nanhai, Gaoming, Sanshui and one city, Zhongshan. Here we are only referring to the city of Foshan and not the large adminstrative region of Foshan City. (This information refers to late 1987, the time of our interviewing programme. Since then Zhongshan City has been transferred out of Foshan's jurisdiction.)

6. Though a lot of new industries such as toys and electronics have been established in Dongguan and Baoan, they are of the processing and assembly type. However, for Shunde, the machine industry and its related industries are built on indigenous technology.

7. Normally enterprises may have to pay up to ten or more different kinds of fees to the local government. The miscellaneous fees include education fees, family planning fees, and welfare fees.

8. The charges for water and electricity are different for different kinds of enterprises. For example, the charges for collective entreprises are 10% higher than those for state-owned enterprises.

Table 6.1
Industrial Profile of Small Towns in the Pearl River Delta

Small Towns of the Xians/Cities	Industrial output average growth rate 1980-84	Industrial output as % of PRD towns in 1984	% distribution of the major industries in the small towns of Xians/Cities in PRD in 1984						Industrial Output as % of Guangdong small towns in 1986	Major Industries
			machinery	construction materials	food processing	textiles	garments	construction		
Poshan	23.2	3.8	2.5*	31.0	1.2	0	-	1.7		construction materials
Zhongshan	26.0	5.8	6.2	3.8	8.2	6.7	5.4	4.1	3.7	food processing, textiles, construction
Nanhai	24.1	14.5	11.7	11.1	1.7	20.8	6.9	7.7	6.2	machinery, garments, textiles
Shunde	28.2	21.8	30.8	7.3	1.3	19.5	28.5	10.4	10.8	textiles
Gaoming	4.3	-	-	-	-	1.5	-	3.0	0.39	
Jiangmen	17.7	-	-	-	-	-	-	-	0.18	
Kaiping	13.3	3.8	4.6	1.9	7.2	0	4.0	8.7	2.3	textile, construction, garments
Xinhui	27.2	12.2	10.4	10.2	9.8	29.3	13.0	14.4	6.9	construction, machinery
Taishan	20.7	7.0	13.7	3.7	7.5	1.4	4.6	17.1	3.6	construction
Heshan	24.1	1.9	-	1.4	2.6	5.4	-	1.6	1.4	
Enping	15.7	2.4	2.3	7.5	1.2	-	1.7	11.3	1.3	
Dongguan	21.6	13.9	5.3	9.4	9.1	14.0	15.0	4.3	3.3	textile and garment
Zengcheng	11.0	2.0	-	3.7	2.5	-	4.6	2.3	0.73	
Baoan	36.5	1.3	3.4	1.8	-	-	-	1.1	1.1	
Doumen	18.0	1.2	-	-	6.3	0	-	1.7	0.85	
Panyu	14.9	7.4	6.1	5.9	5.8	2.0	14.3	10.3	3.6	garments, construction

Notes: The average annual industrial output growth for the Pearl River Delta 1979-84 was 16.5%

* our % means that 2.5% of the machinery output in the Pearl River Delta came from the towns of Poshan.

The total industry output in small towns in Guangdong was RMB 18.6 billion in 1986.

In the following tables, unless it is specified otherwise, Foshan and Jiangmen only include the urban area of the city (not the large administrative region).

Source: Statistical Yearbook of Small Towns in Guangdong Province, 1985, 1987

135

Table 6.2

Foreign Investment in the Small Towns of the Pearl River Delta 1979-1986 (US$10,000)

	Compensation Trade actual amount		Processing Fee		Contractual JV actual amount		Compensation Trade 1979-86	Processing Fee 1979-1986	Contractual JV 1979-86 amount	Contractual JV Contract amount 1979-1986	Small Towns Included in each Xian/City	
	(a) 1979-84	(b) 85-86	(a) 1979-84	(b) 84-86	(a)	(b)	(c)	(c)	(c)	(d)	(a)	(b)
Foshan	31.5	-	15.3	1449.6	-	87				4406.6	2	4
Zhongshan	10	25	1693.5	2026	-	703	35	3709.4	703	6303.6	13	24
Nanhai	332.6	482	1873.1	3366	13.6	805	784.6	5239.1	817.6	1063.0	17	15
Shunde	-	189	2745.3	3433	126.9	930	189	6378.3	1056.9	4971.8	16	12
Gaoming	-	-	-	-	-	313	-	53	313	133.6*	10	10
Jiangmen	-	-	-	-	-	-				3639.7	1	2
Kaiping	-	-	80.6	3412	40.0	775	-	3482.6	815	734.6	3	16
Xinhui	20.4	5	1423.5	1227	27.7	899	25.4	2680.5	926.7	1524.7	17	20
Taishan	46.5	11	305.1	463	465.7	954	57.5	768.1	1419.3	1832	24	24
Heshan	41.9	250	335.0	582	104.3	595	291.9	917	699.3	462.4*	1	9
Enping	-	-	441.9	236	392.7	382	-	638.9	774.4	276.0*	8	17
Dongguan	20	192	1085.28	11076	843.4	1322	212	21928.8	2165.4	2249.5	32	29
Zengcheng	-	296	579.8	567	-	830	286	1146.8	830d	51.5*	6	14
Baoan	47.6	763	1037.3	4764	73.6	1849	810.6	5801.3	1922.6	1594.6*	6	17
Doumen	15.0	-	55.7	189	16.7	203	15	244.7	219.7	1010.8	1	8
Panyu	-	-	3708.7	2724	-	980	-	6432.7	980	755*	22	22
							2717 (total)	59470.2 (total)				

Sources and Notes:

(a) Data obtained from Statistical Yearbook of Small Towns in Guangdong Province, 1985

(b) Data obtained from Statistical Yearbook of Small Towns in Guangdong Province, 1987

(c) = (a) + (b)

(d) Data of the entire xian/city obtained from author's field trip

* includes small towns, but not villages

136

Table 6.3

Distribution of Cooperative Joint Venture Investment by contract value in the Pearl River Delta, 1979–86

(percentage distribution)

	Industry		Building construction, and mining		Agriculture & forestry		Transport, electricity and water		Commerce, tourist trade etc	
	(a)	(b)*	(a)	(b)	(a)	(b)	(a)	(b)	(a)	(b)
Foshan	14.5	24.0	3.4	3.9	9.0	3.8	1.6	1.3	21.6	59.1
Zhongshan	9.1	10.6	16.0	13.0	8.1	2.4	16.8	9.4	33.9	64.6
Nanhai	6.8	46.9	0.7	3.5	-	-	0.5	1.7	3.9	44.2
Shunde	12.9	18.9	49.0	50.4	9.1	3.4	1.2	0.9	9.5	23.0
Gaoming	-	-	-	-	-	-	0.5	14.3	1.0	85.0
Jiangmen	4.9	9.8	5.7	8.0	-	-	70.8	68.7	0.1	0.4
Kaiping	9.9	97.6	-	-	-	-	-	-	0.1	2.4
Xinhui	18.0	86.0	-	-	5.3	6.6	-	-	0.9	7.5
Taishan	-	-	1.5	4.1	35.8	36.5	-	-	9.0	59.1
Heshan	5.0	78.9	-	-	1.1	4.5	-	-	0.1	2.3
Enping	1.8	48.3	1.3	24.5	-	-	-	-	0.6	27.2
Dongguan	4.8	15.5	1.5	3.3	2.7	2.2	7.3	11.3	12.8	68.5
Zengcheng	0.7	100	-	-	-	-	-	-	-	-
Baoan	8.9	40.5	6.0	19.2	18.4	21.6	-	-	1.7	12.8
Donmen	1.7	12.2	1.7	8.4	10.5	19.5	1.3	4.4	4.7	55.0
Panyu	1.0	9.3	13.4	90.7	-	-	-	-	-	-
Total										
(in US$10,000)	7176.8		5115.9		1869.5		3531.2		12024	
(sector as % of total CJV Investment)	(23.5)		(16.5)		(6.0)		(11.4)		(38.8)	

Notes:

(a) As percentage of the total cooperative JV investment in that particular sector in PRD
(b) As percentage of the total cooperative JV investment in that particular xian/city
* The five sectors do not add up to 100% because there are other minor sectors that are excluded from the table

Source: From authors' field trip to China in Summer 1987

Table 6.4
Labour Force and Output Distribution by Form of Economic
Organisation, 1984

Small towns of the xians/cities	State-owned enterprises (%)		Collective enterprises (%)		Individual enterprises (%)	
	labour	output	labour	output	labour	output
Foshan	43.9	47.5	53.6	52.5	1.3	
Zhongshan	11.9	9.3	58.0	86.0	9.8	
Nanhai	23.1	32.5	70.8	67.1	5.0	
Shunde	25.1	16.2	66.6	81.2	5.1	
Gaoming	35.9	63.7	51.4	36.3	6.4	
Jiangmon	7.9	21.8	37.3	78.2	4.5	
Kaiping	46.6	48.1	45.8	51.6	2.7	
Xinhui	28.3	56.0	50.1	43.2	3.4	NA
Taishan	33.8	48.8	47.5	48.0	5.9	
Heshan	54.7	43.9	36.9	55.1	3.4	
Enping	48.4	49.4	40.7	47.3	6.7	
Dongguan	23.3	21.0	52.3	74.2	5.3	
Zengcheng	34.2	25.2	45.3	60.4	8.2	
Baoan	23.7	19.1	47.7	77.7	12.7	
Donmen	58.9	86.4	37.8	13.6	3.2	
Panyu	23.1	19.3	54.8	77.7	3.6	
Guangdong Province	36.2	NA	38.0	NA	7.5	NA

Source: Statistical Yearbook of Small Towns in Guangdong Province, 1985

138

Table 6.5

Percentage Distribution of Cooperative and Equity Joint Ventures
in total Joint Venture investment, 1979-1986 (contract amount)

	Cooperative JV	Equity JV	JV investment in xian/city: Total JV investment (%)
Foshan	67.3	32.7	15.8
Zhongshan	86.8	13.2	17.5
Nanhai	85.5	14.5	3.0
Shunde	96.1	3.9	12.5
Gaoming	100	-	0.3
Jiangmen	86.4	13.6	10.1
Kaiping	39.1	60.9	4.5
Yinhui	97.2	2.8	3.8
Taishan	100	-	4.4
Heshan	100	-	1.1
Enping	28.8	71.2	2.3
Dongguan	47.1	52.9	11.5
Zengcheng	81.1	18.9	0.2
Baoan	60.5	39.5	6.3
Donmen	75.0	25.0	3.2
Panyu	51.1	48.9	3.6
Total	74.6	25.4	100%

Source: From authors' field trip to China in Summer 1987

Table 6.6
Industrial Growth Performance of Foshan City

	Average annual growth rate between 1979-1984	Percentage share of industrial output in Foshan City in 1984
Foshan City*	15.6%	
Zhongshan	15.4%	21.2%
Shunde	14.0%	23.3%
Nanhai	15.2%	17.6%
Sanshui	16.1%	3.7%
Gaoming	6.3%	0.8%
Foshan**	17.4%	33.8%

*   The administrative region of Foshan
** This only refers to the city of Foshan

Source: data obtained from the Statistical Bureau of Foshan City

Table 6.7
Population, Land Area and Construction in Pearl River
Delta Localities

	Year end population in 1987	Non-agricultural population as percentage of total population	Land Area (km²)	Building Area (excluding residential) as percentage of Guangdong small towns total, 1986	Road Construction as percentage of Guangdong small towns total, 1986
Foshan	332837	78.6	77	NA	NA
Zhongshan	1090322	23.3	1683	3.16	3.97
Nanhai	885380	25.3	1152	3.03	2.76
Shunde	872051	28.9	806	2.66	2.25
Gaoming	231861	22.1	955	0.45	0.48
Jiangmen	251861	76.1	NA	NA	NA
Kaiping	612222	20.0	1510	1.81	1.14
Xinhui	842437	24.1	1679	1.33	1.64
Taishan	957027	15.8	3200	1.8	0.86
Heshan	321972	17.5	1108	0.77	0.69
Enping	397840	23.3	1698	1.05	1.34
Dongguan	1248639	22.1	2465	4.81	3.67
Zengcheng	630163	15.0	NA	1.04	1.1
Baoan	269128	22.6	1508	1.12	1.81
Donmen	266366	20.4	928	0.61	0.8
Panyu	707045	23.5	1313	1.5	2.0

Source: Guangdong Statistical Yearbook 1988, for population.
Statistical Yearbook of Small Towns in Guangdong Province, 1986, for building and road construction.
Investment Guide of Pearl River Delta Open Zone, 1986, for land areas

Table 6.8
Communications Profiles of Pearl River Delta
Localities

	distance from Hong Kong by land (km)	distance from Hong Kong by sea (seamiles)	availability of railway	availability of ports	availability of direct telephone link with Hong Kong
Foshan	245	96	Yes	Yes *	Yes
Zhongshan	310	54		Yes *	Yes
Nanhai	250	96		near to Foshan	Yes
Shunde	265^a	69		Yes	Yes
Gaoming	300			will have one later	Yes
Jiangmen	328^a	95		Yes	
Kaiping	370	far			
Xinhui	336	120^b			Yes
Taishan	371	far		to surrounding xians	Yes
Heshan	300	90			Yes
Enping	far	181			Yes
Dongguan	100	47	Yes	Yes *	Yes
Zengcheng	170	70	Yes		Yes
Baoan	40	near	Yes	Yes *	Yes
Donmen	far	^{b}			
Panyu	236	60		Yes *	Yes

Notes:

a   distance from Macau: Shunde - 80km, Jiangmen - 107km, Heshan - 130km.

b   distance from Macau: Xinhui - 60 seamiles, Donmen - near to Macau.

*   have several ports which can ship goods directly to Hong Kong.

Source: Investment Guide to Pearl River Delta Open Economic Zone, 1986,
        (in Chinese)

	agricultural output a (10,000 RMB)	grain production (tons) (A)		industrial output ᵃ (10,000 RMB)	industrial output at or below village level ᵇ (10,000 RMB)	industrial output as percentage of total output
Foshan	3315	-		346488	29169 (8.4)	99.1
Zhongshan*	53418	875413	U	325121	59463 (18.3)	85.9
Nanhai*	40198	358876	D	328344	133722 (40.7)	89.1
Shunde*	37899	96495	D	340008	56194 (16.5)	90.0
Gaoming	12339	136897	U	20109	2371 (11.7)	62.1
Jiangmen	2524	14283	D	167666	13578 (8.1)	98.8
Kaiping	20942	294514	D	91165	21749 (23.9)	81.3
Xinhui	34427	320623	D	187652	24792 (12.5)	85.2
Taishan	34247	441182	U	116905	31279 (26.8)	77.7
Heshan	13270	125861	U	41701	5720 (13.7)	75.9
Enping	20164	195978	D	39306	7469 (19.0)	66.1
Dongguan*	72374	462830	D	298035	100207 (33.6)	80.5
Zengcheng	19841	263171	D	35717	13585 (38.0)	64.2
Baoan	15807	84269	D	87116	9837 (11.3)	84.6
Donmen	17177	111538	D	35624	1283 (3.6)	67.5
Panyu	33189	325661	D	144298	27959 (19.4)	81.3

Notes:

(A) Output compared with 1984 (data for 1984 is from Investment Guide to the Pearl River Delta Open Economic Zone, 1986). U = output up, D = output down.

a   1980 constant prices.

b   including collective enterprises in small towns and private individual enterprises.

Brackets indicate percentage of industrial output generated at or below village level.

*   members of the "four tigers" of Guangdong. The industrial output of the four tigers was almost half of that of the Pearl River Delta.

Source: Guangdong Statistical Yearbook 1988 p.459-463.

7 Summary and conclusions

This research has drawn on material from interviews with over fifty companies operating in the Pearl River Delta. The interviews have not been based on a detailed questionnaire but have been 'open-ended' in the sense that, after basic information about a company's activities has been elicited, the interviewees have been encouraged to lead us into areas of particular interest to their operations. Of course, our interviewing has been informed by theoretical perspectives, and the standard location-specific/firm-specific/internalization advantages approach certainly yields insights. However, the situation in China is greatly complicated by the operation of the economic reforms and we have used existing theory as a starting point rather than a complete framework. Such qualitative research has gained increasing acceptance in other social sciences (see Walker, 1985) and in business studies (see Miles, 1987), and we contend it has a useful role in economic research too.

In the event, and perhaps not surprisingly, our interviews mainly have produced information on "what it is like" to be a foreign-investor in China. Investors' experiences have tended to vary according to the type of contract they have had, and the kind of partner, and these experiences are summarized here first in Sections 1 and 2. In addition, the research does shed light on more general issues of foreign investment and internationalization as illustrated by Hong Kong companies' experience, and on the Chinese economic reforms. These issues are set out under a series of headings in Section 3. Section 4 then looks more generally at the Chinese investment "climate" as of 1987-8, while Section 5 considers questions related to the joint development of Hong Kong and the Pearl River Delta. Finally, Section 6 discusses the effects on the economic reform programme of the austerity measures introduced in autumn 1988, and considers the future in the aftermath of the events of the 4th June 1989.

7.1   Experience of foreign investors with different types of contract

The main types of contract are:

1.   100% Foreign Owned Ventures
2.   Equity Joint Ventures (where some contributions are allowed from the Chinese side in kind, however)
3.   Cooperative (or 'contractual') Joint Ventures (where the Chinese contribution is mainly in kind, normally land and buildings)
4.   Processing and assembly arrangements (for which fees are charged)
5.   Compensation trade (where the foreign side supplies machinery and equipment, and is repaid in instalments of this product)

Our sample covered all the main forms of contract, except for the then (1987) rarely encountered 100% foreign-owned ventures, and material on the equity joint venture companies, contractual joint venture companies, and those in processing and assembly and compensation trade were presented, successively, in Chapters Three, Four and Five. Although it cannot be claimed that the "success" of investment varies systematically with the different types of contract, and although some of the problems investors face are common to all contracts, the idea of tailoring contracts to investors' needs has been an attractive feature of the Chinese scene. In principle they allow a great deal of flexibility about the degree investors commit themselves financially to involvement in China, and the degree they wish to "internalize" the use of their firm-specific advantages (1). In practice they are even more flexible than on paper, and our interviews show this extends to many cases where actual contracts are de facto mixtures of elements from several types. The flexibility is used sometimes, however, as a means of manipulating the economic system and evading controls, and investors do not always get the kind of contract they would most prefer.

Cooperative joint venture contracts are the most popular in Guangdong and the Delta, and cover the widest variety of arrangements. They include cases where the Chinese side contributes only nominally, leaving the foreign partner the opportunity to run a virtually 100% foreign venture, but without the constraint of the usual ten year contract for such operations (Moser, 1987, p.130). In one of our interviews, with a camera factory, both the Chinese officials involved and the Hong Kong businessman were quite explicit about this, and stressed how their operation could be approved at a much lower administrative level than a 100% foreign operation. Similarly, a footwear factory said they would have preferred an equity joint venture, but that would have required provincial level approval, whereas the Hong Kong investor, a former classmate of the county Communist Party secretary, could get approval for a cooperative joint venture at county level, where his personal contact would be effective.

At the other extreme, cooperative joint ventures can be extremely short term. For example, over a contract period of as little as five years, the foreign partner can get his initial investment repaid as a prior claim before the distribution of profits, an arrangement which is not very different from compensation trade. A third of the cooperative joint ventures in our sample had contracts of between five and eight years.

Cooperative joint ventures, however, have less freedom of action in practice, compared to an equity joint venture, particularly with regard to the freedom to import inputs and to retain foreign exchange. For example, a food factory said it needed to get ten different "chops" (authorising stamps) on its documentation before it could import its basic raw materials, a time-consuming process. However, some companies like the footwear company mentioned above and a company making jewellery, claimed to have the same freedom of action as an equity joint venture, and the jewellery company had an arrangement that the assets would be divided among the partners at the end of the contract like an equity joint venture.

Foreign cooperation also offers Chinese companies more freedom of action than they might otherwise enjoy. Thus the food company mentioned above actually made a traditional Chinese food product (smoked dried ducks) for which foreign technology is hardly required. Their reason for seeking a foreign partner was a desire to earn foreign exchange, since they had failed to secure a Chinese export quota as a domestic company, but had succeeded in doing so as a cooperative joint venture.

The equity joint ventures in the sample included several Western multinationals operating through Hong Kong offices. One interesting feature is that approximately a quarter of the sample of equity joint venture companies had had previously a different form of contract (as also had had a quarter of the cooperative joint ventures). Several had moved from processing and assembly arrangements to cooperative joint ventures to equity joint ventures. For a motor vehicle maintenance company the move from a cooperative to an equity joint venture had been a means whereby certain unsatisfactory features of the earlier contract could be renegotiated and a more Hong Kong style of management introduced. A footwear company found that the move from processing and assembly with a state company gave it freedom from interference from the state company' parent body. Some larger Hong Kong companies and the Western multinationals had never considered any arrangement other than an equity joint venture because of its familiarity, its clearer legal position, and its greater freedom of action. Many companies saw equity joint ventures as the only way they could be sure of being able to import capital equipment which was new and of their own choice.

Our interviews have also covered a variety of processing and assembly operations, all of which had <u>lai liao jia gong</u> ("LLJG"- "bringing materials for processing") contracts, the most common type. At one end of the spectrum are factories where the Hong kong investor has brought in the machinery and set up the factory, and the factory works largely under Hong Kong control. These included companies making plastic toys, underwear, and leather goods. The freedom of action given to the investor to control the operation of the factory varies from place to place. The officials in one city said they gave the investor almost complete freedom to hire and fire workers and to manage the factory, and had been criticised by the provincial authorities for doing so, but their success in generating foreign exchange had weakened the criticisms. On the other hand, we found that some Chinese state factories or collectives do short term contract work for Hong Kong, working for a variety of customers for various periods of time, interspersed with work on their own account, sometimes for export but more usually for the domestic market. Most such companies in our sample previously had had "full" LLJG contracts, in the sense that they had worked entirely for one foreign partner and had been completely export-orientated, and this provides an interesting pointer to what may happen as the Chinese acquire expertise themselves and the initial contracts (which are usually three - five years) come to an end. However, we also found companies, in these cases in garments and soft toys, who continued to operate entirely through LLJG, and to continue with the same partner and sometimes others too, long after the original contract expired.

One further feature of LLJG is that it has often been used not only on the initiative of the Hong Kong side, but by existing Chinese factories wishing to update their equipment and secure market access. Usually in our sample they set up totally new factories, and often were collective companies in small towns. Very few complaints were heard from the Hong Kong side about such operations, and the Chinese partners seem to have been far more flexible than the state companies in many equity joint ventures.

The Chinese authorities often argue that processing and assembly operations are but a stepping stone to "closer" forms of cooperation, especially equity joint ventures. As noted above, we did find a number of both equity and cooperative joint venture companies which had developed out of LLJG. However, several companies, and local authority officials, expressed great satisfaction with LLJG, had no wish to move to a joint venture, but saw the LLJG arrangement as continuing long term. Such companies, which were among the largest in our entire sample, stressed the usefulness of LLJG as providing them with high quality raw materials and packaging which, together with the partner's customer contacts, were essential to successful exporting. Local authorities, whose investment companies went into LLJG, stressed how the arrangement economized on expertise and reduced risk for them.

In passing, it is also worth noting that the processing fees paid under LLJG arrangements are also sometimes encountered in cooperative joint ventures, as in the jewellery factory mentioned above, which in other respects said it operated more like an equity joint venture in terms of its freedom of action. Sometimes state factories will undertake LLJG work, like a factory in the sample making gas and water pipes and electrical conduits, and working to high and Hong Kong-validated technical specifications, in the hope that it would lead to contacts out of which an equity joint venture would emerge.

Compensation trade contracts have been most often found in our sample along with other contracts, usually LLJG. For the foreign partner they sometimes have been an opportunity to get rid of old equipment, and sometimes, where there has been new equipment, it has not always been suitable for the Chinese company's needs. Also, even where suitable new equipment is supplied, pure compensation trade contracts raise some problems for the Chinese side. For a reform-minded Chinese management in a state company, partnership with a foreign firm strengthens their hand in introducing change, especially in labour practices. With compensation trade, one company interviewed explained, the foreign side is interested only in the quality of the product, so that it can be repaid in something which it can sell on the world market, and not in costs of production. This company, a brewery, felt it was assigned too many workers by its parent body, and could not resist this, but that a foreign partner could have resisted.

7.2 **Experience with different kinds of Chinese partners**

Although the foreign investment experience did not differ

systematically between the contract types, there was, for equity joint venture companies in particular, a marked difference between ventures undertaken with existing Chinese state companies, and those with collectives owned by local authorities. Although, of course, there were some very reform-minded state companies in the sample, and some local authorities may be unusually incompetent or rapacious, in general cooperation with local authorities was smoother and more successful. In the best of such cooperations, both sides had a genuine interest in making money together, and the Chinese side understood that this meant giving the investor certain freedoms.

7.2.1 Partnerships with state companies

Several examples from our interviews serve to illustrate experience with state companies. In the first case, a Hong Kong removals company had joined with a state transportation company. The synergy between them was not as great as it first seems since the Hong Kong side was performing a personal service. From the Hong Kong partner's view the Chinese side seemed mainly interested in securing foreign exchange in any way it could. Workers were employed through the Chinese partner and paid through the Chinese partner, who insisted on receiving Hong Kong rates of pay in foreign exchange for them. This was in violation of the Joint Venture Law, which stipulates that workers should be paid 20%-50% more than workers doing comparable jobs in state companies. The workers were actually paid by the Chinese side the same as other workers in the state company, and thus the Chinese side creamed off a substantial surplus in foreign exchange. The workers, who were permanent workers assigned from the state company, felt dissatisfied, and especially so since the Hong Kong side expected (unsuccessfully) that they would contribute a Hong Kong style work input. The state company assigned to the venture drivers who could not drive and expected the joint venture to pay for their training.

Problems associated with the use of permanent workers from the Chinese partner also were found in a venture with a Western food multinational working through Hong Kong. Bothered by the lack of motivation and unwillingness to learn that it perceived on the part of its workers, it attempted to employ peasant workers from the local villages, whom it found far more satisfactory. This was a source of continuing dispute. In theory joint ventures are expected to employ workers on contract, but where the partner is a state company, there is little to prevent permanent workers being assigned, who, used to "eating from the <u>da guo fan</u>" (the communal rice pot), may be hard to motivate.

In contrast, a company making shoes, had a manager from the American footwear industry who had a previous contract in China and had managed a shoe factory in Taiwan. The venture was fortunate in having good customer contacts in the USA through the manager so that export sales could be achieved once product quality was assured. Like most of the several footwear manufacturing companies in the sample, the factory used Taiwanese machinery and there was a clear standard against which to judge the factory's labour and capital productivity. Against much opposition from the Chinese side, a genuine incentive system and substantial differentials for supervisory staff were introduced. As export sales started to generate foreign exchange profits, so opposition to the new pay structure and expectations of the workforce fell away.

148

7.2.2 Partnerships with local authorities

In the early years of the Open Policy, and today too to some extent, much of the cooperation between Hong Kong and China involved LLJG contracts with local authorities. These arrangements offered many advantages to county and village governments. The development could bring in capital and employ local workers. Often the investors were relatives of local people. The processing fees earned by the local authorities could be ploughed back into other investment and infrastructure, and the investors normally had no difficulty in exporting their output once quality control was achieved. The use of imported materials also meant that the local authorities did not have to worry about securing domestic supplies of raw materials. LLJG contracts were recorded in Shunde county before the setting up of the Special Economic Zones. While the SEZs were often reluctant to accept this kind of contract seeing it as not sufficiently advanced, many localities welcomed them. Dongguan, reputed to have one of the Delta's best investment climates (about which more later), before the Open Policy was an area known mainly for bananas and lychees, and managed to attract investment by its flexibility and its "one stop" facilities for negotiating contracts. An example of such flexibility in a local authority in practice was recounted by a Hong Kong businessman, who said his local authority in China would encourage him to rename his firm when his contract expired so he could have another tax holiday. Our interviews suggest that such practices are not uncommon.

In the early years there were many problems of wastage of the raw materials, of poor quality and of unreliable delivery times, but these have grown less with experience.

A newer development, which has grown since the mid 1980s, has been the use of local authority investment companies, normally collectives, which can form cooperative or equity joint ventures with overseas partners. Sometimes these are existing companies, whose range of activities can be expanded. Where such a company was originally a state-run company it sometimes, our research has shown, has been reorganized to bring it more directly under local authority control, so as to prevent its foreign exchange earnings being syphoned upwards to higher levels of authority. Sometimes, however, provincial or national bodies (usually specialist trading corporations) joint in as partners, in which case some of the foreign exchange does get syphoned upwards.

A feature of many of these joint ventures has been that they have been able to start with a workforce recruited directly by the joint venture, initially from local workers and increasingly from workers who come to Guangdong from other provinces. Even quite large companies, which the Chinese might have expected to go to Special Economic Zones or large Open Cities, have used these opportunities to locate in smaller places in the Delta, often in areas where they have personal contacts. For equity joint ventures, where the initiative has usually come from Hong Kong side, which then has a good idea of what it wants to achieve, the experience in our sample was generally very positive. Among the cooperative joint ventures, where inexperienced local authorities sought Hong Kong partners from among their relatives and friends, several cases were found (and discussed further at the start of the next section) where ventures encountered problems because the foreign side lacked the necessary expertise.

149

7.3. Issues relating to foreign investment and the economic reforms

7.3.1 The expertise of the Hong Kong partner: firm-specific advantage in practice

The firm-specific advantages of the Hong Kong firms, as was argued earlier, lie in their marketing and management skills and implicitly in their ability to handle technology which, though not generally "advanced" in terms of world best practice, is new to the Delta, and requires substantial reform, especially in local labour and management practices, to carry it through.

Some of the Hong Kong firms in our sample had the intention of relocating either their existing production or (more usually) expansions in production, to the Delta. They sought as partners either experienced state companies who were interested in setting up new production facilities jointly, or open-minded local authorities. In these cases the Hong Kong side normally had all the expertise required, and failures could be blamed mainly on the Chinese side.

In other cases however, state companies or local authorities sought Hong Kong partners in a rather haphazard way, and those they found had only expertise in a limited area. The Hong Kong partner might be a supplier of machinery but with no marketing expertise. The Hong Kong partner in some cases supplied only finance, so that the Chinese side, in effect, had to transfer the technology themselves. Some experienced state companies felt able to try this. One such, a textile company making denim, had branched out into the manufacture of denim clothing, and when interviewed was hoping to overcome problems of product quality so as to achieve its targeted level of exports.

In cooperative joint ventures where the foreign side has a prior claim on profits in order to repay its investment, the ventures may not work out well for the Chinese. A factory making nylon adhesive fastenings had had the problem that its foreign partner proved incapable of getting the machinery operating properly, and was operating at 30% capacity. It also suffered from a shortage of skilled workers in its rural area.

More generally, some of the problems which arise do so out of one side or the other making assumptions which the other does not accept, and which limit their power to carry out the venture as they expected. Learning by experience from other ventures can help in drawing up clearer contracts, which, though no absolute guarantee of harmony, at least provide a better starting point. One such would be the stipulation that the foreign partner has the absolute right to pay the workers directly rather than through the Chinese partner. Experienced foreign investors insist on this, though, even so, difficulties may be experienced about the direct payment of bonuses.

Chinese partners thus need to ensure not only that their Hong Kong partner has access to capital, but also that he can market the output and help with production. Sometimes the Chinese get cheated by firms whose interest lies only in selling machinery, without any channels for marketing the product or really helping with technical production problems. Sometimes, on the other hand, foreign technical workers are unprepared psychologically for the efforts they must make to bring about the changes in attitudes on the Chinese side if the technology is to be introduced successfully.

In passing, it is worth adding that it is equally important for the foreign investor to find out whether the Chinese officials who negotiate the setting up of a project have real authority to carry through their promises.

7.3.2 Taxation and the benefits of foreign investment to the Chinese economy

The very wide variety of tax regimes for foreign companies in China (see Appendix) has caused problems for investors. Equity joint ventures and cooperative joint ventures operating as limited companies are taxed under the Joint Venture Income Tax Law and face a maximum rate of 33% (including 3% points local surcharge) on their profits, and 39.7% if they are remitting them out of China. 100% foreign-owned ventures and cooperative joint ventures acting as partnerships face a maximum of virtually 50% under the Foreign Enterprise Income Tax Law, irrespective of whether the profits are to be remitted abroad. Numerous concessions, especially the 15% flat rate of tax in the Special Economic Zones and the Economic and Technology Development Zones in the Open Coastal Cities complicate matters, but the various tax holidays offered by many areas, including the Zhujiang Delta Open Zone cut across them.

The successful operation of such a system to use tax concessions as an investment incentive, but eventually to yield tax revenue for the Chinese economy, requires considerable ability to fine-tune the tax policy. In practice, considerable anomalies have been created (2). There are also many deductions and exemptions which are subject to the interpretation and discretion of local authorities, so foreign investors have to devote energy and resources to tax planning and negotiations with local tax officials.

The Chinese government acknowledges the deficiences of the tax regime facing foreign investors and is in the process of streamlining it. In the 1988 National Meeting on Taxation, the Ministry of Finance announced its intention to combine the Joint Venture Income Tax and the Foreign Enterprise Income Tax so that foreign enterprises will be subject to the same marginal tax rate, the new tax law to be administered by the central tax authority. At this stage few foreign-invested companies in our sample were paying significant amounts of tax, and the benefits from foreign investment to the Chinese economy must be sought elsewhere (3).

7.3.3 Exporting and foreign exchange

Among our sample of equity and cooperative joint ventures, about half were heavily export-orientated. The rest included companies in service sectors geared to the domestic market (e.g. car servicing, restaurants, a beauty salon), and some companies trying to export more and not succeeding; but others were making an informed choice between exports and the domestic market in the light of the relative domestic and foreign prices on offer.

Success in exporting in industries tranferring labour intensive operations to China is not surprising, although it does mean that adequate product quality has been achieved, and it contrasts with many companies in the Special Economic Zones, whose failure to export has been well-publicized (4). Some ventures' Hong Kong partners, however, did fail to deliver with regard to export orders. A cooperative joint venture with a Hong Kong restauranteur and a Chinese conglomerate to set up a small factory making restaurant equipment failed to get export sales and failed to get local restaurants or hotels to pay in foreign exchange. Export success has normally implied established customer networks. Some industries in Hong Kong which have relocated much of their production to the Pearl River Delta engage mainly in licencing and contract manufacturing for overseas customers. The toy industry, for example, earns almost 80% of its revenue in that way (Far Eastern Economic Review, 25 January 1990), and the footwear and several garments factories in our sample worked in a similar way.

The substantial minority of companies which made a choice to gear more towards the domestic market raise interesting issues. Where there is successful exporting, much of the benefit goes to the Hong Kong side. Some footwear companies were paid commissions by customers outside the joint venture. Many Chinese partners complained they did not know what export prices the Hong Kong side, normally responsible for the marketing, received, or whether they were told the truth about them. For this reason, cases were found where the Chinese side would have preferred domestic sales. Few firms stuck rigidly to the share of exports in total sales (usually 70%) stipulated in their contracts.

Of course, given the isolation of much of the Chinese economy from international trade, domestic prices for some products may be higher than world prices at an equilibrium exchange rate, and have not been competed down by imports. Since both final product and input prices in the Chinese economy are often highly distorted, it could not necessarily be concluded that such goods are not potentially socially profitable exports. However, a more immediate problem is the exchange rate received by companies obviously affects their incentive to export, especially when it is well-known that the free-market rate in China for foreign exchange has usually been at least 50% higher than the official rate. An export-orientated company with a less than 33% profit on sales in Renminbi terms at the free rate would make losses at the official rate (5). Several companies explained that this was crucial to them in practice. Nor does this only affect the Chinese partner. Companies requiring large quantities of Renminbi to purchase local raw materials (and of course labour), like a company interviewed which made fur coats and used Chinese pelts, also depend for the profitability on the exchange rate. Our interviews show an enormous diversity of experience, almost every company having a different arrangement. Although equity joint ventures are in theory free to retain their foreign exchange and there are opportunities for joint ventures with surplus forex to exchange with those in deficit at free rates under the supervision of the authorities(6), we met many cases where the Chinese partner saw little of the foreign exchange (7). Often this was where a higher level authority was a partner to the venture and creamed off much of the forex for itself, but in several cooperative joint ventures firms had difficulty in getting their forex from the Bank of China and got only the official rate. It does appear therefore that the system has a certain anti-export bias especially as far as the Chinese partner is concerned, and this can lead to conflict with the foreign side.(8)

Some LLJG operations also may face problems if they wish to increase their exports. A businessman making leather gloves reported to us that his LLJG factory's expansion had been hampered by an initial failure to secure a larger export quota. On the other hand, LLJG operations are not allowed to sell on the domestic market, and where the Hong Kong investor wished to do so, that was a motive to change to a cooperative joint venture.

7.3.4 Employment issues

A recent World Bank study (Tidrick and Chen, 1987, pp.113-7) has described the Chinese labour market as one of the least reformed parts of the economy. In principle foreign-invested firms can hire and fire workers, and employ them on contract. In practice, as we have seen, a joint venture may often be assigned permanent workers from its partner. These may be virtually impossible to dismiss, whatever their performance. The removals company mentioned earlier said it had succeeded in having only one unsatisfactory worker transferred back to the Chinese partner in the whole history of its operation. Our research suggests that successful foreign investors must be willing to undertake labour market reform themselves, and often in the teeth of opposition, if their venture is to succeed.

It is worth noting that in many of the companies interviewed, particularly in the garment industry, the overwhelming majority of workers were young women, often recruited from outside the area. Although receiving substantially higher wages than in alternative employment, it has been argued that in many factories these workers' conditions of service, and their general lifestyle, is very poor (9). We cannot claim to have noted such poor conditions in our own investigations, and clearly some comparison needs to be made with such workers' previous circumstances.

7.3.5 Management

Hong Kong (and Western) styles of management differ greatly from those of China, where managers are often very conservative and lacking in authority with the workforce. This is especially the case where managers have been appointed on the basis of their personal connections rather than their ability. On the other hand, where the Hong Kong side has a low stake in a joint venture, it may not be keen on being involved in the difficulties of management.

One attractive feature of the Pearl River Delta is its relatively high living standards, and this makes it easier for joint ventures to attract experienced Chinese technical personnel from established industrial areas like Shanghai.

7.3.6 Other operational issues - power and transport

Electricity supply problems, especially frequent, prolonged and unpredictable power cuts are a problem for all industry in China. Foreign ventures are no exception, and localities which generate their own electricity supply can attract foreign investors more easily.

Transport in the Pearl River Delta is often a problem, as rapid development in the area has put a great strain on the road network. Areas close to ports with regular services to Hong Kong, such as Panyu or Zhong Shan are attractive locations.

Vogel (1989, pp.324-7, 373-4) records many instances of local and provincial officials having made far-sighted investment in road transport and power, however. Nor has foreign investment in infrastructure been lacking entirely either. There is, for example, the Hopewell Company of Hong Kong's grand project to link Hong Kong, Shenzhen, Guangzhou, Zhuhai and Macau with modern highways.

153

7.3.7 Bureaucracy

Frequent policy changes and the many layers of bureaucracy in China pose problems for the foreign partner, which an effective and well-connected Chinese partner can greatly relieve. Investors often feel that investing in small places, where the local leadership is sympathetic and especially if it is directly involved in the venture, is wise and worth far more than paper investment incentives (10).

7.3.8 Legal issues

Lack of a legal framework has been a common complaint. The basic legal documents, like the Joint Venture Law of 1979 are short and have required implementing legislation. The 1983 Implementation Act for equity joint ventures did much to encourage joint venture investment after a slow start.

The Law on Enterprises operated exclusively with Foreign Capital did not appear until 1986, and only in 1988 was the Law for Cooperative Joint Ventures promulgated. In all cases there are additional regulations, which are not published and to which foreigners are not allowed access.(11) National authorities, such as tax authorities, do not always accept conditions granted by a local authority. Where a Chinese joint venture partner simply disregards the Joint Venture Law, foreign firms often complain there is little legal redress available to them.

A clearer set of legal guidelines to reduce the scope for arbitrary action, even with regard to equity joint ventures, would be extremely helpful, to say the least.

7.4 **The Chinese investment climate as of 1987-8**

Difficulties encountered by foreign investors had received considerable publicity in the Hong Kong press and overseas well before the autumn 1988 austerity measures (whose effects are discussed in Section 6). Many investors have felt China is unique in the difficulties they encounter. Many problems in fact have sprung from China's being in the middle of economic reform, trying to combine market mechanisms with planning mechanisms, and the Chinese leadership has been well aware of the difficulties. Corruption and the arbitrary actions of officials frequently were criticised in the Chinese press too, and not just in terms of how they affected foreign investment.

Problems with processing and assembly operations have appeared to lessen, as both sides have gained experience. For equity joint ventures, on the other hand, only four or five years experience is available in most cases, and many problems have remained.

The Chinese have made numerous attempts to improve the terms on which foreign investment can be made, particularly the elaborate range of concessions under the Provisions for the Encouragement of Foreign Investment, promulgated by the State Council in October 1986. Besides the extension of tax holidays for export-orientated or technologically advanced ventures, these enterprises also received priority in obtaining the services of public utilities and various other concessions. All joint ventures and wholly foreign enterprises received the right to exchange foreign exchange among themselves, and they were to be subject to simpler export and export licencing procedures. They also received the right to refuse to pay "unreasonable" fees.

The 1986 Provisions, in fact, appear to have been made in response to the fall in foreign investment after the introduction of a set of austerity measures in 1985. The 1985 measures followed gross overheating of the economy in the mid-1980s, when a severe balance of payments problem emerged. The foreign exchange difficulties of several large domestically-orientated joint ventures were well-publicised (Pomfret, 1989,p.41). Reference back to Table 1.1 shows that in 1986 contracted investment virtually had halved, both for China and Guangdong, but picked up considerably by 1987 and 1988. On the other hand, the realized inflow increased steadily, with only a minor fall in Guangdong in 1987.

Although the progress of economic reform, the national legal framework, and macro-economic policy, have been important background factors, our research has shown too that in many respects the foreign investment "climate" is very much of a local affair in China. Even within the Pearl Delta the attractiveness of different locations varies greatly. Firms have been attracted outside the Special Economic Zones, in spite of the SEZs tax privileges, not only by lower wages but by better and more sympathetic attitudes. Also, it seems that, in practice, localities can make themselves competitive on the tax front too. The advantages of geographical location factors such as proximity to Hong Kong and availability of transport may be cancelled out if local power or water supplies are poor, and, above all, if local officials are unhelpful, bureaucratic or corrupt. Many investors wisely look to the experience of other foreign firms in particular locations before making any decision.

There is great competition between localities in the Delta for foreign investment. Shunde, the earliest favoured site for processing and assembly operations, lost ground to Dongguan. Baoan, with insignificant industrial output before 1984, is now well-known for the small industrial villages in most of its towns and has become a major competitor to Dongguan.

As we have seen, joint ventures with established state companies seem more prone to problems than joint ventures with local authorities. In the latter case the investor can "start from scratch" and does not have to carry the burden of reform himself with a workforce and management steeped in the old ways. Shunde, in particular, has stressed a development model based on town and village owned collective enterprises, and has become attractive for joint ventures as well as processing and assembly (12).

In spite of many positive features in the investment climate in the Pearl River Delta, real difficulties remained for foreign investors in China, even before the 1988 austerity measures. Improvements in the investment climate almost certainly will have to await the wider spread of economic reform, at present uncertain.

7.5   The Hong Kong economy and the Pearl River Delta

In popular discussions in Hong Kong, Hong Kong and Guangdong province (and especially the Pearl River Delta) are often linked as if they belong to a single, rapidly growing region. How far has each affected the other's growth? Although our research has focused on the experiences of individual companies, rather than on the general development of the Delta, we feel some observations would be helpful.

Hong Kong, with a population of 5.4 million at the 1986 census (13), more than doubled its real gross domestic product over the 1978-1987 period. This was equivalent to an annual growth rate of 7%, although the rate has fluctuated considerably over the period from a low of 3% in 1982 to a peak of 13.8% in 1987. For Hong Kong, relocation of industries to China is reflected strikingly in a variety of statistics.From 1979 to 1988 Hong Kong experienced a 3.7 fold rise in its total exports (2.3 fold for domestic exports, which are 44% of the 1988 total; and 7.8 fold for reexports, of which roughly half originated in China). Exports are virtually all of manufactures, yet this export growth was achieved with a manufacturing workforce no higher at the end of the period than at the beginning.Textiles and clothing, generating over a third of Hong Kong's domestic exports, achieved this with a more or less constant workforce, as did the electical appliances industry, while plastics employment actually dropped substantially (14).

With continuous rises in factory rents and wages, relocation to China has been the way many Hong Kong companies have tried to maintain their competitive position. Such a large shift of production operations has aroused attention both from government and labour unions. Whether the relocations are a real, long-term advantage to the Hong Kong economy is still uncertain, and depends on whether profits are reinvested in Hong Kong and in what kinds of activity.

Hong Kong has been a labour-intensive manufacturing centre since the 1950s. As it developed into a financial centre in the 1970s wage differentials between the industrial and tertiary sectors widened, and workers were attracted away from industrial employment. The situation has been made worse by the upgrading of the education level, as many high school graduates have not proved interested in blue-collar jobs. The manufacturing workforce peaked in 1981 at 900,000 and has since declined gradually. Although China opened to the outside world in 1978, most production relocations are of more recent origin. The depreciation in real terms after 1985 of the US dollar, to which the Hong Kong dollar is linked, meant that its products have became more competitive in relation to those of neighbouring countries such as Taiwan, South Korea and Singapore. The rapid growth of export demand, and the falling supply of labour to manufacturing, has led to a serious labour shortage. Also, the property boom since 1984 has been instrumental in maintaining factory rents at high levels. With these strong push and pull factors affecting production costs, there has been a rapid shift of production activity to China. The employment figures cited above imply (in the absence of evidence to suggest great technical progress or substitution of capital for labour) that it has been the expansion of production, rather than existing production, which has been relocated to China, although many of our sample companies had reduced (or changed) their activities in Hong Kong too.

The shift of production activities has maintained the profitability of Hong Kong manufactures. However, at the same time it has removed pressure for industrial upgrading, that is, to advance from labour-intensive to technology-intensive industries. As China and other Asian countries such as Indonesia, Thailand and the Philipines enter the world export market for labour-intensive manufactures, Hong Kong will sooner or later lose its competitive advantage if it does not follow the examples of South Korea, Singapore and Taiwan in producing technology-intensive products. This lagging behind is especially marked in the electronics industry. As most of the technology being introduced into the Pearl River Delta by Hong Kong investment is not of an advanced kind, the Chinese may eventually be able to operate it themselves, and Chinese industrialists are likely to become more export-orientated in the coastal regions of China, and especially the Delta. Due to the lack of understanding about doing business in China, many foreign investors have needed to use the services of Hong Kong firms as middlemen. In fact, in some of our interviews, it was the US buyers who persuaded Hong Kong firms to produce in China. This is likely to decline as foreign familiarity with China increases. However, Sino-Hong Kong industrial cooperation has also increased the demand for services such as packaging, quality control, marketing and designing in Hong Kong. In addition, the transportation of goods back to Hong Kong for export and the growing re-export from China have meant that Hong Kong has resumed its role as a trading centre and entrepot.

The relocation to China could be advantageous to Hong Kong in the longer term if it provides profits for reinvestment in industrial upgrading. However, the 1997 issue has affected the long-term investment incentives of Hong Kong industrialists at least since the early 1980s. In our interviews we found some Hong Kong investors were quite pessimistic about the future of Hong Kong. They said they would try to get as much profit from their China operations in a few years, and then emigrate to other countries. Obviously, this tendency will have greatly accelerated in the aftermath of 4th June 1989.

Hong Kong's growth in the last decade has been high by world standards. That of Guangdong and the Pearl Delta has been remarkable. Guangdong, with a population of 58.3 million in 1987 (64.5 million if Hainan island, now a separate province, is included) grew at a real average annual rate of 14% over the 1978-88 period, in terms of its combined agricultural and industrial output (the most commonly used Chinese measure) (Vogel,1989,p.442), a quadrupling of output over the period. The original Pearl River Delta region (refer back to Table 1.3) already had quadrupled its agricultural and industrial real output over the period 1979-86, during which time its industrial output alone rose fivefold.

The growth of the Pearl Delta, and of Guangdong more generally, during the early part of the reform period, clearly was due in part to the reestablishment of earlier patterns of local specialization and trade which had been heavily restricted during the previous thirty years (15). The explosive growth of collectively owned rural industry reflects in part the taking up of surplus agricultural labour following the agricultural reforms. Vogel (1989, Chap.13) records large increases in investment in industry, financed in part from the larger share of funds left to the province after the 1979 "special policy" to stimulate the province's development, under which the central government had given it lower (and fixed) tax obligations, as well as more freedom with regard to its external economic policy. Foreign exchange from the resumption of traditional agricultural products to Hong Kong also generated funds. T.M.H. Chan (1988) is at pains to contradict the popular view that the Pearl River Delta's growth has been led by industrial exports in general and by those from foreign investors in particular, although much of the required data is only available at provincial level. He cites evidence of the lagging of exports behind industrial output. He also notes the high domestic currency costs of foreign exchange generated by exports, because of the high costs of securing raw materials outside state plans; though one might also argue that the situation was as much a reflection of the overvaluation of the Renminbi as of low efficiency (see note 5).

While exports did slow down in the province in the early 1980s, partly as a result of a weak Hong Kong market (three quarters of Guangdong's exports go to Hong Kong) and of temporarily increased central government trade restrictions, they subsequently boomed. By 1987 the share of exports in agricultural and industrial output was up to 18%, quite high by Chinese standards (16), and up to a third to a half for some Delta localities. (Vogel, 1989, Chap.11). However, in 1987 foreign invested enterprises, including processing and assembly, contributed only 16% of the province's overall export earnings, and 53% of that was accounted for by the three Special Economic Zones (17). In particular locations of the Pearl Delta such as Dongguan the foreign share is undoubtedly much higher, but these figures do suggest that Chinese domestic firms' sales to the Hong Kong market and beyond, and domestic growth sources in this large province, still play a much larger role than foreign investment, in spite of the latter's great relocational impact on the Hong Kong economy.

7.6   The current austerity programme and the aftermath of 4th June (18)

By 1988 the need for some reassertion of central macroeconomic control in China hardly could be disputed, if the reform programme was to be preserved. In the 1980s China had experienced an average growth rate in real GNP of about 10% a year, one of the fastest in the world. In 1988 this had risen to 11.2%, and industrial growth was at nearly 18%. Only agriculture lagged, after the initial surge following the post-1979 reforms, and was below the target of 4%. This poor agricultural result reflects grain production having fallen for the fourth successive year, partly due to weather, but also due to a reallocation of land towards industrial uses and a shortage of fertilizer caused by energy shortages. Grain production itself had also fallen because of the competing attraction of other, higher-priced crops.

Our study has highlighted the growing independence of local authorities and the rural (i.e. township and village) industries under their control. One consequence of their independence was a loss of macro control by the central government over investment, with possibly as much as two-thirds of investment being made outside central control. Industrial investment had proceeded without sufficient increases in investment in transportation or power, so that severe infrastructural bottlenecks had emerged, along with considerable inflationary pressure (put at 18% officially for 1988, and unofficially rather higher). Guangdong, as one of the fastest growing areas of China, experienced severe overheating and inflation, and by 1988 the industrial growth rate was 30%. Of course, this was not the first time that the economy had overheated during the reforms. There have been two earlier occasions (in the early 1980s and the mid-1980s) when the government introduced macroeconomic restriction, but the post-1988 measures have been unusually severe.

Problems of the economy also were in part behind the mass demonstrations in Beijing in April and May 1989, prior to the 4th June. Inflation had made life difficult for the many public employees and students on fixed incomes. Growth had led to widening disparities in income, and officials were seen openly to be profiteering and using their economic power corruptly. A new expression, guan dao, entered the language, referring to the propensity of officials to engage in speculative trading. China was becoming a "rent-seeking" society (19);

people were widely dissatisfied and many blamed the Party.

The austerity policy (jinsuo zhengce) was announced in autumn 1988. At the March 1989 meeting of the National People's Congress Premier Li Peng announced that austerity measures would be required for two years, although other pronouncements suggested the period might be longer.

7.6.1 Key features of the austerity policy

--tight credit control, including control over foreign borrowing. In February 1989 the State Council issued a circular restricting overseas borrowing to ten official organizations ("windows").

--increased government conrol over raw material supplies in an attempt to divert resources back to the state sector and away from rural industry and private businesses.

--additional control over rural enterprises, including much closer checking of their tax payments, and attempts to shift workers away from rural enterprise back into agriculture. The Agricultural Bank of China announced it would cut lending to rural enterprises by half and in March 1989 the Agriculture Minister announced plans to cut rural enterprise growth from 30% in 1988 to 15% in 1989.

--attempts to control wage inflation by forcing workers to spend part of their salary on government bonds which are not redeemable for several years. Over the course of 1989 about 10% of workers' basic salaries were clawed back in this way.

--increased centralization of control over foreign trade. The Ministry of Foreign Economic Relations and Trade, for example, stripped Guangdong of the right to issue export licences for a number of commodities.

--increased emphasis on infrastructural investment.

Since June 1989 several new policies have emerged, although it is not always clear which ones already were in the pipeline and have simply achieved greater prominence. One particular change has been a shift from an "area policy" (i.e. a policy favouring coastal areas) to an "industry policy", which implicitly favours inland areas, and perhaps heavy industry at the expense of light industry (20), as well as being intended to promote infrastructural investment. Although many of the tax privileges for coastal areas have remained, especially as they concern foreign investment, there does seem to have been a reallocation of capital spending towards inland areas, according to Chinese economists interviewed in January 1990. At the same time, much lip service, at least, has been paid to the need to continue the Open Policy and attract foreign investment (21).

What have been the effects of the austerity measures on the Chinese economy in general, and on Guangdong in particular? How has the operation of foreign-invested companies been affected? What of new foreign investment, especially that from Hong Kong, and the future of the Chinese economy?

7.6.2 Effects on the Chinese economy

These have mainly worked through credit tightening. In 1989 industrial growth was down to 7%, and the growth rate of light industry fell from 20% per year to about 5%. Industrial growth actually was negative in October 1989, the first time for a decade, and again in January 1990 on a year-on-year basis (The Economist, 17 January 1990). Rural industry has been especially hard hit, and also by difficulties in getting raw materials. 3 million out of a total of 18 million such enterprises have closed or been forced to merge with others, making 8-9 million workers redundant (compared to a total of about 86 million non-agricultural rural workers). The domestic market for consumer durables has collapsed, there has been a large increase in private savings in the face of increased uncertainty, and some 15 to 20 million workers in state and urban collective enterprises have been laid off, out of a total of 135 million. Many state enterprise workers have been laid off on 40-70% of their basic wage, although apparently this policy has been reversed very recently, with the workers going back onto full basic wages to avoid unrest. One hopeful feature has been the improvement in the 1989 grain harvests, and the annual rate of inflation in January 1990 was reported to be down to about 7%.

7.6.3 Effects on Guangdong

Much is often made about Guangdong's inclination and ability to avoid the cutbacks, and provincial officals, while stressing the need for a slowdown, have also made some pleas for Guangdong's special position to be respected. The Financial Times (12 December 1989) carried an interview with the governor of Guangdong, Ye Xuanping, who recently has refused both a high position in Beijing and that of the head of the New China News Agency (the de facto Chinese ambassador) in Hong Kong, in order to stay in Guangdong. Ye strongly reaffirmed his support for reform. In particular, he resists any increased role for the party in enterprise management, and the buying of bonds by workers as forced savings.

Guangdong has been affected by the cutbacks. One particularly harmful aspect during the early period of austerity was the restrictions on food grain imports (and some raw material imports too) from other provinces into Guangdong. In Guangdong, a labour shortage had been met, as we have seen earlier, by the immigration of a million guest workers from other provinces, necessitating food imports. The authorities in other provinces became increasingly unwilling to sell scarce food to Guangdong. Firms with guest workers were unable to buy rice at any price, and rationing was strictly enforced. In consequence, it seemed that at the end of 1988 as many as 30% of the guest workers might have returned home. However, after the Spring Festival (Chinese New Year) in 1989, there was a flood of migrants into Guangdong from other provinces, estimated as over two million, in search of work, following the cutbacks in capital construction and rural industry elsewhere. Restrictions were placed by the provincial authorities on employment of these migrants (principally because of the food supply problem) and many returned. Rail fares were doubled in China in 1989, which has made such migration less easy, but again in 1990 there has been an influx of unemployed migrants into Guangdong, though less than in the previous year. The government also has introduced more supervision of inter-provincial grain trading, where rich provinces like Guangdong might try to secure grain supplies by paying in foreign exchange.

Nevertheless, during 1989 Guangdong's growth was not cut back as much as that as China as a whole. The growth rates of Guangdong and Fujian were reported to be in the 14-16% range, although the Hong Kong press carried stories of Guangdong factories operating at low capacity with raw material and power shortages, and accumulating inventories of unsold goods.

7.6.4 Effects on foreign-invested enterprises

Enterprises selling to the domestic market have been badly affected. The large investors in the motor industry - Volkswagen in Shanghai, American Motors in Beijing, and Peugeot in Guangzhou -have all been reported as experiencing great difficulties and to be suffering from the inability of officials to take decisions, especially about their production quotas. A small firm interviewed in Shenzhen in January 1990, which had larger domestic than overseas sales in 1988, said that it now relied entirely on overseas sales for its profits. One interesting feature, which may be a continuation of a trend, but also could be a response to the present internal difficulties, is that the export performance of joint ventures seems to have improved greatly. Provincial officials in Guangdong (interview, January 1990) said that the exports of joint ventures and 100% foreign companies had risen from US$1 billion in 1988 to US$2.2 billion in 1989 (and that the province's exports from such companies constituted two-thirds of those for China as a whole).

For joint venture investment, the credit restrictions have greatly reduced the ability of existing Chinese partners to find finance for expansion, or indeed for working capital, and of prospective Chinese partners to raise funds for new ventures. One response of the government, starting with a speech by Zhao Ziyang in late 1988, has been to encourage 100% foreign-owned ventures. The provinces of Guangdong and Fujian, together with Hainan and the open coastal cities, have been given the right to approve such projects up to US$30 million, unless they are subject to licencing restrictions.

Rural industries under local authority control have been effective joint venture partners in many of our interviews. At the start of the austerity policy rural enterprises in China were employing 20% of the country's workforce, and generating 20% of China's national output (China News Analysis, 1 March 1989) and 15% of her export earnings. It was reported that the credit squeeze was hampering rural enterprises from forming new joint ventures (Wen Wei Po, 15 February 1989), but economists and officials interviewed in China in January 1990 were of the opinion that existing joint venture operations with rural industry partners were not being affected. However, there is some evidence to the contrary, and even of firms with established customer contacts overseas being forced to give them up in the aftermath of 4th June (22).

7.6.5 Hong Kong investment in China

The general effects on the Hong Kong economy of the prospect of its reintegration into China in 1997 as a Special Administrative Region with freedom to operate a capitalist system for fifty years are well-known. The brain drain has been running at an annual rate of approximately 1% of the total population. Since this emigration is heavily concentrated on professional people and middle managers, staff shortages are severe in many parts of the economy. The 4th June, with its tremendous shock to the people of Hong Kong, has accelerated this tendency, and the loss of confidence behind it.

Since the June events, much press coverage has been given in Hong Kong to the likelihood of Hong Kong firms relocating away from China, especially towards South East Asian countries. Thailand and Malaysia are the most frequently cited beneficiaries of such moves (23). A well-publicised example is the decision by the Hong Kong Electronics

Manufacturers Association to abandon plans to set up an "electronics city" in the Shenzhen Special Economic Zone, and to build it in Bangkok instead. However, it seems that, rather than coming from the Hong Kong manufacturers themselves, much of the pressure for moving out of China has come from overseas customers, fearful of future trouble in the Chinese economy, and in protest at the 4th June. A plastics manufacturer (interview, January 1990) said he visited Thailand at the prompting of his American customers, but still felt Guangdong had a much better investment environment. Officials, fearful of a loss of investment, sometimes were more helpful than in the past. The toy industry, though sourcing some 60% of its production in Guangdong, actually has moved only about 2% of its production to Thailand (24).

7.6.6 Recent policy changes and the future

There can be little doubt that the strengthening of the conservative faction in the Chinese leadership after 4th June led to the austerity policy being pursued with renewed vigour. Obviously, this was not necessarily to lay the foundations for further future reform. It is worth observing that it is not only Deng Xiaoping in the present leadership who has encouraged economic reform in the past, but the gap between leaders such as the economist Chen Yun and more clearly reformist elements in the Party is considerable. Such reformists now must be biding their time, in the hope that things will change in their favour when the present old leaders die and in the belief that not much can be done until then.

The rapid industrial expansion of the economy, often based on borrowed funds, has made growth very sensitive to macroeconomic restriction. But there have been both political and economic dangers in the policy of restriction and recentralization on to the state sector. Rural enterprises during the 1980s generated well in excess of 40 million new jobs compared to 20 million in the state sector, and estimates have been made that there will be 100 million new jobs required during the 1990s as children born during the baby boom of the early 1970s enter the labour force. Unemployed workers, and those who have been laid off on reduced basic wages, are a powerful source of discontent, and this has probably been behind the recent decision to pay laid-off workers full basic salaries again, provided apparently that they report in to their places of work (interviews, January 1990). Forcing people back into agricultural employment is unlikely to be popular either.

The Chinese stress that the policy of economic reform is being continued. The central government's Economic Reform Commission (Jingji Tizhi Gaige Weiyuanhui - or Ti Gai Wei for short), having officially been cleared of "counterrevolutionary" activity, is now back in operation. Price reform, in particular, however, is difficult to envisage in present circumstances. Recentralization of resources in favour of state companies will make it harder to end the dual (or "two-track") price system, where a portion of supply is cleared at free market prices and which has given such scope for speculation; unless all supplies were to be recentralized, which is unlikely.

In late 1989 and early 1990 certain policy changes have occured. The 21% devaluation of the Renminbi in December 1989 has brought the official rate nearer to the free rate (25). The Economic Reform Commission's January meeting produced a statement suggesting that sectors other than the state sector should be fostered, the first such comment made so far. Credit contol has been slackened somewhat too.

Recently reported figures for the inflow of contracted foreign investment to China suggest that the level for the whole of 1989 is about the same as for 1988 for contractual and equity joint ventures and 100% foreign ventures as a group (US$5.3 billion); although, of course, contracted investment is less likely to materialize in present circumcumstances.

Some further improvements in conditions for foreign investors have been made. Changes in the law on joint ventures have given the foreign side more freedom to manage, and the chairman of the board can now be a foreigner. Yet successful foreign investment depends to a great extent on the continuation of economic reforms. Without these, labour practices will be more difficult to improve, domestic suppliers of inputs are less likely to produce products of acceptable quality or reliable delivery, and foreign firms in joint ventures will be thrown back on partnerships with state companies who have proved so much less flexible and innovative than the collective sector (26). Also, the aims of the Chinese government in attracting foreign investment are by no means clear; nor the role that Special Economic Zones are meant to play now that many other locations have been opened to foreign investment. The total inflow of actually-used direct foreign investment of all kinds over the 1979-88 period was equivalent to only 3.1% of China's total domestic investment in state-owned fixed assets (Beijing Review, 6-12 March 1989), and by the late 1980s the stock of Chinese investment in Hong Kong was greater than that of Hong Kong in China. High technology investment, so often stressed, could be attracted by China's huge domestic market, but the tightness of recent macroeconomic control has greatly reduced effective demand for goods with a high income elasticity of demand. Besides, there is the high cost of remitting abroad, as foreign exchange, profits made in Renminbi, especially at a time of great foreign exchange shortage. At the same time, China has discouraged foreign investment in a number of products, including many consumer durables (27), and there are frequent comments suggesting that processing and assembly investment is merely tolerated. Our interviews have shown, however, that China has received much genuine transfer of technology from labour-intensive, export-orientated activities, and that these have been profitable for the investors too.

Recent events in China greatly have increased political risk as perceived by foreign investors. Even though one may feel that the home-grown nature of Chinese communism makes unlikely any repetition, in China, of the overthrow of the Rumanian communist government in late 1989, there are clear dangers of political instability in any power struggle after the death of Deng Xiaoping and other aged leaders. In any case, whoever is in power will face serious problems in the economy. "Restructuring", even if genuinely a preliminary to more reform, brings great dangers of discontent if unemployment continues to rise and many people's real income fall in the short term, and this may be behind the easing of credit restriction in early 1990. Discontent will be worsened unless corruption and nepotism are brought under more obvious control. Agricultural problems are emerging too, after the great early successes of the agricultural reform programme, including a lack of agricultural infrastructure investment. Attempts to shift farmers out of well-paying cash crops back into grain production, while simultaneously restricting rural industries, are likely to prove unpopular, as has been the government's decision to pay peasants for wheat and other crop deliveries partly in credit notes. Many investors feel that, especially after 4th June, the "China decade" is over. No longer will they be willing to accept the frustrations of operating in China in the expectation of future profits in the hope that the reforms will proceed further, that the domestic market will become more accessible and that profits will become easier to remit. There is a widespread view that China will have to compete more on genuinely equal terms with other host countries if it is to secure further foreign investment, especially investment from Western countries and Japan.

NOTES

1. An offshoot from the present research is to investigate choice of contract in relation to the desire by the firms involved to minimise transactions costs (see Williamson, 1985), a preliminary attempt at which is Leung et al (1989). One area which would be worth exploring with a larger (and quantitative) data set would be contract choice in relation to industry and other structural characteristics, as well as (as our work implies) in relation to the preferences of the partners about risk and involvement. This would derive from the approach used by Casson (1987, ch 5). However, in the Pearl River Delta, the various Hong Kong industries are rather similar to each other in the sense that they produce mainly labour-intensive light consumer goods. Also, the fact that a number of our sample companies had had different contracts in the past may suggest that industry characteristics (such as the specificity of the capital equipment) will be less important in contract choice in the Delta than in China more generally or in other countries. (Casson notes too, p.35, with some justification, that there are objections to the idea that it is firm-specific advantage which is " internalized", along lines suggested by Dunning, e.g. 1985, rather than markets.)

2. In most investing countries, foreign investment profits remitted home by domestic companies are taxed, although usually foreign tax paid is credited against home tax liability under double taxation agreements. Thus the relevant tax for the foreign investor is whichever is the higher of the domestic and the foreign rate (see Kwon, 1989, p.253). In Hong Kong, company profits on overseas direct investment in general are not taxed. See Hong Kong Inland Revenue Ordinance Chapter 112 of the (1986) revised edition of Ordinance No.20 of 1947. I am grateful to Fergus Wong of the Hong Kong Baptist College Accounting Department for this information. Kwon (1989, p.267) estimates that there are large differences in the effective tax burden on direct foreign investments in China according to location and type of contract.

3. Our research has been preliminary in the sense of covering the widest range of issues associated with foreign investment, and quantitative data has not been generated to appraise the net benefits from foreign investment. Our interviews suggest that few local materials are purchased, so few backward linkages are generated, in part because of local supply constraints but also

because of poor local quality. However, the economic structure associated with foreign investment can 'deepen' with time (see Weisskopf and Wolff, 1977), and as foreign firms try to develop their own local supply sources. For the moment, the use of imported materials and components often facilitates rapid export expansion. The main economic benefit, then, at present is the generation of employment, and the foreign exchange equivalent of the wage bill, the gains from which are represented by the excess of the wage bill generated in foreign exchange earnings or savings over the social opportunity cost of labour. Externalities include labour training effects as trained workers move from foreign to domestic enterprises and the diffusion of management and technical skills. The sheer exposure to foreign standards of product quality and work input will have been especially instructive. To investigate these issues further would involve taking related industries, breaking down (in more detail than we have been able to do) the payments made out of their income from sales, and tracing the location of their expenditure. For examples of this kind of appraisal of the benefits from foreign investment (applied in this case to primary commodity export industries) see Thoburn (1977, 1981); and Warr (1984 and 1987) on free trade zone investments in Korea and Malaysia. Studies of the effects of foreign investment in China before the Second World War, the only point of comparison with investment under the Open Policy, are surveyed in Dernberger (1975), and a particularly useful one is Hou (1965). Most such investments were trade-related, rather than in manufacturing. Dernberger's conclusion is that, although the backward and forward linkages of manufacturing investments were slight, the overall impact of foreign investment was positive and worked mainly through indirect effects such as the introduction of new technology.

4. See Thoburn (1986). However, since the mid-1980s, there seems to have been some improvement in Shenzhen's export performance from foreign-invested ventures. Pomfret (1989, p.47) cites export/output ratios of over 50% for Shenzhen in 1987 and an estimated 64% by end-1988. The figures are made difficult to interpret by the large numbers of domestic enterprise in the Shenzhen Special Economic Zone, but Shenzhen's exports from foreign-invested ventures in 1988 were 45% of the national total of foreign-invested ventures' exports.

5. For example, consider a company in China producing a product at a unit cost of RMB50, which it can sell in Hong Kong at HK$100. If it receives the "free market" rate of exchange of 75 RMB per HK$100 it makes a profit on turnover of 33% per unit. If it receives the (then) official exchange rate of RMB47 it makes a loss. John Kamm (in Vogel, 1989,Chap.11) records that many goods were procured for export by official agencies from domestic companies at costs in RMB which were substantially greater than the RMB value, at the official exchange rate, of the foreign exchange earned from those exports. T.M.H. Chan (1988, pp.25-7) also discusses this problem, and draws the conclusion that the Pearl Delta suffers from an export disadvantage relative to the rest of China. Kamm (in Vogel,1989, p.379) argues that the RMB losses involved were a major factor explaining the large

extension of export licencing in 1986-7. Of course, since so many domestic prices are distorted, the RMB cost of foreign exchange cannot be regarded as a true measure of the opportunity cost of domestic resources. For a convenient discussion of the use of domestic resource cost as a form of economic appraisal see Roemer and Stern (1981,pp.153-5)

6. These are the Foreign Exchange Adjustment Centres, which have been established since November 1985, and now are in operation in a large number of locations. One equity joint venture investor (interviewed in Shenzhen in January 1990), and who had both domestic and export sales, complained that if he brought in foreign exchange the authorities would try to make him exchange it at the official rate, but he would have to buy at the free rate if he wished to exchange RMB into forex.

7. John Kamm's contribution in Vogel (1989, Chap.11) gives a very detailed account of changing practices in foreign exchange retention practices. He shows how these have varied over time, and from place to place and industry to industry.

8. The existence of anti-export bias working through the exchange rate and forex retention provisions was also emphasized by the World Bank's 1986 "country study" for China, recently published. (See World Bank, 1988).

9. See Leung Wing Yue (1988), reviewed in China Now, Spring 1989.

10. There are some counter-stories, however. One very experienced China trader and investor (interviewed in Hong Kong in January 1990), who had had five processing and assembly factories in various locations in Guangdong, had moved all his operations to the Guangzhou Economic and Technology Development Zone. In part this was to secure a more reliable supply of electric power, but also to escape what he described as the arbitrary use of power by officials in small localities, and the absence of the rule of law there. Indeed, he had split his original operations between five locations to spread such risks.

11. In other words, the regulations are often neibu. See Moser (1987, p.102).

12. See Vogel (1989, Chap.5) for an excellent account of economic policy and development in the various local authorities in the Inner (i.e. based on 1985 boundaries - see our Table 1.3) Pearl River Delta.

13. Unless otherwise stated, data on Hong Kong and Guangdong in this section come, respectively, from various issues of the Hong Kong Annual Digest of Statistics and the Guangdong Statistical Yearbook.

14. According to Hong Kong (1989,p.76) 74% of Hong Kong's 1988 domestic exports and 69% of its industrial employment came from the textiles, clothing, electronics, plastics products, electrical appliances, and watches and clocks industries.

15. For a convincing picture of the social and economic isolation of village life during the Maoist era, and the associated decline in local trade and specialization, see Chan, Madsen and Unger (1984). Rural handicrafts, and small-scale industries producing light consumer goods in small towns like today's "rural" industries, were also a prominent feature of Chinese economic growth before the Second World War (See Dernberger, 1975, pp.39-42).

16. The ratio of exports to gross domestic product for China was 13% in 1987, according to the World Bank's 1989 World Development Report. However, one would expect the share of exports in GDP, ceteris paribus, to be lower than in combined industrial and agricultural output, since GDP contains the services and government sectors, whose outputs are largely non-traded.

17. The share of the SEZs in Guangdong's processing and assembly earnings was 35.6%, and the combined share of SEZ equity and cooperative joint ventures and 100% foreign owned firms in the provincial total was 63.9%.
Foreign invested enterprises of all kinds generated 39.5% of the SEZs'own 1987 export earnings, indicating how much domestic investment has been attracted there.

18. These comments are based on further visits to China by Thoburn, Chau and Tang in January 1989, and by Thoburn in January 1990, and on following the Hong Kong press. To avoid an excessive number of citations in the text, recent material on policy and statistics is taken, unless otherwise stated, from the South China Morning Post, the Far Eastern Economic Review, or the 12 December 1989 Financial Times supplement on China. Also useful is the thoughtful commentary on the 4th June events by Nolan (1989). Anita Chan (1989) gives an incisive account of the causes of popular dissatisfaction with the reform programme.

19. For an analysis of "rent seeking" see Krueger (1974). Peter Nolan has put the point to us strongly that rent-seeking was also very much a feature of the Maoist period.

20. Kueh (1989, p.440) argues that, following an initial adjustment towards light industry in the late 1970s, heavy industrial growth has kept up with that of light industry. He is also concerned with what he sees as the starvation of agriculture of investment funds as a result of the reforms.

21. Of particular interest here is the statement issued after the 5th Plenum of the 13th Central Committee of the Chinese Communist Party in November 1989, published in the People's Daily, overseas edition, 10 November 1989 (translated in Inside China Mainland, December 1989). Besides stating that the "restructuring" of the economy now would last three years or more, it reaffirmed the need to continue to "open" to the outside world for foreign investment and technology. It also stated that the "basic policies" of the Special Economic Zones and coastal regions would remain in force.

22. An RTHK (Radio Television Hong Kong) television programme "Days of Economic Restriction", broadcast in Cantonese on 30 November 1989 in a well-known documentary series, carried interviews with officials and managers in a town (Pingzhou, between Foshan and Guangzhou) which had had considerable rural industry development. Pingzhou was said to have suffered a 70% cut in its industrial output since the start of the austerity policy. The manager of a sports shoes factory, which had been set up to service an American buyer, said that he had been forced to give up this "contact with foreigners" after 4th June. Others spoke of the severe effects the credit restrictions had had on their working capital, although, well before 4th June, they were also being hampered by severe shortages of electicity. Workers were worried that if they were forced back into agricultural employment their earnings would be much lower. (A brief description of Pingzhou, once a model commune, is given in Vogel,1989,pp.1-2.)

23. See for example Ming Bao, 12 January 1990.

24. I am grateful to Diane Yowell of the Hong Kong Bank for this point. She should not, however, be held responsible for any view expressed here.

25. Free rates in Guangzhou in January 1990 were about 6 RMB = US$1, compared to the official rate of 4.7 RMB = US$1.

26. Although our interviews have led us to form a generally favourable view of rural collective industrial enterprises, Chinese economists also have suggested that they are by no means all economically efficient. Their apparent competitiveness relative to the state sector sometimes is the result of the fact that they have been able to avoid tax and thereby keep prices low.

27. See Far Eastern Economic Review, 2 March 1989 for a list.

Appendix: The taxation of foreign investment in China

A.1. Introduction (1)

Preferential tax treatment has been one of the incentives used by China to attract foreign investment.   Before the 1979 Open Policy, China's tax system was developed within the context of a socialist economy.   Since 1979, China's tax system has evolved to implement a tax scheme applicable to foreign investments and other types of Chinese-foreign cooperative business activity. In addition, the new tax scheme is also used as a regulatory tool for the realisation of China's macroeconomic policy objectives.

Foreign investment in China is subject to the following principal taxes: individual income tax (IIT), joint venture income tax (JVIT), foreign enterprise income tax (FEIT), consolidated industrial and commercial tax (CICT), real estate tax (RET), vehicle and vessel licence tax (VVLT), customs duties (CD), etc. Section two of this Appendix will discuss in detail the nature and scope of the above taxes, with special emphasis on preferential treatments given to foreign investments.   Section three will discuss the tax policy practised in Special Economic Zones (SEZs), the fourteen coastal cities, and subsequently designated open areas such as the Pearl River (Zhujiang) Delta Open Economic Zone.   Section four will give a brief description of the tax treaty on double taxation.   The last section will discuss tax performance and the recent development of tax laws on foreign investments.

A.2 The principal Chinese taxes

A.2.1 The individual income tax (IIT)

The individual income tax law (2) was promulgated in 1980.   The IIT is levied on individuals, regardless of citizenship, according to their residence and the source of their income.   The residence rules can be summarized as follows:

1.   Individuals who are not residents of China are subject to IIT only on income gained within China.

2.   Individuals who reside in China for less than 90 consecutive days are exempt from IIT on this compensations for services performed within China provided that such compensation is paid by an employer outside China and is not borne by an establishment of that employer inside China.

3.   Individuals who reside in China for less than one year are subject to tax only on income gained within China.

4. Individuals who reside in China for one year or more are subject to tax on all their income, whether such income is gained within or outside China. But this rule is subject to two preferential treatments: First, if an individual resides in China for one year or more but not exceeding five years, income gained outside China will be subject to tax in China only if it is remitted to China. All income earned by an individual residing in China for more than five years is subject to taxation from the sixth year onward, irrespective of whether non-China source income has been remitted to China. Secondly, foreign personnel working in Chinese-foreign joint ventures, in co-operative joint ventures, in branches in China of foreign enterprises and other economic organisations, so long as they are in China merely on duty for one year or more but not exceeding five years and have no intention to reside in China permanently, are exempt from taxation on that part of their income which is generated outside China irrespective of whether or not it has been remitted to China.

The IIT rates are classified into two categories: First, regular income including wages, salaries and other constant income, after deducting RMB 800 allowances, is taxed monthly at the following progressive rates:

Range of Monthly Income	Marginal Tax Rate %
For RMB below 15000	5%
RMB1501 - 3000	10%
RMB3001 - 6000	20%
RMB6001 - 9000	30%
RMB9001 - 12000	40%
RMB12001 and above	45%

Secondly, income from personal services, royalties, interest, dividends, bonuses, lease of property, and other kinds of income, after a 20% deduction (or a reduction of RMB800 for income below RMB4000), is taxed at a flat rate of 20%.

Because of the recent high levels of inflation (3) eroding the purchasing power of the RMB, and the devaluation of RMB, the State Council announced that the IIT levied on the wages and salaries of foreign personnel (including overseas Chinese personnel and personnel from Hong Kong and Macau) working in China was to be reduced by 50% effective from 1 August 1987, i.e. the taxpayer pays only half of tax payable calculated according to the above schedule.(4)

A.2.2 The joint venture income tax (5) (JVIT)

The JVIT applies to all equity joint ventures in China. The JVIT is levied on the income derived from production, operation and other business undertakings of joint ventures in China, including income of their branches and subsidiaries inside and outside China.

After deductions of allowances costs, expenses and losses, the net taxable income is subject to the following two tax rates: Firstly, a national tax at a rate of 30% is imposed on the world-wide net taxable income of a joint venture company. Secondly, a local surcharge of 10% of the amount of the national tax is levied by the local government.

The two tax rates form a sum total of 33% on net taxable income. When the foreign party's share of the after-tax net profit is remitted outside China, it is subject to a remittance tax at a rate of 10%.

A.2.2.1 Preferential tax provisions The following preferential tax treatments have been made to attract foreign investment:

1. A newly-established joint venture which is to operate for a period of 10 years or more, is eligible for a total tax exemption for the first two years of its first profit-making year, and the 50% reduction is available in the three subsequent years. The statutory tax holiday provisions apply both to the national JVIT and the local surtax.

2. Joint ventures may apply to the local tax authorities for reductions of, or exemptions from, the 10% local surtax in years beyond the fifth year.

3. Joint ventures engaged in low-profit operations such as farming and forestry or located in remote, economically underdeveloped, outlying areas may be granted a 15% to 30% reduction in JVIT for ten years following the expiry of the five years statutory exemption and reduction period.

4. Joint ventures engaged in a harbour construction project with a term of 30 years or longer are eligible for a variety of tax advantages including accelerated depreciation, a reduced tax rate of 15%, and an exemption from the remittance tax on individuals.

5. A foreign partner in a joint venture who reinvests his share of profits in China for a period of not less than five years may obtain a rebate of 40% of the income tax paid on the reinvested amount.

6. Joint ventures which have Hong Kong, Macau, or overseas Chinese investors may apply for an extension of the period of tax exemption from two to three years commencing with the first profit-making year, and the period of 50% of tax reduction from three to four years following the first three years of tax exemption. Joint ventures engaged in low profit business may also be eligible for a 20% to 40% reduction in tax for a further period of 10 to 15 years after the expiry of the original tax exemption and reduction period.

7. An equity joint venture which qualifies as an Export Enterprise can enjoy the following tax incentives:

   (a) The foreign party will be exempt from the remittance tax levied on dividends remitted abroad.
   (b) After the statutory tax reduction and exemption period has expired, if during a particular year the value of the products exported by the joint venture is 70% or more of the value of its total production, then the joint venture will enjoy a 50% reduction of the applicable income tax rate in that year (but not below 10 per cent). If this joint venture is already entitled to the reduced 15% tax rate by virtue of being established in a Special Economic Zone or an economic and technological development zone,

then it will be subject to tax at 10% in any year in which it satisfies the foregoing export ratio.

(c) If the foreign party in a joint venture reinvests its share of the joint venture's profits in an Export Enterprise in China for not less than five years, it will receive a full refund of the income tax previously paid by the joint venture on the reinvested profits.

8.   An equity joint venture which qualifies as a Technologically Advanced Enterprise can enjoy the following tax incentives:

(a) The foreign party will be exempt from the remittance tax levied on dividends remitted abroad.

(b) After the statutory tax-exemption and reduction period has expired, the joint venture will enjoy a 50% reduction of the applicable income tax rate (but now below 10%) for another three years.

(c) If the foreign party in a joint venture reinvests its share of the joint venture's profits in a Technologically Advanced Enterprise in China for not less than five years, it will receive a full refund of the income tax previously paid by the joint venture on the reinvested profits.

A.2.3 The foreign enterprise income tax (7) (FEIT)

Except for equity joint venture investments, all other types of foreign companies, enterprises including cooperative joint ventures, and other economic organisations, are subject to the foreign enterprise income tax. Taxable income includes income derived from production and business, and other sources of income. The former includes income from the production and business operations of foreign enterprises in industry, mining, communications, transportation, agriculture, forestry, animal husbandry, fisheries, poultry farming, commerce, service, and a wide range of other trades. Income from other sources includes dividends, interests, income from the sale or lease of property, income from the transfer of patents, technical know-how, trade mark rights, and other non-business income.

A progressive tax schedule is applicable on net income of these foreign investments with establishments in China which engage in production and business operations there. The tax rate scheduled of FEIT ranges from 20% to 40%.

Range of Annual Income	Marginal Tax Rate %
Below RMB250,000	20%
RMB250,001 to 500,000	25%
RMB500,001 to 750,000	30%
RMB750,001 to 1,000,000	35%
RMB1,000,001 and above	40%

In addition to the above progressive rates, a foreign enterprise with an establishment in China is also subject to a 10% local income tax surcharge on its net taxable income. On the other hand, a foreign enterprise with no establishment in China is subject to a 20% withholding tax which is imposed on income derived from Chinese sources in the form of dividends, interest, rentals, royalties, and other types of income designated as taxable by the Ministry of Finance.

A 2.3.1 <u>Preferential tax provisions for foreign enterprises with establishment(s) in China</u>

(1)   Foreign enterprises engaging in farming, forestry, animal husbandry, and other low profit operation with a scheduled term of operation of ten years or more may be exempt from FEIT in the first year of profitable operation and allowed a 50% reduction in the second and third years. A 15% - 30% reduction in FEIT may be allowed for a period of ten years following the expiry of the term for exemptions and reductions.

(2)   Foreign enterprises engaged in small-scale and low-profit production with annual income less than RMB 1 million may be allowed exemption from or reduction in local income tax upon approval by the local tax authorities.

(3)   Income from interest on loans given to the Chinese government or China's state banks by international financial institutions is exempt from FEIT.

(4)   Co-operative joint ventures and wholly foreign-owned enterprises may enjoy the same tax incentives on Export Enterprise and on Technologically Advanced Enterprise as given to equity joint ventures.

A.2.3.2 <u>Preferential tax provisions for non-establishment foreign Enterprises</u>

(1)   Income from interest on loans given at preferential interest rates by foreign banks to China's state banks and/or to Chinese trust and investment corporations authorized by the State Council to handle foreign currency business may be exempt from FEIT.

(2)   Foreign banks with grant loans to the China National Offshore Oil Corporation at interest rates not higher than the preferential rates given by international banks may obtain tax exemption on the interest gained.

(3)   Foreign banks and individuals opening accounts in Chinese state banks at an interest rate lower than in saving banks or lower than the interest rate on deposits in their own countries may have that part of the interest exempt from FEIT.

(4)   Chinese companies, enterprises and other units which import technology, equipment or goods on credit provided by the sellers' governments, and pay interest to the sellers at a rate not higher than the buyers' deferred credit payment, may have the interest exempt from FEIT.

(5)   Foreign firms which provide Chinese companies and enterprises with equipment and technology and receive payment from the Chinese side by way of goods produced, processing of imported materials or assembling of ready-made parts may have their payment (principal and interest) exempt from FEIT.

A 2.4 The consolidated industrial and commercial tax (CICT)

The consolidated industrial and commercial tax was introduced in 1958 and applied to all enterprises in China, including both state owned enterprises and foreign companies. In 1984, the CICT was divided into a number of separate taxes.(8) As a result, the CICT applies only to joint ventures and foreign enterprises operating in China, and is no longer applicable to domestic enterprises.

Basically the CICT is a broad-based turnover tax levied at various stages of economic activity upon the transfer of taxable goods and services from one entity to another. The tax is imposed on sales by producers of goods as well as on sales by wholesalers to retailers. The tax is levied at the retail level when goods and services are sold to consumer.

The tax rates of CICT are classified in accordance with different products and trades. There are 104 categories of taxable industrial products. Forty-two tax rates have been laid down in accordance with the principle that tax rates for necessities should be lowered than those for non-necessities, and those for materials used in production on capital goods should be lower than those for consumer goods. The rates for most goods are below 20%. The maximum rate is 69% on cigarettes and the lowest rate is 1.5% on grey cotton cloth.

A 2.4.1 <u>Preferential tax provisions</u> The CICT law and regulations provide for various tax reductions and exemptions. Exemptions are granted for the business income of state banks, insurance companies, agricultural machinery stations, and medical and health services as well as the proceeds from experiments conducted by scientific research institutions. In addition to these statutory exemptions, the Ministry of Finance has issued many supplementary regulations giving exemptions in certain types of transaction involving foreign enterprises. For example, equity joint ventures are exempt from the CICT on imports of the following goods: (9)

(a)   Machinery, equipment, parts, and other materials contributed by the foreign party as part of its capital contribution pursuant to the joint venture contract;

(b)   Machinery, equipment, parts, and other materials acquired with funds originally contributed as part of the joint venture's capital;

(c)   Machinery, equipment, parts and other materials which are acquired with the joint venture's additional capital and the production and supply of which cannot be guaranteed from sources in China.

For cooperative joint ventures, exemption from CICT is given to imported advanced machinery and equipment provided that China is unable to supply and that they are required for building factories and installing and reinforcing machinery and equipment in the following areas (10): basic construction of energy development, railways, highways, and harbours; industry; agriculture; forestry; animal husbandry; aquatic breeding; deep-sea fisheries; scientific research; education and medicine and health. There are also other preferential provisions for foreign enterprises engaging businesses in offshore oil, consignment sales and centers, contracted projects, etc.
A 2.5 The real estate tax (RET)

The real estate tax is imposed on the owners of land and buildings in urban areas. The tax is levied either on the owner at 1.2% of the value of the property as determined by a local real estate appraisal committee, or 18% of the rents received by the owner from a lessee. As far as foreign investment is concerned, the RET applies primarily to equity joint ventures and wholly foreign owned enterprises. Under existing Chinese law, an enterprise with foreign investment is permitted to own buildings but not the underlying land. Usually, a foreign enterprise obtains the right to use the underlying land for a period coterminous with the life of the enterprise. Thus, foreign enterprises are subject to the RET with respect to buildings but not the underlying land.

A 2.6 The vehicle and vessel licence tax (VVLT)

The vehicle and vessel licence tax is levied on vehicles and small power-boats and sailing-boats owned by persons or organisations in China. The tax is imposed at the discretion of local governments, upon approval by the provincial government authorities. There is no preferential tax provisions given to foreign enterprises.

A 2.7 Customs duties (11) (CD)

All goods imported into and exported out of China are subject to import and export duties, with some exceptions stipulated by the government. The tariff rates fall into two categories: general tariff rates and low tariff rates. The general tariff rates apply to imports originating from countries with which China has not concluded trade treaties on reciprocal favourable terms; the low tariff rates apply to imports originating from countries with which China has concluded trade treaties on reciprocal terms. Under the current system, goods are classified into 99 main categories and various subcategories. The average import tariff rate is about 10%. For the purpose of encouraging export, a majority of goods are exempt from export tariff except for a few such as coal and Chinese herbal medicine. The following goods imported by equity ventures, co-operative joint ventures and wholly foreign owned enterprises are exempt from customs duties:

(a)   equipment for production and management, and building materials contributed as an investment;

(b)   raw and semi-processed materials, components, parts and packing materials, automobiles for private use, and office equipment imported for the manufacture and export goods;

(c)   reasonable quantities of household articles and automobiles for private use imported by foreign technicians and other employees;

(d)   export products from these foreign enterprises are exempt from export duties.

Table A.1 summarizes the salient features of the taxes applicable to foreign investments.

Table A.1 Taxes Applicable to Foreign Investments (Sheet 1)

Taxes	Application	Tax coverage	Tax rate schedule	Tax exemptions	Tax reductions
1. Individual Income Tax (IIT)	Levied on individuals, regardless of citizenship, according to their residance status.	1. Regular income such as wages, salaries and other constant income. 2. Income from personal services, royalties, etc.	1. For regular income, the marginal rate schedule is as follows: Monthly Income (RMB) Rate below 1500 5% 1501 - 3000 10% 3001 - 6000 20% 6001 - 9000 30% 9001 - 12000 40% 12001 and above 45% 2. Income from personal services in taxed at a flat rate of 20%. 3. In SEZs and 14 coastal cities, a flat rate of 10% is levied on incomes other than wages and salaries.	Individuals who reside in China for less than 90 consecutive days are exempt from tax.	1. Other preferential tax provisions are given to individuals who reside in China for more than one year but less than five years. 2. Because of recent inflation, the IIT levied on regular income of foreign personnel working in China was reduced by 50% effective from 1 August 1987.
2. Consolidated Industrial and commerical Tax (CICT)	Levied on joint ventures and foreign enterprises in China.	Applied to various stages of economic activities upon the transfer of taxable goods and services.	There are 104 categories of taxable industrial products with 42 tax rates ranging from the minimum 1.5% to the maximum of 69%.	1. Under certain conditions, equity and cooperative joint ventures are exempt from the tax on imports of parts, offshore oil, and other materials 2. Foreign companies undertaking contracted projects in China may be exempt from the tax.	Various reductions in and exemption from the tax are granted to enterprising operating in the SEZs and the 14 coastal cities.

176

Table A.1   Taxes Applicable to Foreign Investments (Sheet 2)

3. Real Estate Tax (RET)	Levied on all types of domestic and foreign enterprises.	Foreign enterprises are subject to the tax with respect to buildings but not the underlying land.	Levied on the owner at 1.2% of the value of the property, or 18% of the rents received by the owner from a leasee.	Nil	Foreign enterprises may apply for exemption from or reduction in the tax from local authorities.
4. Vehicle and Vessel Licence Tax (VVLT)	Levied on all types of domestic and foreign enterprises and persons.	Vehicle and small power boats and sailing boats.	The tax rate is determined by local authorities.	Nil
5. Customs Duties	Levied on all types of domestic and foreign enterprises.	All goods imported into and exported out of China, except for those stipulated otherwise by the government.	Goods are classified into 99 main categories and various subcategories with import tariff ranging from the minimum 3% to the maximum 80%.	1. Export products from foreign enterprises are exempt from export duties. 2. Certain imported goods such as advanced machinery which are not available in China are exempt from import duties for all foreign enterprises engaging in certain industries. 3. Certain imported goods which are part of the foreign party's capital contribution to the joint venture in accordance with the stipulations of the joint venture contract are exempt from the tax.	Foreign enterprises may apply for exemption from or reduction in the tax.

177

Table A.1 Taxes Applicable to Foreign Investments (Sheet 3)

Notes:

Sources: Details of Joint Venture Income Tax and Foreign Enterprise Income Tax which are also applicable to foreign investments are given in Table A.6.

(1) Income Tax Law of the People's Republic of China concerning Joint Ventures Using Chinese and Foreign Investment, adopted at the Third Session of the Third Session of the Fifth National People's Congress and promulgated on 10 September 1980.

(2) Detailed Rules and Regulations for the Implementation of the Income Tax Law of the People's Republic of China concerning Joint Ventures Using Chinese and Foreign Investment, approved by the State Council on 10 December 1980 and promulgated by the Ministry of Finance on 14 December 1980.

(3) Individual Income Tax Law of the People's Republic of China, adopted at the Third Session of the Fifth National People's Congress and promulgated on 10 September 1980.

(4) Detailed Rules and Regulations for the Implementation of the Individual Income Tax Law of the People's Republic of China, approved by the State Council on 10 December 1980 and promulgated by the Ministry of Finance on 14 December 1980.

(5) Income Tax Law of the People's Republic of China concerning Foreign Enterprises, adopted at the Fourth Session of the Fifth National People's Congress on 13 December 1981.

(6) Detailed Rules and Regulations for the Implementation of the Income Tax Law of the People's Republic of China concerning Foreign Enterprises, approved by the State Council on 17 February 1982 and promulgated by the Ministry of Finance on 21 February 1982.

(7) Provisional Regulations of the State Council of the People's Republic of China on Reduction and Exemption of Enterprise Income Tax and Consolidated Industrial and Commercial Tax for Special Economic Zones and the Fourteen Coastal Port Cities, promulgated by the State Council on 15 November 1984.

(8) Measures on Readjusting Land Use Fees and Preferential Reduction and Exemption of Land Use Fees in Shenzhen Special Economic Zone, promulgated by Shenzhen Municipal People's Government on 25 December 1984.

(9) Detailed Rules and Regulations on Encouragement of Foreign Investment in People's Republic of China, promulgated by the State Council on 11 October 1986.

A.3   Taxation in China's special investment areas

This section describes the preferential tax treatments applied in the
Special Economic Zones,the Fourteen Coastal Cities, and Open Economic
Areas.   The Special Economic Zones were established in 1980 by order
of China's State Council in the municipalities of Shenzhen, Shantou,
and Zhuhai in Guangdong Province, and in Xiamen in Fujian Province.
Foreign enterprises established in the Special Economic Zones enjoy a
variety of investment incentives, the most attractive of which has
been their liberal tax rules.   Encouraged by the success of the
Special Economic Zones in attracting foreign investment, China's State
Council announced on 6 April 1984 that fourteen coastal port cities
would be designated Open Cities offering investment incentives to
foreign enterprises.   Different preferential tax treatments are
granted to foreign enterprises depending on their location within the
cities, i.e. in the Economic and Technological Development Zones or in
the old districts of the cities. The subsequently designated Open
Economic Areas, such as the Pearl River Delta Open Economic Zone,
receive the same preferences as the areas in the Open Cities outside
their Economic and Technological Development Zones.   Table A.2
describes major differences in tax treatment of foreign enterprises
established in these special investment areas.

Table A.2 Major Differences in Tax Treatment of SEZ Enterprises, ETDZ Enterprises, Open Economic Zone and Open City Enterprises (Sheet 1)

	Special Economic Zones	Economic and Technological Development Zones of the Fourteen Coastal Port Cities	Open Economic Zones, Original Urban Areas of the Fourteen Coastal Port Cities and the Urban Areas of Shantou, Zhuhai and Xiamen
1. Industrial Income Tax	(1) For wages and salaries income, the marginal rate schedule is as follows: Monthly Income (RMB) / Rate 801 - 1500 / 3% 1501 - 3000 / 7% 3001 - 6000 / 15% 6001 - 9000 / 20% 9001 - 12000 / 25% 12001 upwards / 30% (2) Income from personal services and other incomes are taxed at a flat rate of 15%. (3) Deductions are treated in the manner specified in the National Individual Income Tax Law. (see Table A-1).	(1) For wages and salaries income, the marginal rate schedule of National Individual Income Tax applies: Monthly Income (RMB) / Rate 801 - 1500 / 5% 1501 - 3000 / 10% 3001 - 6000 / 20% 6001 - 9000 / 30% 9001 - 12000 / 40% 12001 upwards / 45% (2) Income from dividends, interest, rentals, royalties and other sources of outside investors who have not set up establishments in China, except in the cases in which tax exemption is granted according to law, shall be taxed at a reduced rate of 10%.	Same tax treatment as in the Economic Technological Development Zones.
2. Enterprise Income Tax	(1) The income of equity joint ventures, cooperative joint ventures, and wholly foreign owned enterprises established in the SEZs are taxed at a reduced rate of 15%.	(1) The income of equity joint ventures, cooperative joint ventures, and wholly foreign owned enterprises established in the ETDZs that are of productive nature and operated in the ETDZs are levied at a reduced rate of 15%. (2) ETDZ enterprises engaged in advanced technology and exporting production shall be taxed at a reduced rate of 10% on enterprise income tax.	(1) The income of equity joint ventures, cooperative joint ventures, and wholly foreign owned enterprises (OT enterprises) operating within the confines of the original urban area of the fourteen coastal port cities or the urban area of Shantou, Zhuhai and Xiamen that are technology or knowledge-intensive, or have foreign investments exceeding US$30 million and require a long period of capital recovery, or belong to the fields of energy, communication and port construction.

Table A.2 Major Differences in Tax Treatment of SEZ Enterprises, ETDZ Enterprises, Open Economic Zone and Open City Enterprises (Sheet 2)

(2) SEZ enterprises engaged in productive trades such as industry, communication and transportation, agriculture, forestry and livestock breeding, etc., and scheduled to operate for a period of ten years or longer, may be exempted from income tax for two years commencing from the first profit-making year and allowed a 50% reduction from the third to the fifth year inclusive.

(3) SEZ enterprises engaged in service trades with foreign investments exceeding US$5 million and a scheduled period of operation of ten years or longer, may be exempted from income tax in the first profit-making year and allowed a 50% reduction in the second and third year.

(4) SEZ enterprises engaged in exporting production, after expiry of the tax exemption scheme stipulated in (2), are allowed a 50% reduction of the current rate of Enterprise Income Tax, if the value of exports is above 70% of the value of their total production in that year.

(3) The ETDZ enterprises scheduled to operate for a period of ten years or longer may be exempted from income tax for two years commencing from the first profit-making year and allowed a 50% reduction from the third to the fifth year inclusive.

(4) Same tax treatment as stipulated under (4) of the first column for the SEZ enterprises

(2) For OT enterprises in certain fields of operations that are not entitled to tax reduction as prescribed in (1), a 20% reduction in the existing enterprise income tax may be allowed.

(3) Same tax treatment as stipulated under (4) of the first column for the SEZ enterprises.

Table A.2 Major Differences in Tax Treatment of SEZ Enterprises, ETDZ Enterprises, Open Economic Zone and Open City Enterprises (Sheet 3)

	SEZ Enterprises	ETDZ Enterprises	Open City Enterprises
	(5) SEZ enterprises engaged in service trades with foreign investments exceeding US$5 million and a scheduled period of operation of ten years or longer, may be exempted from income tax in the first profit-making year and allowed a 50% reduction in the second and third year.		
3. Local Surtax	The grant of local surtax reduction or exemption to SEZ enterprises, if necessary, shall be decided upon by the people's government of the SEZs.	The grant of local surtax reduction or exemption to ETDZ enterprises, if necessary, shall be decided upon by the people's government of the city where the ETDZ locates.	The grant of local surtax reduction or exemption to OT enterprises, if necessary, shall be decided upon by the people's governments of the cities.
4. Consolidated Industrial and Commercial Tax	(1) Except in the case of imported mineral oils, cigarettes and wines on which the tax rate shall be 50% of the rate as prescribed in the tax law, all other imports shall be free from CICT. A reasonable quantity of self-use cigarettes, wires, checked-in articles and home appliances brought in by outside investors may be exempted from CICT. (2) CICT shall be exempted on export products made by SEZ enterprises, except those on the state restriction list or otherwise provided. (3) For products made by SEZ enterprises and sold in the same SEZ, except for various mineral oils, cigarettes, wines and a few products, shall be exempted from CICT.	(1) CICT shall be exempted on building materials, production equipment, raw and other materials, spare parts and accessories, components and elements, means of transport and office supplies imported by ETDZ enterprises for self use. In case products made from tax-exempt imported raw and other materials, accessories, components and elements are sold domestically by ETDZ enterprises, the tax on such imported items shall be paid retroactively in accordance with the tax law. (2) CICT shall be exempted on export products made by ETDZ enterprises, with the exception of those on the state restriction list. Product sold in domestic market shall be subject to CICT as prescribed by the tax law. (3) A reasonable quantity of home appliances, household articles and vehicles brought in for personal use by outside investors and their staff working in ETDZ enterprises or residing in ETDZ may be exempted from CICT.	(1) CICT shall be exempted on production equipment, business equipment and building materials imported by OT enterprises as investment by outside investors or as additional investment of the enterprises, as well as on vehicles and office supplies imported for their own use. (2) CICT shall be exempted on export products made by OT enterprises, except those on the state restriction list. Products for domestic sale shall be taxed according to the tax law. (3) CICT shall be exempted on raw and other materials, spare parts and accessories, components and elements and packing materials imported by OT enterprises for making export products; but those imported for making products for domestic market shall be taxed according to the tax law. (4) A reasonable quantity of home appliances, household articles and vehicles brought in for personal use by outside investors and their staff working in OT enterprises or residing in the OT shall be exempted from CICT.

Table A.2 Major Differences in Tax Treatment of SEZ Enterprises, ETDZ Enterprises, Open Economic Zone and Open City Enterprises (Sheet 4)

(4)	CICT shall be levied at the rate as prescribed in the tax law for SEZ enterprises on their income derived from commercial, communication and transportation and service undertakings.		
5. Remittance Tax	In the case of an outside investor in a joint venture in a SEZ remitting abroad its profit derived therefrom, the income tax on the remitted amount shall be exempted.	In the case of an outside investor of a joint venture in a ETDZ remitting abroad its profit derived therefrom, the income tax on the remitted amount shall be exempted.	To be decided upon by the people's government the cities.
6. Land Use Fees	There are various measures on readjusting land use fees and preferential reduction and exemption of land use fees in Shenzhen SEZ.	To be decided upon by the people's government of the ETDZs.	To be decided upon by the people's government of the cities

Source: Adapted from Shenzhen Special Economic Zone Yearbook (1985) and China's Open Cities and Special Economic Zones (1986). See also sources to Table A-1.

A.4 **Tax treaties --- protection from double taxation**

China has signed taxation agreements on avoiding double taxation and guarding against tax evasion with a number of countries. The articles on taxation agreements are drawn up through negotiation with countries that have economic contacts with China. They are worked out in accordance with local conditions, and with special reference to the model treaty of 1977 drafted by the United Nations and the Organisation of Economic Cooperation and Development.

The scope of a tax treaty usually covers types of tax, activities of taxpayers and source of income. The main points of tax agreements are in general as follows:

(1) The agreements are generally at governmental level. On the Chinese side, an agreement must be approved by the State Council before it becomes law.

(2) For China, the taxation agreement covers individual income tax, joint venture income tax, and foreign business income tax. The foreign side should apply the agreement to the same or similar taxes. Other taxes are not included in taxation agreements.

(3) China in principle adopts international definitions of a wide variety of economic and accounting terms. However, because of different taxation laws in different countries, specific clauses may vary to a certain extent in different agreements.

A.5 **Tax performance and recent development of tax laws on foreign investment**

The joint venture income tax law and the foreign enterprise income tax for the Special Economic Zones were enacted in 1980, and the foreign enterprise income tax for those foreign investment other than equity joint venture types and outside the Special Economic Zones was enacted in 1982. Since 1980, the total industrial and commercial tax figure has included revenues from foreign investment. For example, in Table A.3, the total industrial and commercial tax in China includes equity joint-venture income tax, foreign enterprises income tax, individual income tax and value added tax. Separate data on tax revenue from foreign investment are not available, however. It is not possible to tell from Table A.3 the profitability of foreign investments in China. Even Guangdong Province, which absorbs the largest share of foreign investment in China, does not differentiate its sources of tax revenues from domestic enterprises and foreign investment.

Table A.3 Tax Revenues of the Central Government of the PRC
(in million RMB)

Year	Total Industrial & Commercial Tax	Growth Rate of Total Industrial & Commercial Tax (%)
1979	47269	
1980	50135	6.06%
1981	53840	7.39%
1982	60459	12.29%
1983	65781	8.8%
1984	77051	17.13%
1985	119700	55.35%
1986	129969	8.58%
1987	138538	6.59%
1988	157716	13.84%

Notes: In 1985, the Ministry of Finance implemented the second step of substituting taxation for enterprise income submission, and also reformed the system of industrial and commercial taxes. Thus the 1985 figure is not comparable with the previous figures. Also the drastic increase in 1987 is mainly because of the higher inflation rate in that year.

Source: China Statistical Yearbook, various issues.

Fortunately, Shenzhen, the largest Special Economic Zone, publishes separate data on tax revenue from foreign enterprises (see Table A.4). The Shenzhen Special Economic Zone levies foreign enterprise income tax, individual income tax, consolidated industrial and commercial tax, real estate tax, and vehicle and vessel licence tax on foreign enterprises and personnel.

185

Table A.4 Tax Revenues of the Shenzhen Special Economic Zone
(in million RMB)

Year	Tax Revenues from Foreign Enterprises (1)	Growth Rate of Tax Revenues from Foreign Enterprises (2)	Total Individual & Commercial Tax Revenues (3)	(1) --- (3)
1980	1.1		27.2	4.2%
1981	5.7	418.2%	83.1	6.8%
1982	12.0	110.5%	81.3	14.8%
1983	17.1	42.5%	131.5	13.0%
1984	24.9	45.6%	263.0	8.4%
1985	66.4	166.7%	593.0	11.2%
1986	66.3	-0.2%	650.8	10.2%
1987	84.8	27.83%	774.9	19.1%

Source: Shenzhen Special Economic Zone Yearbook, various issues.

Foreign enterprises enjoy preferential tax provisions on foreign enterprise income tax, individual income tax and consolidated industrial and commercial tax. Tax revenues from foreign enterprises are grouped under the heading of total industrial and commercial tax revenues, which also include product tax, value added tax, turnover tax enterprise income tax, individual income tax, real estate tax, urban maintenance and repair tax, and vehicle and vessel licence tax levied on domestic enterprises operated in the Shenzhen Special Economic Zone. The ratio of tax revenues from foreign enterprises to total industrial and commercial tax revenues in the Shenzhen SEZ has remained at an average of 12.8% between 1982 to 1987. But there is no detailed breakdown of the above five taxes on foreign enterprises, and we know nothing about the amount and growth rate of the foreign enterprise income tax. Thus it would not be possible to tell from Column 1 of Table A.4 the profitability of foreign enterprises in the Shenzhen SEZ. The high growth rate in tax revenues from foreign enterprises in 1981 and 1982 was probably due to increased revenues from real estate tax, the vehicle and vessel licence tax, and the consolidated industrial and commercial tax levied on an increasing number of foreign enterprises invested and established in the Shenzhen SEZ during that time period. On the other hand, the sharp increase in 1985 may due to the end of the three-year tax holidays for many firms established in the early eighties.

Local tax officials are very reluctant to publish separate figure on each tax on foreign enterprises fearing that a low rate of return and/or a small proportion of profitable foreign investments as implied by these tax figures may deter new foreign investments coming into the Shenzhen SEZ. On the other hand, in view of increasing competition from the Pearl River Delta Open Zone, the Shenzhen SEZ has to offer more favourable tax incentives to attract and to retain foreign investments. Thus, tax expenditure has been increasing in the whole Pearl River Delta region and the Special Economic Zones.

Depending on the types of contract, foreign investors pay either the joint venture income tax or the foreign enterprise income tax. In general, preferential tax provisions are more favourable under the joint venture income tax than under the foreign enterprise income tax.

For example, joint venture income tax allows two years tax holidays, while the foreign enterprise income tax gives one; joint venture income tax has an effective rate of 33%, while the maximum marginal rate for foreign enterprise income tax is 40%.

Table A.5 Average Rates for Foreign Enterprises Income Tax

Annual Taxable Income	National Tax Rate	National + Local Tax Rate
(RMB)	(%)	(%)
250,000	20.0%	30.0%
500,000	22.5%	32.5%
750,000	25.0%	35.0%
1,000,000	27.5%	37.5%
1,250,000	30.0%	40.0%
5,000,000	37.5%	47.5%
10,000,000	38.75%	48.75%
100,000,000	39.87%	49.87%

Table A.5 gives the average rates for foreign enterprises income at various income levels. At income level up to half a million, the tax rate for foreign enterprises is lower than that for joint ventures. If we consider both the national and local taxes, the two types of foreign investment have the same tax rate of 33% at an annual income of RMB535,714. If all profits are remitted out of China, then the maximum rate an equity joint venture has to pay is 39.7% (i.e. 33% + 10%(100% - 33%)). But the maximum rate for a foreign firm under the foreign enterprise income tax is 49.87%, irrespective of whether profits are remitted out of China.

There are also differences in deductions and exemptions which are subject to interpretation and approval of local authorities (see Table A.6). These differences in tax provisions often cause difficulties to foreign investors because they have to devote energies and resources to tax planning and negotiations with local tax officials.

The Chinese government acknowledges the deficiencies of the present tax system involving foreign investment and is now in the process of streamlining it so that it can be a more effective instrument in attracting foreign investment. In the 1988 National Meeting on Taxation, the Ministry of Finance announced its intention to combine the joint venture income tax and the foreign enterprise income tax so that foreign enterprises will subject to a unique and same marginal rate schedule and tax law. The new tax law will be administered by central tax authority. Details of the new tax on foreign enterprises have not been announced yet and it would not be too unrealistic to predict that more favourable tax provisions would be proposed. It is expected that a flat tax rate of 30% will be applied.

Table A.6 Differences in Tax Treatment
of Joint Ventures and Foreign Enterprises

	Joint Venture Income Tax	Foreign Enterprises Income Tax
1. Tax Coverage	World-wide income	Chinese source income only
2. Tax Rate	30%	Annual Income (RMB) / Rate below 250,000 — 20% 250,001 - 500,000 — 25% 500,001 - 750,000 — 30% 750,001 - 1,000,000 — 35% 1,000,001 and above — 40%
3. Local Surcharge Tax Rate	10% of the assessed income tax	10% of taxable income
4. Tax Rate on Remitted Profit	10% of the remitted amount	Nil
5. Tax Exemption	Exemption from income tax in the first two profit-making years for a joint venture scheduled to operate applies to local surcharge tax.	Exemption from income tax in the first profit-making year for a foreign enterprise in a low-profit industry such as farming, forestry and animal Exemption also applies from local surcharge tax for small scale or low profit enterprises.
6. Tax Reduction	Reduction in income tax by 50% in the 3rd to 5th profit-making years for a joint venture scheduled to operate for over 10 years, and for those joint ventures, after expiry of the tax exemption scheme, if the value of the exports are above 70% of the value of their total production in that year. Reduction also applies to local surcharge tax.	Reduction in income tax by 50% in the 2nd and 3rd profit-making years for a foreign enterprise in a low-profit industry and scheduled to operate for over 10 years, and for those joint ventures, after expiry of the tax exemption scheme, if the value of the exports are above 70% of the value of their total production in that year. Reduction also applies in local surcharge tax for small scale or low-profit enterprises.
7. Further Tax Reduction	Further reduction in income tax by 15% - 30% for 10 more	Further reduction in income tax by 15% - 30% for 10 more years for a foreign

	years for a joint venture in a low profit industry or located in a remote, economically under-developed area, following the expiry of the 5-year statutory exemption and reduction period. May apply to the local tax authorities to receive reduction to, or exemption from the 10% local surcharge tax in years beyond the fifth year.	enterprise in a low profit industry. Reduction in local surcharge tax also applies for small scale and low profit enterprise.
8. Tax Refund on Reinvested Profit	Refund of 40% of the income tax paid on the amount of profit reinvested in China for a period of 5	Nil.
9. Special Provisions to Encourage Foreign Investment	Special tax preferences are granted to joint ventures which qualify as export enterprises or technologically	Same as those granted to joint ventures.

Source: Same as Table A.1

NOTES

1. Major references for the various tax laws referred in this Appendix are: <u>Shenzhen Special Economic Zone Yearbook</u> (Economic Information Agency, 1985); <u>China's Open Cities and Special Economic Zones</u> (1986); <u>The China Investment Guide</u> (Longman, 1986 and 1989); Moser and Zee (1987); and Easson (1988, 467-470).

2. The Individual Income Tax Law was passed by the Third Session of the Fifth National People's Congress on 10 September 1980, and the Detailed Rules for the Implementation of the Individual Income Tax Law was approved by the State Council on 10 December 1980 and promulgated by the Ministry of Finance on 14 December 1980.

3. The inflation rates were 8.8%, 6.0%, 7.3% and 17.8% in 1985, 1986, 1987 and 1988 respectively. The 1988 figure was a preliminary estimate (see <u>China Statistical Yearbook</u>, various issues).

4.   The State Council announced on 8 August 1987 that effective from
       1 August 1987 there would be a 50% reduction in tax for foreign
       personnel.

5.   The Joint Venture Income Tax Law was adopted at the Third
       Session of the Fifth National People's Congress on 10 September
       1980 and the Detailed Rules for the Implementation of the Tax
       was approved by the State Council on 10 December 1980.

6.   On 11 October 1986 State Council promulgated the Foreign
       Investment Encouragement Provisions which grant special tax
       preferences to joint ventures which qualify as "export
       enterprises" or "technologically advanced enterprises".

7.   The Foreign Enterprises Income Tax Law was passed at the Fourth
       Session of the Fifth National People's Congress on 13 December
       1981, and the Detailed Rules for the Implementation of the Tax
       was approved by the State Council on 17 February 1982. Both the
       Law and the Implementations were put into effect as of 1 January
       1982.

8.   The Consolidated Industrial and Commercial Tax was created in
       1958 by integrating four previously separate levies, i.e. the
       Commodity Tax, the Commodity Circulation Tax, the Business Tax,
       and the Revenue Stamp Tax, into a single tax structure.   In
       1984, the   Chinese tax authorities reorganised the tax system
       applicable to domestic enterprises, including converting the
       existing Consolidated Industrial and Commercial Tax into a
       number of separate taxes which was similar to that which
       prevailed prior to 1958.

9.   The preferential tax treatment given to equity joint ventures
       for the importation of goods was specified in the "Regulations
       Regarding the Supervision and Control of and the Law of and
       Exemption from Tax on Goods Importation and Exported by Chinese
       Foreign Joint Ventures" which was put into effect on 1 May 1984.

10.   The preferential tax treatment given to co-operative joint
       ventures for the importation of goods was specified in the
       "Regulations Regarding the Supervision and Control of and the
       Levy of and Exemption from Tax on Goods Imported and Exported by
       Chinese-Foreign Co-operative Ventures" which was put into effect
       on 1 February 1984.

11.   The Regulations on Import and Export Duties was approved by the
       State Council on 7 March 1985, and the Customs Law was enacted
       on 22 January 1987 by the Standing Committee of the National
       People's Congress.

12.   These fourteen coastal cities are Tianjin, Shanghai, Dalian,
       Qinhuangdao, Yantai, Qingdao, Lianyangang, Nantong, Ningbo,
       Wenzhou, Fuzhou, Guangzhou, Zhanjiang, and Beihai.

13.   It was reported in late 1988 (see Hong Kong Economic Journal, 12
       December 1988) that the new tax law unifying the Joint Venture
       Income Tax and the Foreign Enterprise Income Tax would be

discussed and passed in the 1989 March Annual Session of the National People's Congress. However, because of the austerity measures used in early 1989 to cool down the economy, the amendment of foreign investment tax law has to be delayed. Chinese officials said that some crucial issues had still to be worked out before it could be submitted to the National People's Congress for discussion and approval. In view of recent developments in China, it is anticipated that it might be shelved for the time being. (see also Hong Kong Economic Journal, 25 April 1989).

Bibliography

Amcham (1988), Doing Business in Today's Hong Kong, Oxford University Press, for American Chamber of Commerce, Hong Kong

Beijing Review (1989), "The Utilization of Foreign Capital, 1979-88", 6-12 March

Campbell, N. (1989), A Strategic Guide to Equity Joint Ventures in China, Pergamon Press, Oxford

Campbell, N. and P. Adlington (1988), China Business Strategies, Pergamon Press, Oxford

Casson, M. (1987), The Firm and the Market. Studies on Multinational Enterprise and the Scope of the Firm, Basil Blackwell, Oxford

Caves, R.E. (1982), Multinational Enterprise and Economic Analysis, Cambridge University Press, Cambridge.

Chai, J. (1983), "Industrial Cooperation between China and Hong Kong", in Youngson (ed) (1983).

Chai, J. and C.K. Leung (eds) (1987), China's Economic Reforms, Selected Seminar Papers on Contemporary China, VII, Centre of Asian Studies, University of Hong Kong.

Chan, A. (1989), "The Challenge to the Social Fabric", in Goodman and Segal (eds) (1989)

Chan, A., R. Madsen, and J. Unger (1984), Chen Village. The Recent History of a Peasant Community in Mao's China, University of California Press, Berkeley

Chan, T.M.H. (1988), The Development and Prospects of the Zhujiang Delta Open Zone, China Economic Papers series, Friedrich Ebert Foundation, Shanghai, May

Chen, E.K.Y. (1981), 'Hong Kong Multinationals in Asia:Characteristics and Objectives' in Kumar and McLeod (eds) (1981).

Chen, E.K.Y. (1983), 'Multinationals from Hong Kong' in Lall (ed) (1983).

China (various years), Almanac of China's Foreign Economic Relations and Trade, Beijing.

China (1986), China's Open Cities and Special Economic Zones, Economy and Science Press, Beijing.

China (various years), Statistical Yearbook, Beijing (in Chinese).

192

Dernberger, R.F. (1975), "The Role of the Foreigner in China's Economic Development,1840-1949", in Perkins (ed) (1975)

Dunning, J.H. (ed), (1985), Multinational Enterprises, Economic Structure and International Competitiveness, Wiley, London.

Easson, A. (1988), "People's Republic of China: Tax Incentives for Foreign Investors", Bulletin for International Fiscal Documentation, November.

Economic Information Agency (1985), Shenzhen Special Economic Zone Yearbook, Hong Kong.

Feuchtwang, S., A. Hussain and T. Pairault (eds) (1988), Transforming China's Economy in the Eighties, Vol.I The Rural Sector, Welfare and Employment; Vol.II Management, Industry and the Urban Economy, Zed Books, London.

Forestier, K.(1989), The Hong Kong Connection: Doing Business in Guangdong Province, American Chamber of Commerce, Hong Kong

Fransman, M. and K. King (eds) (1984), Technological Capability in the Third World, Macmillan, London.

Frobel, F., J. Heinrichs and O. Kreye (1980), The New International Division of Labour. Structural Unemployment in Industrialized Countries and Industrialization in Developing Countries, Cambridge University Press, Cambridge (originally published in German by Rowohlt, Hamburg, 1977).

Goodman, D., and G. Segal (eds) (1989), China at Forty. Mid-Life Crisis?, Clarendon Press, Oxford

Guangdong Province (1986), Investment Guide to the Pearl River Delta Open Zone, (in Chinese).

Guangdong Province (various years), Statistical Yearbook, Guangzhou (in Chinese).

Guangdong Province (various years), Statistical Yearbook of Small Towns in Guangdong Province, Guangzhou (in Chinese).

Hang Seng Bank (1987), "Industrial Processing in China", Hang Seng Bank Economic Monthly, Hong Kong, April.

Hennart, J-F (1986) 'What is Internalization?', Weltwirtschaftliches Archiv, 122,4.

Hong Kong (various years), Annual Digest of Statistics, Census and Statistics Department

Hong Kong (1989), Hong Kong 1989, Government Information Service

Hou Chiming (1965), Foreign Investment and Economic Development in China, 1840-1937, Harvard University Press, Cambridge, MA.

Jenkins, R. (1987), Transnational Corporations and Uneven Development: The Internationalization of Capital and the Third World, Methuen, London.

Kaplinsky, R. (1984), "The International Context for Industrialization in the Coming Decade", Journal of Development Studies, 21, 1.

Katz, J.M. (ed) (1987), Technology Generation in Latin American Manufacturing. Theory and Case Studies Concerning its Nature, Magnitude, and Consequences, Macmillan, London.

Krueger, A.O. (1974), " The Political Economy of the Rent Seeking Society", American Economic Review, June

Kueh, Y.Y.(1989), "The Maoist Legacy and China's New Industrialization Strategy", China Quarterly, September

Kumar, K. and M.G. McLeod, (eds) (1981), Multinationals from Developing Countries, Lexington Books, Lexington, MA.

Kwon, O.Y. (1989), "An Analysis of China's Taxation of Foreign Direct Investment", The Developing Economies, September

Lall, S. (ed) (1983), The New Multinationals: The Spread of Third World Enterprises, Wiley, London.

Lall, S. (1987), Learning to Industrialize. The Acquisition of Technological Capability by India, Macmillan, London, for the World Bank.

Lei Qiang (1988), "New Progress in Hong Kong and Pearl River Delta Industrial Co-operation", Hong Kong and Macau Research, Zhong Shan University, Guangzhou (in Chinese).

Leung, H.M., E. Chau, and J.T. Thoburn (1988) "Industrial Cooperation between Hong Kong and China: some Interview Results and Theoretical Analysis" in Y.C. Jao and K. Lai (ed), The Transition Period in China-Hong Kong Economic Relations, Joint Publishing Co, Hong Kong (in Chinese).

Leung, H.M., J.T. Thoburn, E. Chau and S.H. Tang (1989) "Contractual Relations, Foreign Direct Investment and Technology Transfer: The Case of China", National University of Singapore, mimeo.

Leung Wing Yue (1988) Smashing the Iron Rice Pot: Workers and Unions in China's Market Socialism, Asia Monitor Resource Centre, Hong Kong.

Little, I.M.D. and J.A. Mirrlees (1974), Project Appraisal and Planning for Developing Countries, Heinemann, London.

Longman (1986 and 1989), The China Investment Guide, Longman, Hong Kong.

Miles, R.H. (1987), Managing the Corporate Social Environment: A Grounded Theory, Prentice Hall, New Jersey.

Moser, M.J. (ed), (1987), Foreign Trade, Investment, and the Law in the People's Republic of China, Oxford University Press, Hong Kong, 2nd ed.

Moser, M.J. and W. K. Zee (1987), China Tax Guide, Oxford University Press, Hong Kong.

Nolan, P. (1983), Growth Processes and Distributional Change in a South Chinese Province: the Case of Guangdong, Contemporary China Institute, School of Oriental and African Studies, Research Notes and Studies No.5, London.

Nolan, P. (1988), The Political Economy of Collective Farms: An Analysis of China's Post-Mao Rural Reforms, Polity Press, Oxford.

Nolan, P. (1989), "History, Democracy and Economic Change", China Now, No.131

Ozawa, T. (1979), 'International Investment and Industrial Structure: New Theoretical Implications from the Japanese Experience', Oxford Economic Papers.

Pack, H. (1987), Productivity, Technology, and Industrial Development: A Case Study in Textiles, Oxford University Press, New York, for the World Bank.

Perkins, D.H. (ed) (1975), China's Modern Economy in Historical Perspective, Stanford University Press, Stanford

Perkins, D.H. (1988), "Reforming China's Economic System", Journal of Economic Literature, June.

Perry, E.J. and C. Wong (eds) (1985), The Political Economy of Reform in Post-Mao China, Harvard University Press, Cambridge, MA.

Pomfret, R. (1989),"Ten Years of Direct Investment in China", Asian Perspective, Fall/Winter

Reuber, G.L. (with H. Crookell, M. Emerson and G. Gallais-Hamouno) (1973), Private Foreign Investment in Development, Clarendon Press, Oxford, for OECD Development Centre.

Reynolds, B.L. (1987) (ed). Reform in China: Challenges and Choices, M.E. Sharpe, New York.

Riskin, C. (1987), China's Political Economy. The Quest for Development since 1949, Oxford University Press, New York.

Roemer, M. and J.Stern (1981), Case Studies in Economic Development: Projects, Policies and Strategies, Butterworths, London

Sit, V.F.S. and S.L. Wong (1988) "Hong Kong Manufacturing: Growth and Challenges of an Export - Oriented System Dominated by Small and Medium Industries", mimeo, University of Hong Kong.

Sit, V.F.S. (1989) "Hong Kong's Industrial Out-Processing in the Pearl River Delta of China", mimeo, Centre of Asian Studies, University of Hong Kong.

Tang, K. and M. Lau (1988), An Introduction to Foreign-Related Tax Laws in China, Kaitin Publishing, Shenzhen (in Chinese)

Thoburn, J.T. (1977), Primary Commodity Exports and Economic Development: Theory, Evidence and Study of Malaysia, Wiley, London.

Thoburn, J.T. (1981), Multinationals, Mining and Development: A Study of the Tin Industry, Gower, Aldershot.

Thoburn, J.T. (1986) "China's Special Economic Zones Revisited", EuroAsia Business Review, October.

Thoburn, J.T., S.H. Tang and E. Chau (1989), Hong Kong Investment in the Pearl River Delta, China Economic Papers series, Friedrich Ebert Foundation, Shanghai, January.

Thoburn, J.T., E. Chau and S.H. Tang (1990) "Industrial Cooperation between Hong Kong and China: The Experience of Hong Kong Firms in the Pearl River Delta", in E.K.Y. Chen (ed), The Future of Industrial and Trade Development in Hong Kong, Hong Kong University, Centre of Asian Studies, forthcoming.

Tidrick, G. and Chen Jiyuan (eds) (1987), China's Industrial Reform, Oxford University Press, for World Bank, New York.

Tsim, T.L. and B.H.K. Luk (eds.) (1989), The Other Kong Kong Report, Chinese University Press, Hong Kong

Usher, D. (1977), "The Economics of Tax Incentives to Encourage Investment in Less Developed Countries", Journal of Development Economics, No.4.

Vogel, E.F. (1989), One Step Ahead in China: Guangdong under Reform, Harvard University Press, London

Walker, R. (ed) (1985), Applied Qualitative Research, Gower, Aldershot.

Wang, G.G. (1988), China's Investment Laws, New Directions, Butterworths, Singapore.

Warr, P. (1984) "Korea's Masan Free Export Zone: Benefits and Costs, The Developing Economies, June.

Warr, P. (1987), "Malaysia's Industrial Enclaves: Benefits and Costs", The Developing Economies, March.

Weigt, V. (1988), German Currency Reform in China? An Investigation into Two Countries and Two Reforms, China Economic Papers series, Friedrich Ebert Foundation, Shanghai, December.

Weisskopf, R. and E. Wolff (1977) "Linkages and Leakages: Industrial Tracking in an Enclave Economy", Economic Development and Cultural Change, July.

Wells, L.J. jnr (1983), Third World Multinationals: the Rise of Foreign Investment from Developing Countries, MIT Press, Cambridge, MA.

Williamson, O.E. (1985), The Economic Institutions of Capitalism. Firms, Markets, Relational Contracting, Free Press, New York.

World Bank (1988), China: External Trade and Capital, Washington, D.C.

World Bank (1989), World Development Report 1989, Washington, D.C.

Youngson, A.J. (ed) (1983), China and Hong Kong: The Economic Nexus, Oxford University Press, Hong Kong.